Knitting Know-How

*This book is dedicated to **Bob** and to **Philippe**. You are our reasons for being.*

Knitting
Know-How

Dorothy T. Ratigan
& Judith Durant

Krause Publications
Cincinnati, Ohio

Contents

Introduction

Dorothy and Judith met in the mid 1990s, when Judith was book editor at Interweave Press and Dorothy worked as a freelance technical editor for Interweave's knitting books. When *Interweave Knits* magazine was launched in 1996 with Judith as co-editor, Dorothy was a big part of the enterprise, both as technical editor and writer of the "Beyond the Basics" column. And, of course, we both contributed designs. Although Judith had been knitting for more than thirty years, it wasn't until knitting became a big part of her working life that she realized how much she didn't know.

Early on in the relationship, Judith saw the potential for gathering Dot's knitting knowledge into a book to share with the world. The problem was finding the time to do it. While Dot had gathered an enormous amount of knitting know-how, it wasn't collected and filed in any particular order. Some things were written down; many things were not. No disrespect intended, but Judith likes to say that each bit of Dot's information is stored on a sticky note in her brain; you never know which sticky note may fall out at any given time, and there's no way to easily access the one you want. We tried to start pulling it together a while back, but the need to work on other projects to pay the bills kept us from completing the task.

When F+W Media offered us a contract to do the book, we finally had no choice but to get to it. Judith caught Dot's sticky notes as they dropped and made a list. We then added some of Judith's know-how to the list and came up with a master plan. As we worked through our outline, we remembered questions frequently asked by our students and made sure we answered every one of them. And as we worked through the chapters, we realized once again that knitting is an ever-evolving craft, and that there is almost always more than one way to solve a problem. So, rather than just present a dictionary of techniques, we chose to include only those that have worked best for us over the years. And we've done our best to describe why we've chosen these methods over others.

The book you hold in your hands represents a combined 100+ years of knitting and 50+ years of teaching experience. We don't know everything, but we do know a lot and hope that this know-how will help you become a better knitter and get even more pleasure than you already derive from our favorite craft.

Part I
Materials and Tools

Knitting has come a long way since its beginnings in the thirteenth century, and we're lucky to have a huge variety of yarns, needles and other tools to work with.

Chapter One discusses yarn in detail: what it's made of, how it's twisted, the various weights available and how it's sold. Here you'll learn how to read a yarn label and how to use that information to substitute one yarn for another. Also included is a chart for estimating how much yarn you'll need for sweaters of various sizes, which is handy to know when you encounter a "must-have" yarn but have no idea what you'll be knitting with it.

    Chapter Two covers needles and needle sizes. There are choices to be made in materials, lengths and shapes: straight versus circular and even round versus square. Needle choice, like most things in knitting, is a matter of preference. But once you've tried various tools, you may find that with needles, you get what you pay for. If you're into knitting for the long haul, use the best tools you can afford.

    In Chapter Three we discuss perhaps the most important tool for most knitters: the pattern. The most luscious cashmere yarn knitted on solid-gold needles will not yield a good result if you don't know how to follow the pattern. You'll learn about measurements, yarn requirements and required tools. We also provide a list of the most commonly used abbreviations in both text and chart form. We explain what those parentheses mean and how they differ from brackets, and if you've wondered what those asterisks are doing in most patterns, the answer is here.

① Yarn

Yarn for knitting is spun (or not) from a veritable plethora of fibers: some are organic, some are synthetic and many are a blend of several materials. Some yarns are so fine they seem appropriate for cobwebs, while others are bulky enough to make into rugs. Yarns are packaged in several standard weights (with exceptions, of course) but the yardage varies greatly between the packages. This chapter will help you find your way through the yarn maze.

How Yarn Is Sold

Yarn for handknitting is most commonly sold in **balls**, **skeins** or **hanks**. Ribbon and other novelty yarns are often sold on **spools**. Yarn for machine knitting and weaving is usually sold on **cones**, though this yarn can also be used for handknitting. It's not clear to us why or how manufacturers choose which way to package their yarns for retail. You can find wool, cotton and other fibers presented in all these forms. It's interesting to note, though, that luxury yarns are almost always sold in hanks.

FINDING THE CENTER PULL

To find the end at the center of a ball or skein, insert your thumbs and index fingers into opposite sides so they meet in the center. You should feel that one side of the center hole is looser or more open than the other; the yarn end should reside in the more open part of the hole. Fish around until you feel the end and gently pull it from the center and out of the more open end. It's not always possible to find the very end, but you can usually locate the initial wraps and pull out a few yards to begin.

Spool

Cone

Skein

Ball

Hank, twisted

Balls of yarn are just what the name implies: The yarn is wound into a round shape that usually weighs 50 or 100 grams (1.75 or 3.5 ounces). Yarn wound into a ball is ready to knit, and most balls are wound so you can pull from both the center or the outside. This is handy when you want to knit with two strands held together.

The terms **skein** and **hank** are often used interchangeably, but they're not actually the same thing. A **skein** is yarn that's been wound similarly to a ball, except the shape is oblong. Like balls, yarns wound into skeins are ready to knit, and most of them can also be worked from the center or from the outside.

A **hank** is a loosely wound circle or ring of yarn tied in one or more places. Hanks are usually twisted for retail sale. Yarn sold in a hank needs to be wound into a ball before it can be knit.

A ball of yarn

A skein of yarn

A hank of yarn, untwisted

SWIFT AND BALL WINDER

Two of the best tools a knitter can own are a swift and a ball winder. While you can hang a hank of yarn over the back of a chair or employ the arms and hands of a willing friend, a swift will hold the yarn securely while you wind it into a ball. A swift looks something like an umbrella frame, and it can be adjusted to hold hanks of various sizes. From the swift you can wind a ball by hand or employ a ball winder. These handy items clamp on to a table edge and wind a nice, neat ball of yarn that can be knit from the inside or the outside.

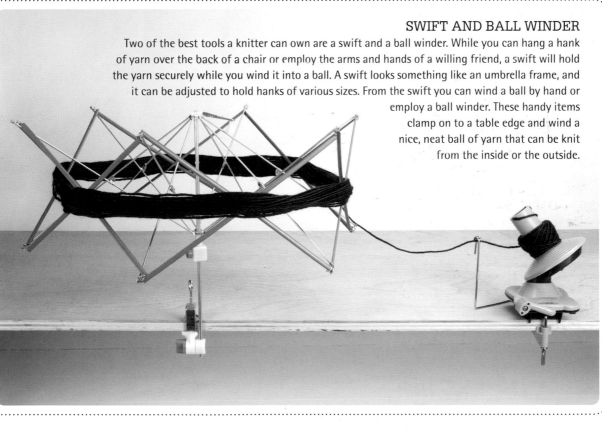

WINDING A CENTER-PULL BALL

If you don't have a swift and ball winder, winding a center-pull ball is the next best solution. The center-pull ball allows you to knit without worrying about your ball of yarn rolling all over and possibly falling on the floor.

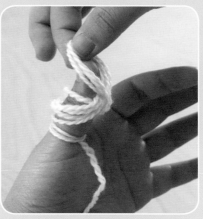

1 Wrap the end of the yarn around your thumb four times. With your palm facing up, work a figure eight between the thumb and little finger four times.

2 Take the wraps off the little finger and fold them onto the wraps on the thumb.

3 Remove the wraps from the thumb and, keeping the initial wraps around the thumb, rest the thumb on the index and middle fingers. Wrap the yarn loosely around the initial wraps and three fingers about thirty times.

4 Keeping the thumb in the center of the ball and in contact with the initial wraps, remove the yarn from the fingers and rotate the ball about 90 degrees. Wrap the yarn around the wound yarn and all fingers about thirty times.

5 Repeat Step 4 until all the yarn is wound and tuck in the tail.

6 Remove the thumb with the initial wraps from the center of the ball. This becomes the end you can begin knitting with.

Spooled yarn is wound around a cardboard cylinder and can be worked from the outside only.

Coned yarn for machine knitting is wound very tightly and is usually lightly treated with an oily or waxy substance so it moves through the machine without getting caught on any of the parts. If you want to handknit this yarn, it's best to rewind it into hanks and wash it before starting. Using cotton waste yarn and a figure-eight tie, bind the hank in four areas. Wash the

hank in mild soap and then rinse until all the soap is removed. Gently squeeze out most of the water. Roll the hank in a towel and press gently to remove more water. Place a dry towel over a shower curtain rod or the back of a chair and drape the yarn over the towel. Move the hank about 45 degrees every few hours or when it begins to feel dry at the top. Do not hang anything on the wet skein—this will stretch the yarn. When completely dry, wind the yarn into balls for knitting.

How to Read a Yarn Label

Yarn labels come in different formats. The labels from one company will have more or less information than those from another company, and the information may be presented in various ways. Here are a couple of examples.

In the first example (below, left), the Craft Yarn Council (CYC) symbol for yarn weight (see chart on page 19), which in this case is 3 Light, is included. The gauge and care instructions are written in text form.

In the second example (below, right), no yarn weight is given, but you can deduce that from the recommended gauge. In this case the gauge is presented as a grid showing the number of rows and stitches per 4" (10cm), and the recommended needle size in metric and US sizes is given below the grid. In this case the recommended gauge is twenty-two to twenty-three stitches per 4" (10cm) on a US 4 needle, putting the yarn in the 2 Fine category. Recommended gauge could put this yarn in the 3 Light category, but considering recommended needle size, we'd categorize it as 2 Fine. Care instructions are given in symbols indicating that the yarn can be machine washed at 104 degrees Fahrenheit (40 degrees Celsius) but cannot be washed with bleach. After washing, the label instructs to lay the knitted piece flat to dry and to press with a cool iron.

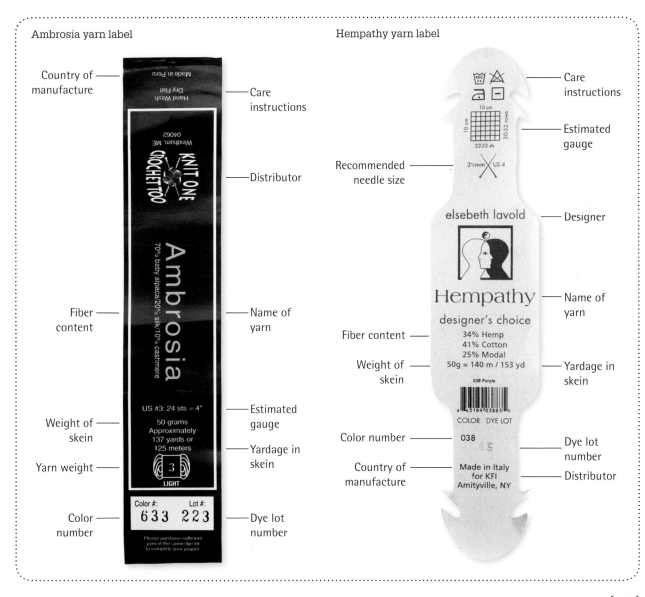

Ambrosia yarn label

- Country of manufacture
- Care instructions
- Distributor
- Fiber content
- Name of yarn
- Weight of skein
- Estimated gauge
- Yardage in skein
- Yarn weight
- Color number
- Dye lot number

Hempathy yarn label

- Care instructions
- Estimated gauge
- Recommended needle size
- Designer
- Name of yarn
- Fiber content
- Weight of skein
- Yardage in skein
- Color number
- Dye lot number
- Country of manufacture
- Distributor

What Yarn Is Made From

Yarn was traditionally made of two types of fiber: animal or plant. The nineteenth century saw the introduction of cellulosic fibers, which are made from plant materials processed down to a liquid solution that then hardens into a spinnable fiber. Synthetic and manmade fibers such as nylon and acrylic were introduced at the beginning of the twentieth century, and the start of the twenty-first century has seen the introduction of alternative fibers made from unlikely materials such as chitin (shrimp and crab shells), milk and jade.

Animal Fibers

Wool should be last in this alphabetic list of animal fibers, but because it is the most widely used knitting yarn, we're placing it first. Wool comes from the fleeces of a large variety of sheep breeds and is produced in many countries. Wool has many qualities that make it the ideal fiber for handknit clothing. It is a warm fiber that can absorb up to 30 percent of its weight in moisture without feeling cold and clammy, which is great if you're caught in a sudden snowstorm. Wool fibers have a lot of memory, meaning they won't stretch out of shape over time. When you wash a wool garment and lay it out flat, you can push everything back into shape, even manipulating the overall garment size if necessary, and once it dries it will remember this shape and hold on to it. Wool is also naturally flame retardant. The length of the fiber (staple length) determines the quality of wool: Its softness increases, and its strength and elasticity decrease as the fiber gets shorter. Most wool yarns are a blend of fibers from different breeds, though some are breed-specific, such as merino and Icelandic.

Lambswool comes from the first clippings of baby lambs and is very fine and highly valued.

Merino wool   Lambswool   Alpaca   Cashmere

Many wool yarns now come in a machine-washable variety known as superwash. **Superwash wool** has been processed to prevent shrinkage when machine-washed on a gentle cycle, but you should still lay your garment flat to air dry.

Alpaca yarns are spun from the long hairs harvested from one of two types of this South American member of the camel family: suri and huacaya. This lustrous and soft fiber is very warm and similar to wool in its ability to hold a fair amount of water and remain warm and comfortable to wear. Alpaca is a durable fiber, and because it contains no lanolin, it's a good option for those with wool sensitivities or allergies.

Cashmere yarn comprises the short hairs that form the downy undercoat of the cashmere goat. It's beautifully soft, lustrous and smooth, and though it's much lighter than wool, it's extremely warm. Because the downy fiber is only less than half the goat's fiber, production is low and processing is labor intensive, which means it's very expensive. If not prepared properly, cashmere yarn will pill. Blending with wool makes it cheaper and stronger but detracts from its softness.

Mohair comes from the Angora goat (not to be confused with angora yarn, which comes from a rabbit). The fibers are long, lustrous, smooth, elastic and strong. While very light, mohair is also very warm and hard-wearing. Mohair yarn can be curly like a **bouclé** or **brushed** into a yarn with a "halo." It comes in various weights and is often blended with wool and nylon or silk.

Silk usually used for knitting yarn is produced by the domesticated Bombyx silkworm, which feeds on mulberry leaves. The filament is spun in a single long strand by the caterpillar and is pure white with a very high luster. It is soft, fine, incredibly strong and fairly elastic. **Tussah silk** is produced by undomesticated silkworms. Because they feed on leaves other than mulberry, the color is often brownish and uneven, and the fibers are thick and thin. Silk yarn can be smooth and shiny, dull and nubbly, or in the form of bouclé.

Brushed mohair   Mohair bouclé   Silk   Silk bouclé

[15]

Plant Fibers

Cotton yarn is made from the fibers that grow around the seedpod of the plant. As with wool, the length of the fiber determines the quality and the price of the cotton, as its strength and softness increase with length. Most prized are Egyptian and Pima cottons. Cotton is a cool, comfortable fiber, ideal for warm weather. Available in a variety of finishes and textures, it can be dyed in a wide range of colors. Cotton garments may stretch with wear but also may shrink when washed.

   Hemp is produced with the stems of the Cannabis sativa plant. It is very strong and shares most of the characteristics of linen.

   Linen, made from the stalks of flax plants, is a durable fabric that is somewhat harsh in the skein but softens and shines with handling and wear. It wicks moisture from the skin, so it is often worn in warm climates. Like cotton, it lacks elasticity.

Cellulosic Fibers

Bamboo yarn is marketed as an earth-friendly yarn because it comes from a highly sustainable plant. It's strong, flexible and can be softer than silk when spun into yarn. One of its highly prized characteristics is that it's antibacterial, even after multiple washings. It's cool, drapey and silky soft.

   Corn fiber is made from cornstarch. It, too, is marketed as an earth-friendly yarn. It looks and feels much like mercerized cotton.

| Cotton | Hemp | Linen | Bamboo | Corn |

Rayon was one of the first "industrial" fibers used for yarn and is produced from highly processed wood pulp. It can be spun into many types of yarn, from smooth and silky to highly textured. "Viscose rayon" is named for the viscose process used to produce it. While rayon is manmade, its ancestry is traced back to trees, so we put it in the cellulosic category.

Soy yarns are produced with the waste left over from tofu production, making it environmentally friendly. It produces a very soft and breathable fabric that is good for warm-weather wear.

Synthetic Fibers

Acrylic fibers, produced from synthetic polymers, are durable and can be made to look like wool. Unlike wool, they don't absorb moisture, so they wick and dry quickly. They are not as warm and insulating as wool, and because they don't "breathe" they can be uncomfortable in warm weather. They also conduct static electricity.

Nylon is produced from petrochemicals. Because it is equally strong when wet or dry and is very durable, it's often blended with wool to produce sock yarn. Nylon conducts static electricity and, like other synthetics, can be a dust magnet. It's often used in ribbon and other novelty yarns.

Polyester, made from polymers of polyethylene and polypropylene, shares many characteristics with nylon, though it's somewhat softer and warmer. It's very strong but susceptible to damage under high heat. Polyester is usually plied with other fibers to strengthen the yarn.

| Rayon | Soy | Acrylic | Nylon |

Ply and Twist

Z-twist   S-twist

For conventional ply, fiber is spun into yarn in one of two directions: clockwise or counterclockwise. Depending on that direction, the resulting yarn has either a Z twist or an S twist. In a Z-twist yarn, the direction of the twist is from right to left, the same direction of the line in the letter Z. In an S-twist yarn, the direction of the twist is from left to right, the same direction of the line in the letter S. Generally, though not always, a Z twist is used to spin a single strand of yarn. This yarn is called a single and can be knit as is or plied with two, three or more singles. An S twist is used to ply Z-twist singles together. If you look closely at a three- or four-ply wool yarn, usually you'll see it has an S twist. If you untwist the four plies and examine one of the singles, you'll see that it was spun with a Z twist.

Cable and multistrand yarns go one step further by plying together four or more conventional ply strands.

A cable yarn, often made of cotton, uses a Z twist to ply together four 4-ply S-twist strands. This alternating of twist, from the Z-twist singles to the S-twist four-ply to the Z-twist cable, creates a strong and balanced yarn. Multi-strand yarns are made by plying together any number of S-twist plied strands in the same direction with another S twist.

So why is this important? It's not really, except in a couple of instances. First, if you're working with a singles yarn spun with an overly tight twist, it'll tend to lean or bias when knitted in Stockinette stitch. This problem can't be corrected by blocking, so you'll have to work this yarn in a combination of knit and purl stitches. Secondly, if your yarn coils and kinks after you've wound it into a ball, you've probably wound it against the twist. Check the twist in your yarn before winding it. If you've got an S twist, wind the yarn in a clockwise direction, which is the same direction of the twist. If you've got a Z twist, wind in a counterclockwise direction.

In addition to plying, there are other ways to construct yarn. Cotton is often woven in tubular fashion to form a cordlike yarn, and there are many novelty yarns such as ribbon, eyelash and ladder yarns that are woven or tied.

Weight, Gauge and Hand

* **Yarn weight** refers to the heft or thickness of the yarn.
* **Gauge** is the number of stitches and rows or rounds in 1 knitted square inch (2.5 square centimeters) of the yarn.
* **Hand** is used to express the drape, firmness and feel of the fabric knitted from the yarn.

Weight

There was a time when the ply indicated the weight of yarn. For example, two-ply referred to fingering or baby weight, three-ply indicated sport weight, etc. This is no longer the case, and you can find ten-ply fingering weight or two-ply bulky weight yarns. This is important to note if you're using some vintage patterns that use this designation. To choose the right yarn, use the indicated gauge to determine the correct weight.

Yarns come in a weight range from lace to super bulky. Gauge comes into play when determining the weight of a yarn because each weight of yarn covers a small range of gauges. The Craft Yarn Council (CYC) has categorized seven numbered categories of yarn weights as indicated in the chart on the next page. Some yarn manufacturers print these designations on the yarn label.

Not all yarns fit neatly into these categories. In addition to the note about lace yarn in the chart, novelty yarns are often uneven strands that are not meant to be knit on their own but are paired and knitted together with smoother, more stable yarns.

CYC Standard Yarn Weight System

Yarn Weight Symbol & Category Names	0 Lace	1 Super Fine	2 Fine	3 Light	4 Medium	5 Bulky	6 Super Bulky
Type of Yarns in Category	Fingering, 10-count crochet thread	Sock, Fingering, Baby	Sport, Baby	DK, Light Worsted	Worsted, Afghan, Aran	Chunky, Craft, Rug	Bulky, Roving
Knit Gauge Range* in Stockinette Stitch to 4 inches	33–40 sts**	27–32 sts	23–26 sts	21–24 sts	16–20 sts	12–15 sts	6–11 sts
Recommended Needle in Metric Size Range	1.5mm–2.25mm	2.25mm–3.25mm	3.25mm–3.75mm	3.75mm–4.5mm	4.5mm–5.5mm	5.5mm–8mm	8mm and larger
Recommended Needle in US Size Range	000 to 1	1 to 3	3 to 5	5 to 7	7 to 9	9 to 11	11 and larger
Crochet Gauge* Ranges in Single Crochet to 4 inch	32-42 double crochets**	21–32 sts	16–20 sts	12–17 sts	11–14 sts	8–11 sts	5–9 sts
Recommended Hook in Metric Size Range	Steel*** 1.6–1.4mm Regular hook 2.25mm	2.25mm–3.5mm	3.5mm–4.5mm	4.5mm–5.5mm	5.5mm–6.5mm	6.5mm–9mm	9mm and larger
Recommended Hook US Size Range	Steel*** 6, 7, 8 Regular hook B–1	B-1 to E-4	E-4 to 7	7 to I-9	I-9 to K-10½	K-10½ to M-13	M-13 and larger

* **GUIDELINES ONLY:** The above reflect the most commonly used gauges and needle or hook sizes for specific yarn categories.

** **Lace weight yarns** are usually knitted or crocheted on larger needles and hooks to create lacy, openwork patterns. Accordingly, a gauge range is difficult to determine. Always follow the gauge stated in your pattern.

*** **Steel crochet hooks** are sized differently from regular hooks—the higher the number, the smaller the hook, which is the reverse of regular hook sizing.

Gauge

Gauge refers to the number of stitches and rows or rounds in an inch (2.5cm) of knitted fabric. If there is no weight designation on a label, there is almost always a statement regarding the recommended gauge. Gauge is most commonly given as the number of stitches (and sometimes rows) in 4" (10cm) worked on a specific needle size. So, for example, if a label says "20 stitches = 4" (10cm) on US 7 (4.5mm) needles," you can refer to the chart and determine that the yarn is 4 Medium (worsted, afghan, Aran) weight. Not all yarn fits neatly into these categories, however. A label may read "22 stitches and 24 rows = 4" (10cm) on US 4 (3.5mm) needles." Referring to the chart, you can see that the stitch gauge puts the yarn into the 3 Light category, but the recommended needle size appears in the 2 Fine category. Ultimately it's the stitch count and not the needle size that's important here, so the yarn in question will work for a pattern that calls for twenty-two stitches in 4" (10cm), or five and a half stitches per inch (2.5cm). For a full discussion of gauge as it relates to garment fit and drape, see Chapter Twelve.

Hand

The way a yarn looks, feels and drapes when it has been knitted up is called the hand. A yarn that feels good, looks good and is appropriate to the project is what we're striving for, and the weight and gauge specifications are used merely as a guide to finding the right yarn for a project. If a label recommends the yarn be knitted at five stitches per inch (2.5cm), but your swatch at that gauge feels very dense and stiff, you probably won't be happy with an afghan knitted at that gauge. So you can either knit your afghan at fewer than five stitches per inch (2.5cm) or use the yarn at five stitches per inch (2.5cm) for a rug or a place mat.

How to Substitute Yarns

Armed with the information above regarding weight, gauge and hand, you can now choose a yarn to knit with other than the one specified for a particular pattern. You should always knit a swatch in your chosen yarn to be sure it produces a fabric you like for the project. Even though two different yarns knit to the same gauge, the resulting fabrics may differ in density. (See more on this subject in Chapter Twelve.)

Another consideration is fiber content and how the yarn behaves. If you have a pattern for a cabled and bobbled wool sweater with a gauge of five stitches per inch (2.5cm), you may not be happy with that sweater knitted in bamboo yarn, which doesn't have the same memory as wool and will not hold its shape like wool.

Always be sure to compare the yardage of your chosen yarn against that of the recommended yarn. The label will state how much the ball or hank weighs and how many yards it contains. But the yardage can be vastly different from one yarn to the next. For example, one DK yarn knits at five and a half stitches per inch (2.5cm) on size 6 (4mm) needles, is composed of 85 percent wool and 15 percent polyester, and has 202 yards per 100 grams; another that knits at the same gauge on the same size needles is composed of 50 percent acrylic, 40 percent wool and 10 percent nylon and has 288 yards per 100 grams. The physical weight of the fibers differs between compositions and therefore one has more yardage than the other; be sure you buy enough to complete the project. In general, a difference of fewer than 10 yards (9m) per ball or hank will yield enough yarn on the same number of units.

CONVERTING YARDS TO METERS

Most, but not all, yarn labels give the length in both yards and meters. If the yarn you're eyeing doesn't have the conversion and you don't have a calculator handy, here's a quick way to estimate; the results will not be precise, but they'll be accurate enough for our purposes. Note: The number of yards or meters must be 100 or more.

METERS TO YARDS: Add the number of the first two digits to the whole number. For example, 165 meters: 165 + 16 = 181 yards. The exact conversion is 165 meters = 180.44 yards.

YARDS TO METERS: Subtract the number of the first two digits from the whole number. For example, 181 yards: 181 − 18 = 163 meters. The exact conversion is 181 yards = 165.5 meters.

Estimating Yardage

The best way to buy yarn is with a particular project in mind, with the pattern that lists the yarn used and the amount needed for your size in hand. However, this is not always possible because you never know when you'll be confronted with an "I don't know what I want to make out of it, but I simply must have it" yarn.

The amount of yarn needed to complete a given project depends on many variables including the size and style of the garment, the stitch pattern and the yarn weight and density. We've seen many charts that give guidelines for how much yarn is required for a particular project. While these can be helpful, there are so many variables that amounts needed are difficult to determine. Charts for estimating sweater yardage usually assume a long-sleeved pullover or cardigan and are based on chest measurement. However, a chart published in 1965 would suggest different requirements than one published in 2012 because clothes were worn tighter than they are now. Looking at four charts to estimate yardage for a woman's 36" (91.5cm) sweater yields the following results: 1,090 yards, 1,100 to 1,400 yards, 1,120 yards and 1,370 yards. With that much variation, you could easily come up one or more hanks short. That said, here are some rough guidelines for sweaters with 2" (5cm) of ease. If possible, buy some extra for safety.

Child Sweaters

Chest size	22" (56cm)	24" (61cm)	26" (66cm)	28" (71cm)	30" (76cm)
Gauge (sts per inch [2.5cm])					
Fingering (6.5 to 7 sts)	570 yds 520m	750 yds 690 m	800 yds 730m	950 yds 870m	1,200 yds 1,100m
Sport (5 to 6 sts)	500 yds 460m	600 yds 550m	720 yds 660m	820 yds 750m	975 yds 890m
Worsted (4 to 4.5 sts)	420 yds 385m	500 yds 460m	650 yds 595m	800 yds 730m	950 yds 870m
Bulky (3 to 3.5 sts)	350 yds 320m	375 yds 340m	490 yds 450m	650 yds 595m	750 yds 685m

Adult Sweaters

Chest size	32" (81cm)	36" (91cm)	40" (102cm)	44" (112cm)	48" (122cm)	52" (132cm)
Gauge (sts per inch [2.5cm])						
Fingering (6.5 to 7 sts)	1,500 yds 1,370m	1,800 yds 1,970m	2,000 yds 1,830m	2,400 yds 2,200m	2,700 yds 2,450m	3,000 yds 2,740m
Sport (5 to 6 sts)	1,300 yds 1,200m	1,500 yds 1,370m	1,700 yds 1,550m	1,950 yds 1,780m	2,200 yds 2,000m	2,400 yds 2,200m
Worsted (4 to 4.5 sts)	1,100 yds 1,000m	1,250 yds 1,150m	1,400 yds 1,280m	1,600 yds 1,450m	1,850 yds 1,700m	2,100 yds 1,920m
Bulky (3 to 3.5 sts)	900 yds 820m	970 yds 890m	1,050 yds 960m	1,200 yds 1,000m	1,350 yds 1,230m	1,500 yds 1,370m

② Needles

There are many styles of needles made from a variety of materials. Most knitting needles are cylindrical with points that can range from dull or rounded to very sharp and pointy. Like most things in knitting, needle selection comes down to personal preference. Here is some information that can help in making choices.

Needle Composition

Needles are made from many different materials, from bamboo and wood to metal and plastic to a milk protein called casein.

Bamboo

Bamboo needles are lightweight and warm. Because there is a bit of surface friction, these work well with very slippery yarns such as silk tape or mercerized cotton. This also makes them good for beginners because they slow the knitting a bit. Bamboo needles can break if you're too rough with them.

Casein

These needles are environmentally friendly in that they're made from a nontoxic milk protein and are biodegradable. Because of their warmth, they're often preferred by those with arthritis. They're slicker than wood and bamboo but not as slippery as metal. They are very slightly pliable, which will keep them from snapping while performing complicated knitting tricks.

Metal

Aluminum needles are lightweight and smooth, allowing the knitting to speed along. They are cold to the touch and click loudly while knitting, two traits that some knitters find annoying.

Nickel-plated aluminum needles are an entirely different story. They're even slicker than unplated aluminum and allow for the fastest knitting with any type of yarn. They make a little less noise than aluminum but are also cold to the touch.

Smooth steel needles are most common in very small sizes used for lace, but they're also available in standard sizes.

Brass needles are usually coated with a fine resin, which imposes a slight bit of friction on the surface. This slows the knitting ever so slightly, which can be a good thing for control with lace and other intricate designs.

Plastic

Warm to the touch, lightweight and smooth, plastic needles are often used by arthritic knitters who want more speed than they can get from bamboo or wood. Some plastic needles have a steel wire core to prevent bending.

Wood

Needles are made from a variety of woods including birch, ebony, cherry, tulipwood, black walnut, maple and more. Like bamboo, wood is lightweight and warm to the touch. Many knitters love the feel of exotic wood, and the needles improve over time, reacting with oil from the skin.

Needle Types

Needles come in three basic styles: straight, double point and circular. Traditionally needles have been perfectly round, but square needles came on the scene in the early 2000s and are especially suited for people with arthritis and others who have trouble holding round needles. The style you choose depends on what you're knitting.

Straight Needles

Straight needles have a point on one end and some kind of stopper on the other end; the stopper keeps the stitches from sliding off the needle as you work. Straight needles are used for flat work, and if you knit a sweater with them you will usually make the front, back and sleeves separately and then sew them together. The needles come in various lengths from 9" to 16" (23cm to 40cm), and you can choose the length that most suits your project. Some knitters like to tuck the right needle under their right arm and opt for long needles.

Circular Needles

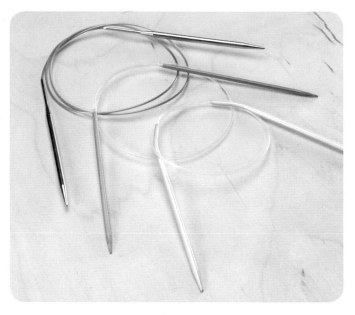

Circular needles have two short, straight needles with pointed tips connected by a nylon cable. The length of the needles can vary from about 3" to 5" (7.5cm to 12.5cm), but the overall length of needles plus the cable is used to categorize the different lengths, which range from 8" to 60" (20cm to 152cm). Circular needles are made for knitting in the round, forming a tube without seams. The shorter ones are used for socks and gloves, medium lengths are for hats and scarves, and the long ones work for sweaters and other large items. Circular needles can also be used when there are too many stitches to fit on a straight needle. Many knitters use circular needles for all flat work because most of the weight is carried on the cable, which means the fabric can rest in your lap. Because nothing protrudes from the work, circulars are great for knitting in tight spaces like airplanes, trains and buses. Knitters have developed new ways to use circular needles, including knitting one sock on two circular needles and two socks on one long circular needle. Interchangeable circular needle sets come with a range of needle sizes that attach to different cable lengths.

Double-Point Needles

Double-point needles are also made for working in the round, and they come in sets of four or five. Stitches are divided evenly and carried on three or four needles, and you knit with the fourth or fifth. Double-point needles come in lengths from 4" to 16" (10cm to 40cm), made for knitting everything from the fingers of gloves to full-size shawls. Some Shetland knitters wear a knitting belt into which they insert one end of a double-point needle. This is said to steady the needle and speed up the work; the belt also enables one-handed knitting. If you're going to do any knitting in the round, you'll need double-point needles. Even if you knit a hat on a 16" (40cm) circular needle, you'll need double-point needles for the very top of the crown, which will have too few stitches to fit on a circular needle.

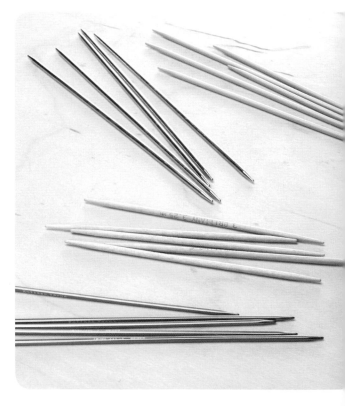

A SMOOTH CABLE JOIN
The most important thing to look for in circular needles of any kind is the quality of the join between the needle and the cable: It must be strong and absolutely smooth so the knitting doesn't get hung up as it moves from the cable to the tips.

Needle Sizes

Straight, circular and double-point needles all come in a huge range of sizes from 8/0, which are as thin as sewing needles and used for very fine lacework, to 50, which are as thick as tree trunks and often used in conjunction with super-bulky yarns or pencil roving. There are four different sizing systems for needles: US sizing, UK sizing, metric sizing and Japanese sizing, and not all sizes convert accurately between the different systems. The metric system is the most straightforward: The needle size is the exact millimeter measurement of the needle's diameter. US sizing has changed over the years, and a size 6 needle manufactured in 1950 probably won't be the same size as a size 6 needle manufactured in 2012. Sizes have also varied between manufacturers, probably because the size number does not represent a specific measurement. US size numbers go up as the diameter increases, and UK size numbers move in reverse. Japanese sizes are based on metrics, but they change in 0.3mm increments. The most important thing is to choose a needle that yields the correct gauge necessary for the project at hand. Here is a conversion chart for the four sizing systems.

US sizes	UK/Canadian/Australian sizes	Metric sizes (mm)	Japanese sizes
00000000		0.5	
000000		0.75	
0000		1.0	
0000		1.25	
000		1.5	
00		1.75	
0		2.0	
			0 (2.1mm)
1	13	2.25	
			1 (2.4mm)
1½		2.5	
			2 (2.7mm)
2	12	2.75	
2½	11	3.0	3 (3mm)
3	10	3.25	
			4 (3.3mm)
4		3.5	
			5 (3.6mm)
5	9	3.75	
			6 (3.9mm)
6	8	4.0	
			7 (4.2mm)
7	7	4.5	8 (4.5mm)
			9 (4.8mm)
8	6	5.0	
			10 (5.1mm)
			11 (5.4mm)
9	5	5.5	
			12 (5.7mm)
10	4	6.0	13 (6.0mm)
			14 (6.3mm)
	3	6.5	
			15 (6.6mm)
10½	2	7.0	7mm
11	1	7.5	
	0	8.0	8mm
13	00	9.0	9mm
15	000	10.0	10mm
17		12.0	
19		16.0	
35		19.0	
50		25.0	

③ Working with Patterns and Charts

Just as there are many ways to knit a garment, so there are many ways to write a pattern. Over time, designers and publishers have come together to try to standardize verbiage, abbreviations and symbols, but as yet there's no universal way to present a knitting pattern. Some patterns give both imperial and metric measurements, while others don't. That said, here are some guidelines for working with patterns and charts.

How to Read a Pattern

Before beginning any project, it's a good idea to read through the entire pattern to be sure you understand all the terms and abbreviations and that all the necessary information is there. Here's what to look for during your initial read.

Sizes

If you're knitting a garment, the first thing to look for is the size to be sure the pattern is appropriate for the intended wearer. The pattern should include both the finished measurements and the size of the person it's meant to fit. A typical presentation for a sweater looks like this:

> To fit bust sizes: 30–32 (33–35, 36–38)" (76–81 [84–90, 91–97])cm
> Finished bust measurements: 34 (37, 40)" (86 [94, 102])cm

In this example, the pattern is written in three sizes. The first size will fit a bust of 30" to 32" (76cm to 81cm) and is followed by two progressively larger bust sizes in parentheses. The finished bust measurement, also shown as the first size followed by the two progressively larger sizes in parentheses, tells us that the sweater fits with 2" to 4" (5cm to 10cm) of ease between body measurement and finished garment.

Baby clothing usually gives the age of the child and the finished measurements.

> To fit 12–18 months, approximately 22" (56cm) chest circumference

Sizes for a hat pattern may look like this:

> To fit most adults, approximately 20" (51cm) circumference, unstretched.

Patterns for scarves, afghans and other nonwearables usually give finished measurements:

> Finished size: 6" (15cm) wide and 66" (167.5cm) long

KEEPING TRACK
Once you have purchased your pattern, make a photocopy and highlight the stitch counts for your size so you don't accidentally use the wrong one.

Yarn Requirements

Usually the exact yarn that was used in the photographed model will be listed here. The yarn specifications, color and amount should all be included.

> America's Favorite Yarn (50% wool, 50% cotton; 200 yds [183m] per 3.5 oz [100g]): 3 (3, 4) hanks of no. 001 red, 2 (3, 3) hanks of no. 002 white and 2 (2, 3) hanks of no. 003 blue

Needles

Some projects require only one size and type of needle, while others require more than one size or more than one type.

> Here are a few examples:
>
> US 6 (4mm) and US 8 (5mm) straight needles
>
> US 4 (3.5mm) and 5 (3.75mm) straight needles and one US 5 (3.75mm) circular needle 16" (40cm) long
>
> One US 4 (3.5mm) circular needle 16" (40cm) long and a set of four US 4 (3.5mm) double-point needles

Needle size is often followed by a statement such as "Adjust needle size if necessary to obtain the correct gauge." You are hereby advised to heed this message.

Gauge

The required gauge is given in Stockinette stitch, pattern stitch or both. If the project uses stitch patterns other than Stockinette stitch, yet only a Stockinette stitch gauge is given, it's assumed that if you get the stated gauge in Stockinette stitch, you'll get the correct gauge in pattern.

> Some possible examples:
>
> 18 stitches and 22 rows = 4" (10cm) in color pattern on larger needles
>
> 18 stitches and 22 rows = 4" (10cm) in Stockinette stitch, 21 stitches and 24 rows = 4" (10cm) in pattern on larger needles

The gauge is often followed by a statement such as "To save time, take time to check gauge." You are hereby advised to heed this message. Again. For more information about gauge and how it affects garment fit, see Chapter Twelve.

Other Supplies

A good pattern will also list any other supplies you'll need to work and complete the project, such as stitch markers, stitch holders, buttons or a crochet hook.

Abbreviations

It's very important that you have the definition of all abbreviations used in the pattern. If you're working from an individual pattern leaflet, all abbreviations should be listed with the pattern. If you're working from a pattern in a book, abbreviations that are common to several patterns may be listed in an appendix, with only special abbreviations used exclusively with your pattern listed on its page. Be sure that all abbreviations are defined because they do not always mean the same thing from one designer or publisher to another. See page 29 for a list of the most common abbreviations.

Pattern Stitches

Some patterns also list the various stitch patterns before the instructions begin and then refer to them by name within the instructions. For example, Seed Stitch may be listed as a pattern stitch. If there is a complicated sixteen-stitch and twelve-row pattern called Leaf and Vine that is worked within the instructions, the row-by-row instructions and/or a chart may be given outside the instructions. Within the instructions you may see something like this:

> **Row 1:** K1, inc 1, k6, seed 6, p2, C4B, p2, work Leaf and Vine over next 16 sts, p2, C4F, p2, seed 6, k6, inc 1, k1.

The Instructions

Patterns will begin with instructions for casting on and will be followed by some row-by-row directions and some instruction in plain-text form. Abbreviations abound, and punctuation may look peculiar.

Parentheses

As previously noted, parentheses are used to separate different sizes. Instructions for casting on may look like this:

With smaller needles, cast on 66 (74, 82) sts.

You'll cast on sixty-six stitches for the smallest size, seventy-four for the medium size or eighty-two for the largest size.

When the stitch count varies for the different sizes, these will appear in parentheses as follows.

Row 1: K1, inc 1, k6 (7, 8), seed 6 (6, 7), p2, C4B, p2, work Leaf and Vine over next 16 sts, p2, C4F, p2, seed 6 (6, 7), k6 (7, 8), inc 1, k1.

In addition to separating stitch counts for multiple sizes, parentheses are used to contain a set of instructions that will be worked more than one time. For example:

Row 1: K4, (yo, ssk) 3 times, k4.

This means that you knit four stitches, yarn over, slip slip knit, yarn over, slip slip knit, yarn over, slip slip knit, knit four.

You may have parentheses for both stitch repeats and sizes in the same row.

Row 1: K4, (yo, ssk) 3 (4, 5) times, k4.

Brackets

If a series of instructions to repeat contains a parenthetical repeat as described above, the whole series will be enclosed in brackets followed by the number of times to work it.

Row 1: K4, [p1, k1, p1, (yo, ssk) 3 (4, 5) times] twice, k4.

Here you repeat the yo, ssk the indicated number of times for each of the two times you work all the instructions within the brackets.

Asterisk

The asterisk is yet another device used to indicate a repetition of instructions.

Row 1: *K4, [p1, k1, p1, (yo, ssk) 3 (4, 5) times] twice; repeat from * to last 4 sts, k4.

This means that once you've worked the instructions between the brackets twice, you begin again at the asterisk.

Common Abbreviations

As previously noted, there's no absolute standard for abbreviations, so be sure to check for the specific meaning in the pattern you're using. Here are some common abbreviations and meanings.

alt	alternate	pfb	purl into the front and back of the same stitch
approx	approximately	pm	place marker
beg	begin/beginning	p2tog	purl two stitches together—one stitch decreased
BO	bind off	prev	previous
CA	color A	psso	pass slipped stitch over
CB	color B	pwise	purlwise
CC	contrasting color	rem	remain/remaining
cm	centimeter(s)	rep(s)	repeat(s)
cn	cable needle	rev St st	reverse Stockinette stitch
CO	cast on	RH	right hand
cont	continue	rnd(s)	round(s)
dec	decrease/decreases/decreasing	RS	right side
dpn	double-point needle	sk	skip
foll	follow/follows/following	skp	slip, knit, pass stitch over—one stitch decreased
g	gram	sk2p	slip one, knit two together, pass slipped stitch over the k2tog—two stitches decreased
inc	increase/increases/increasing		
k or K	knit	sl	slip
kfb	knit into the front and back of the same stitch	sl st(s)	slip stitch(es)
k2tog	knit two stitches together—one stitch decreased	sl 1k	slip one knitwise
kwise	knitwise	sl 1p	slip one purlwise
LH	left hand	sm	slip marker
M1	make one knit stitch	ssk	slip, slip, knit these two stitches together
M1L	make one left-leaning stitch	sssk	slip, slip, slip, knit these three stitches together
M1p	make one purl stitch	St st	Stockinette stitch
M1pL	make one left-leaning purl stitch	st(s)	stitch(es)
M1pR	make one right-leaning purl stitch	tbl	through back loop
M1R	make one right-leaning stitch	tog	together
m	meter(s)	WS	wrong side
MC	main color	wyb	with yarn in back
mm	millimeter(s)	wyf	with yarn in front
oz	ounce(s)	yd(s)	yard(s)
p or P	purl	yfwd	yarn forward
patt(s)	pattern(s)	yo	yarn over

Reading Charts

Many knitters, including us, prefer to work with charts rather than written-out instructions whenever possible. Charts are used for colorwork, pattern and cable work, and lace. A chart reflects what the actual knitting looks like, so if you lose your place, you can easily find it by comparing the two. Knitting progresses from the bottom up, so you begin working a chart with the bottom-most row. If you're working flat (back and forth), you'll read right-side rows from right to left and wrong-side rows from left to right. If you're working circularly (in the round), you'll read all rows of the chart from right to left.

TRACKING CHART PROGRESS
Sticky notes come in very handy for keeping your place on a chart. Stick the note on the chart so it's just above the row you're about to work. Placing the note above the worked rows rather than below allows you to compare the chart to the actual knitting.

Beady Cable chart

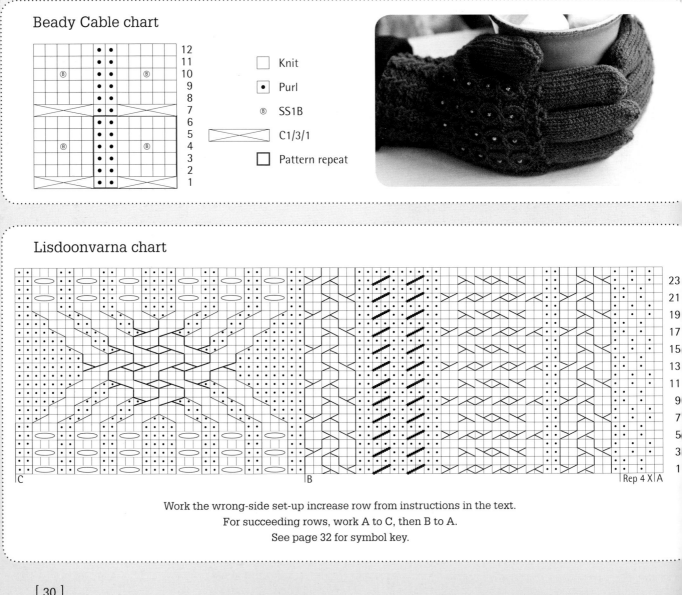

Knit

Purl

Ⓑ **SS1B**

C1/3/1

☐ **Pattern repeat**

Lisdoonvarna chart

Work the wrong-side set-up increase row from instructions in the text.
For succeeding rows, work A to C, then B to A.
See page 32 for symbol key.

Charts can be used to plot out a stitch pattern that will be worked within an otherwise simply knit piece, such as the Beady Cable chart (on previous page), a large segment of a garment such as a sweater front or back from seam to seam, such as the Lisdoonvarna chart (on previous page), or even a whole garment. Pattern repeats will usually be indicated with bold lines forming a box around the repeat or on either side of the first and last stitches of a repeat.

Charts for Colorwork

Charts used for colorwork are most often presented in color, where each color closely resembles the color of yarn used for that stitch. However, if printing in color is not an option, each color will be represented by a different symbol.

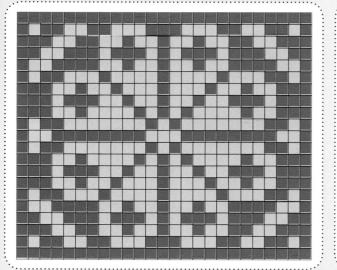

Colored color chart

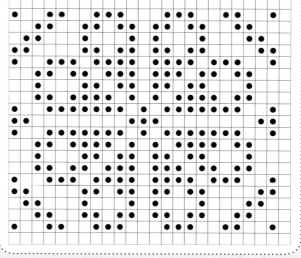

Symbol color chart

CHECKING A CHART FOR YOUR SIZE

To be sure that the number of stitches given in a chart is correct for your size, count the stitches outside the pattern repeat and subtract them from the total number of stitches indicated for your size. Divide the remainder by the number of stitches in the pattern repeat. The result is the number of times you'll work the pattern repeat in the row. If the result isn't a whole number, there's a problem. Be sure you've located the correct starting and ending point for your size.

Common Chart Symbols

Charts used for stitch work use a series of symbols that represent one or more stitches. As for written abbreviations, there's no absolute standard for these symbols, but here we'll present commonly used symbols.

	K on RS, p on WS
•	P on RS, k on WS
O	Yarn over (yo)
/	K2tog on RS, p2tog on WS
\	Ssk on RS, ssp on WS
	Right-slanting increase
	Left-slanting increase
	Right-slanting purl increase
	Left-slanting purl increase
	Slip 2 tog pwise, k1, pass 2 slipped stitches over
	Slip 1, k2tog, pass slipped stitch over
	K1tbl on RS, p1tbl on WS
V	Slip 1 pwise with yarn on WS
	Slip 1 pwise with yarn on RS
●	Bobble
■	Stitches do not exist in these areas of the chart
	Bind off
	Pattern repeat

	2/2 right cable
	2/2 left cable
	K2/p2 right cable
	K2/p2 left cable
	2/1 right cable
	2/1 left cable
	K2/p1 right cable
	K2/p1 left cable
	1/2 right cable
	1/2 left cable
	K1/p2 right cable
	K1/p2 left cable
	3/3 right cable
	3/3 left cable
	K3/p3 right cable
	K3/p3 left cable
	3/1 right cable
	3/1 left cable
	K3/p1 right cable
	K3/p1 left cable
	1/3 right cable
	1/3 left cable
	K1/p3 right cable
	K1/p3 left cable

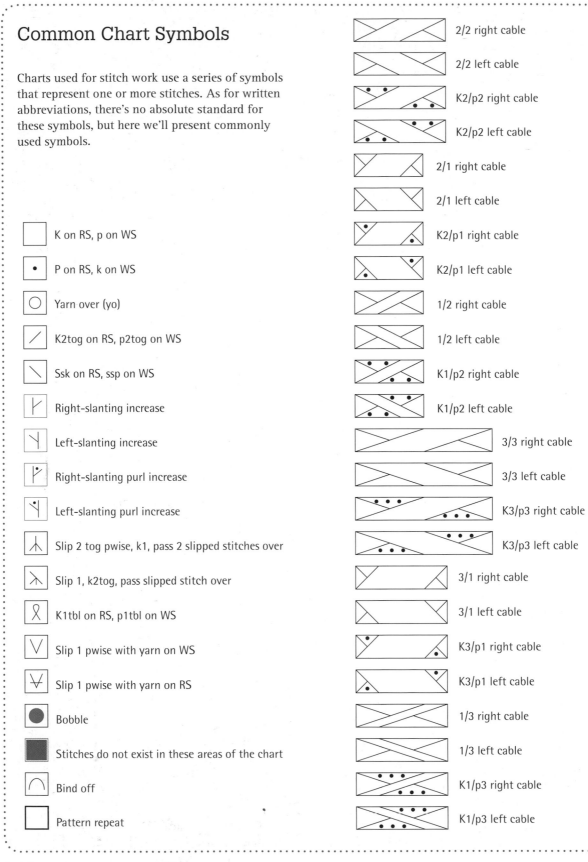

Part II
The Basics

We've both said many times that all you have to know in order to work a project is how to knit and how to purl, but you'll see in this next section that there's actually a bit more to it.

In Chapter Four we begin with these two simple stitches and then show you what happens when you alter the way they're made, combine the two or alter and combine them. You'll see the difference between Continental and English knitting styles, how to start new yarns and weave in ends and how to fix mistakes.

Every knitted piece (hold on—in deference to the enormous amount of creativity out there in the Knitting Queendom, let's say most knitted pieces) has at least two edges: a cast-on edge and a bound-off edge. Pieces that are knit back and forth, as opposed to in the round, also have selvedge edges. In Chapter Five we discuss various ways of forming these edges and the properties of each. It's our hope that you'll experiment with different methods and become comfortable enough with them to incorporate them into any pattern.

Chapter Six addresses the techniques used for shaping knitted pieces: increasing, decreasing and using short rows. There are many, many ways to get from the beginning to the end of every knitting project, but armed with the knowledge of how the various methods affect the results, you're free to be the perfectionist you've always wanted to be. Many knitting patterns don't specify a particular method to use when increasing and decreasing, so if you can make informed choices, you can raise the bar of knitting excellence.

In Chapter Seven we examine flat and circular knitting and the special requirements for each. For example, if you're knitting a sweater in four pieces—back, front and two sleeves—you'll have to seam those pieces together. Believe it or not, it's best to decide before you even cast on which method you'll use for seaming so you can create the appropriate edges as you work. Circular knitting has some special requirements, from joining the stitches to forming a round to making steeks, and we cover those techniques here.

4 The Stitches

K nitted fabric is made one stitch at a time. The two basic stitches are knit and purl—once you've mastered these, you can put them together in various ways to create a boundless library of textures and patterns.

The Knit Stitch

A knit stitch looks like the letter V. On the needle it's a loop coming out of a V in the row below. With a regular knit stitch, the front of the stitch will be slightly to the right of the back of the stitch.

1 Insert the right needle into the front of the stitch on the left needle from front to back.

2 Wrap the yarn under and around the right needle from back to front.

3 Move the right needle to the front, bringing a loop of yarn forward, and then drop the stitch from the left needle. You now have one new knit stitch on the right needle.

The Purl Stitch

A purl stitch looks like a bump. On the needle it's a loop coming out of a horizontal bar at its base. With a regular purl stitch, the front of the stitch will be slightly to the right of the back of the stitch.

1 With the yarn forward, insert the right needle into the front of the stitch on the left needle from back to front.

2 Wrap the yarn over and around the right needle from back to front.

3 Move the right needle to the back, bringing a loop of yarn backward, and then drop the stitch from the left needle. You now have one new purl stitch on the right needle.

Twisting Stitches

Knit and purl stitches can be altered for decorative effect. One way to do this is to twist the stitch.

Twisted stitches are tighter than regular stitches, and if you work them at the same spot on every row, they stand up and get noticed. Twisted stitches are used decoratively in ribs, patterns and outlines and also in certain decreases—the latter will be covered in Chapter Six.

Regular knit stitch

Twisted knit stitch

Twisted Knit Stitch

When you knit a stitch through the back loop, the resulting stitch is twisted at the base and leans to the left.

1 Insert the right needle into the back of the stitch on the left needle from front to back.

2 Wrap the yarn under and around the right needle from back to front, as for a regular knit stitch.

3 Move the right needle to the front, bringing a loop of yarn forward, and then drop the stitch from the left needle.

4 Notice that the front of the loop is slightly to the left of the back of the loop.

Twisted Purl Stitch

You can also purl a stitch through the back loop on the wrong side to get a twisted stitch.

1 With the yarn forward, insert the right needle into the back of the stitch on the left needle from back to front.

2 Wrap the yarn over and around the right needle from back to front, as for a regular purl stitch.

3 Move the right needle to the back, bringing a loop of yarn backward, and then drop the stitch from the left needle.

4 The stitch will appear twisted on the right side.

Slipping Stitches

Slipping a stitch means simply moving a stitch from the left to the right needle.

Slip stitches are used to make various texture and color patterns, as well as for parts of some decreases. These will be covered in the appropriate chapters.

Slipped stitches purlwise

Slipped stitches knitwise

Slipped Stitch Purlwise

1 Insert the right needle as if you were going to purl the stitch.

2 Transfer the stitch from the left needle to the right needle. The stitch will be in the regular orientation, with the front of the stitch being slightly to the right of the back of the stitch.

Slipped Stitch Knitwise

1 Insert the right needle as if you were going to knit the stitch.

2 Transfer the stitch from the left needle to the right needle. The stitch will be twisted, and what was the front of the stitch is now at the back.

Combining Knits and Purls

Here's where the fun begins. Combining knits and purls in a planned way makes different stitch patterns.

Garter Stitch

If you knit all the stitches on both right- and wrong-side rows, the result is garter stitch—all the stitches have a horizontal bar at the bottom. Garter-stitch rows are compressed, and the resulting fabric is thicker than Stockinette stitch. You will get the same result if you purl all the stitches. To work garter stitch in the round, alternate one round of knit stitches with one round of purl stitches.

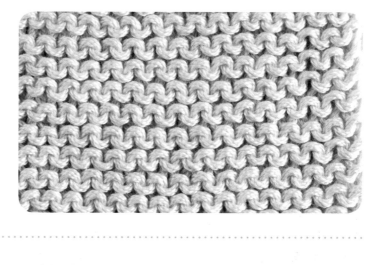

Stockinette Stitch

This is probably one of the most widely used stitch patterns. The result is a fabric that's smooth—on the right side all the stitches look like Vs, and on the wrong side all the stitches look like interlocking Us. To work Stockinette stitch back and forth, alternate one row of knit stitches (the right side) with one row of purl stitches (the wrong side). To work Stockinette stitch in the round, knit all stitches in all rounds.

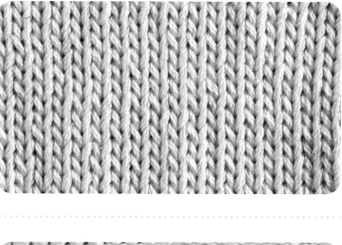

Reverse Stockinette Stitch

Reverse Stockinette stitch is the same as Stockinette stitch but using the purl side as the right side of the work. Reverse Stockinette stitch is often used as a background for cables and other textured designs.

Ribbing

Ribbing involves making columns of knit and purl stitches. The purl stitches will lie recessed between the knit stitches, and the fabric will collapse accordion style. Ribbings are often described as 1/1, 2/2, 3/1, etc. For a 1/1 rib, knit one, purl one and repeat. For a 2/2 rib, knit two, purl two and repeat. For a 3/1 rib, knit three, purl one and repeat. You can also use twisted stitches for decorative effect.

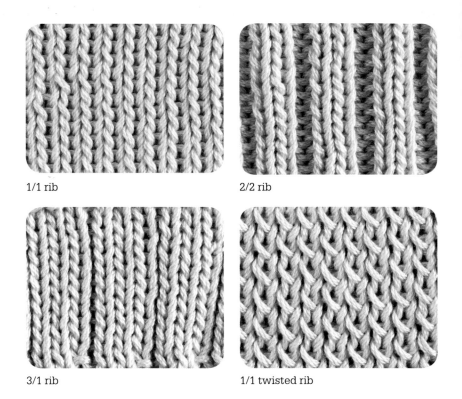

1/1 rib

2/2 rib

3/1 rib

1/1 twisted rib

Seed Stitch

This stitch is essentially a checkerboard of knit and purl stitches. To work the first row, knit one, purl one and repeat to the end of the row. On subsequent rows, knit the stitches that look like purls and purl the stitches that look like knits. This puts a purl on top of a knit and a knit on top of a purl on both sides.

From here the possibilities are endless. By strategically placing knit and purl stitches according to a plan, you can create all kinds of textured and graphic fabric.

Other Ways to Manipulate Stitches

Knit and purl stitches can be crossed to produce traveling stitch patterns and cables.

Right Cross

In a right cross, two stitches are crossed so the front stitch slants from left to right.

Left cross

Right cross

1 Pass in front of the first stitch on the left needle and insert the right needle into the second stitch.

2 Knit this stitch but leave it on the needle.

3 Insert the right needle into the first stitch on the left needle.

4 Knit this stitch and drop both stitches from the left needle.

Left Cross

In a left cross, two stitches are crossed so the front stitch slants from right to left.

1 Pass behind the first stitch on the left needle and insert the right needle into the back loop of the second stitch.

2 Knit this stitch but leave it on the needle.

3 Insert the right needle into the front loop of the first stitch on the left needle and knit this stitch.

4 Drop both stitches from the left needle.

Cables

Cables involve crossing two or more stitches over other stitches. Some knitters advocate doing this without a cable needle; we both feel that the time and effort involved, coupled with the risk of dropping stitches, makes a cable needle an essential tool.

Cable crossings are often described as 2/2L (two over two left), 3/2R (three over two right), etc. The first number is the number of stitches that will cross in front; the second number is the number of stitches you'll be crossing. The L or R indicates whether the front stitches will cross from right to left (L) or left to right (R). You will sometimes also see a P in the formula, in which P stands for "purl" and the knit stitches will be passing over the purl stitches.

For a more in-depth conversation on cables, see Chapter Nine.

2/2 Left Cable

In a 2/2 left cable, the two front stitches will cross from right to left over the two back stitches.

1 Slip two stitches (without twisting them!) onto a cable needle and hold them to the front of the work.

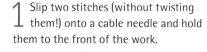

2 Knit two stitches from the left needle.

3 Knit the two stitches from the cable needle.

NOTE: *You may place the two stitches from the cable needle onto the left needle and knit them from there, or knit them directly from the cable needle.*

3/2R Cable
In a 3/2R cable, the three front stitches will cross from left to right over the two back stitches.

1 Slip two stitches (without twisting them!) onto a cable needle and hold them to the back of the work.

2 Knit three stitches from the left needle, then knit the two stitches from the cable needle.

NOTE: *Here we find it easier to place the stitches from the cable needle back onto the left needle and then knit them from there.*

Drop Stitches

While usually we try very hard not to drop any stitches while knitting, you can plan to do this for an openwork pattern. This usually involves wrapping the yarn one or more times around the needle (this is a yarn over [yo]) in one row and then dropping the yarn-over loops from the needle in the next row. In this example (below, left), two yarn overs are worked between the knit stitches on a right-side row, and then the wrong-side row is purled, dropping the yarn-over loops from the needle. Another possibility is to drop and unravel stitches down over more than one row, usually down to where a yarn over was placed (below, right).

Dropped yarn over pattern

Raveled drop-stitch pattern

Styles of Knitting

While there is no absolutely right or wrong way to knit, the most common is the Western style, which uses stitches formed as described on pages 36 and 37. Western knitting can be done by "throwing" or "picking." A few other methods follow these basics.

English Knitting, or "Throwing"

This is the style of knitting used by most of the American knitters we've met. The working yarn is held in the right hand and wrapped or "thrown" around the needle to form a stitch. Wrap the working yarn loosely around your right pinkie, about 3" to 4" (7.5cm to 10cm) from the work. This will keep some tension on the yarn as you work. To form a stitch, insert the right needle into the stitch on the left needle, move your right hand to wrap the yarn around the needle in the appropriate way and finish the stitch.

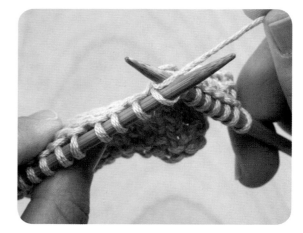

Continental Knitting, or "Picking"

This is the style of knitting used by many knitters with western European roots. The working yarn is held in the left hand, and you use the right needle to "pick" a loop of yarn to form a stitch. Wrap the working yarn loosely around your left index finger or around your left pinkie and over the top of your left index finger. To form a stitch, insert the right needle into the stitch on the left needle and then move the right needle around the yarn coming off the index finger to grab a loop to pull through and finish the stitch.

Crossed Knitting

We've seen knitters who work every stitch through the back. Working Stockinette stitch this way makes the stitches look a little smaller and the running thread between them a little larger. We're not recommending this method but just letting you know we've seen it.

Eastern Knitting

Eastern knitting also involves knitting and purling into the backs of stitches, but in addition the yarn is worked around the needle in the opposite direction from English and Continental. Stockinette stitch worked this way looks very similar to English or Continental Stockinette stitch, but the stitches are more compact. Again, we're not recommending this method. If a compact fabric is desired, we recommend working on smaller needles.

Eastern Knit Stitch

To work a knit stitch, insert the needle from front to back through the back of the stitch and then bring the yarn over the top of the needle from back to front and finish the stitch.

Eastern Purl Stitch

To work a purl a stitch, insert the needle from back to front through the back of the stitch and then bring the yarn under and around the needle from front to back and finish the stitch.

COMBINING METHODS
It's possible to work one row in the English or Continental style and the next in the Eastern style. This method is used for bead knitting to keep the fabric from biasing (see Chapter Eleven).

LEFT-HANDED KNITTING
We've seen some very interesting methods employed by our left-handed knitting friends! Because we live in a right-handed world, it's best if lefties can work the same way as outlined for either the English or Continental methods. At the very least, lefties must work in the same direction, from right to left, in order to follow patterns and charts.

Starting a New Yarn and Weaving in the Ends

If you're working on a piece that will be seamed, it's easiest to begin a new yarn at the beginning or the end of a row and then weave the ends into the seam allowance. However, if you're working in the round or on a piece with finished edges such as a scarf, you'll need to start the new yarn in the body of the knitting.

Split-Ply Method

The split-ply method is the best way to weave ends into a Stockinette-stitch piece that's worked without seams; it's nearly invisible to both sight and touch.

If you're working with a singles yarn you can't split into plies, carefully separate the single into two or more strands, keeping the original twist in each strand. If you're working with a novelty tape or cord, consider using scissors to split it in half before weaving. If you're faced with a yarn you can't split, you have no choice but to weave in the full tails.

1 Work until you have about 6" (15cm) of yarn left and drop the yarn tail in the back of the work. Pick up the new yarn, leaving a tail about 6" (15cm) long at the back, and work a few stitches. Return to the two tails, cross one over the other and make a half knot.

2 Snug the knot to the needle and make a slipknot. This will hold the yarn firmly in place as you continue. You can return to this area to weave in the ends after working a few rows or wait until you are finished knitting.

3 Release the slipknot and split the yarn into plies. Depending on how many plies are in the strand, thread one or two at a time onto a tapestry needle and weave them into the back of the work, following the curve of the stitches, working each ply into a different row and working the new and the old yarn in opposite directions.

Full-Strand Method

If you're working cables or another highly textured pattern, you can probably weave in full strands, or at least half strands, without affecting the density of the fabric. As with the split-ply method, follow the curve of the stitches and work the new and old yarns in opposite directions.

Fixing Mistakes

The best way to ensure accurate knitting is to count off a pattern as you work and to stop often and admire what you've done. This way you can either prevent the mistake from happening in the first place or find the mistake before you've gone too far to fix it.

....

Backing Up to Fix a Stitch in the Current Row

If you're paying really close attention as noted earlier, chances are good you'll recognize a mistake very soon after you've made it. In this case, you can back out of the row to the mistake, fix it and move on.

However, if you do make a mistake, here's a mantra to keep in mind: "You can't knit without a crochet hook." The hook is the tool for fixing mistakes, which usually requires picking up dropped stitches or dropping down to an incorrectly worked stitch, making the correction and working it back up.

Undoing a Knit Stitch

1 Insert the left needle from left to right into the right loop below the most recently made knit stitch.

2 Drop the stitch from the right needle and pull the working yarn to remove the loop.

....

Undoing a Purl Stitch

1 Insert the left needle from front to back into the loop below the most recently made purl stitch.

2 Drop the stitch from the right needle and pull the working yarn to remove the loop.

Picking up Dropped Stitches

If your stitch count is wrong or you discover a hole in the knitting that was not intentionally made with a yarn over, you may have dropped a stitch. Check the knitting carefully and look for a loose loop that's not worked into the rest of the knitting.

If the dropped stitch is many rows back and you've somehow managed to keep in pattern, you can tie the stitch off with a short length of yarn and weave the ends into the back.

1 If the stitch is three or fewer rows down from the top, you can usually pick it up with a crochet hook and work it back up.

2 Working on the right side of the Stockinette stitch, hook the stitch from front to back.

3 Pick up the bar above the stitch and pull it through to make a new stitch.

4 Snug the stitch up and continue until you can place the stitch back on the needle.

Picking Up a Dropped Edge Stitch

If you look closely at a Stockinette-stitch swatch, you'll see that the edge stitches comprise a series of loops and knots. When knitting a right-side row, a knot forms below the first stitch, and a loop forms below the last stitch. The same thing happens when purling a wrong-side row; a knot forms below the first stitch, and a loop forms below the last stitch. If you drop an edge stitch, you'll need to re-create this series.

1 If your dropped stitch went down four rows, you'll have a vertical loop at the bottom, which is the stitch, and a larger horizontal loop above it—the bottom of this loop comes from one row, the top from another. Note that the stitch has a knot at the base.

2 Insert a crochet hook from front to back into the stitch and then insert the hook from back to front into the large loop and pull it through the stitch.

3 Remove the crochet hook and insert it through the stitch just formed from back to front and then from front to back through the large loop again. Pull the loop through the stitch.

4 Leave the stitch on the hook and draw the working yarn through the last loop and place it on the needle. Our example shows a stitch dropped four rows—the method would be the same for more rows.

Fixing an Incorrectly Worked Stitch

If you find a stitch many rows back that should have been purled instead of knit or vice versa, it may be possible to ravel down to the stitch, rework it and then work back up to the top.

1 The purled stitch that should have been knitted is clearly visible.

2 Follow the mistake up the column to the needle. Drop the stitch at the top of the column off the needle and ravel it down through the error.

3 Correct the stitch and work it back up the ladder.

Ripping Out

To be a flawless knitter, you have to be willing to unknit. Some mistakes just can't be fixed without going back to the error and starting over from there. If you have many rows to unravel, mark the row where you want to restart the knitting, drop all the stitches from the needle and unravel to the row above the marked row. Remove the last row stitch by stitch, placing the stitches as they're unworked back onto the needle. If you've somehow ended up with a twisted stitch on the needle, there's no need to move it into the correct position—simply work it through the back loop, and it will twist back into the correct position.

If the raveled yarn isn't too kinky, go ahead and reknit with it the way it is. However, if the knitting was done some time ago, chances are the yarn has kinked, and this will cause the new knitting to have ridges in it. So what do you do with all that kinky yarn? Cut the yarn from the garment, leaving a 6" (15cm) tail to weave in later. Wind the yarn around your elbow and your thumb, making large loops. When all the used yarn is wound, remove the loop from your arm and tie a couple of scraps of yarn around the hank to keep it together. Now you can steam out the kinks in one of two ways: Place the yarn in a vegetable steamer with 1/2" (13mm) of water in the pot. Make sure the water doesn't touch the yarn. Place a double layer of paper towels over the top of the steamer and put a lid on the pot. The paper towels will absorb condensation and keep the yarn dry. Steam over low heat, checking often to add water if necessary or replace paper towels when they're too wet, until there are no more kinks. You could also place the yarn on a flat surface and steam it with steam from your iron, holding the iron at least 4" (10cm) away to keep from saturating the yarn. If the kinks don't come out with steam, immerse the yarn in water, gently squeeze to remove the excess and allow it to dry.

5 The Edges

Although the edges make up a minimal part of a knitted project, they can often determine the degree of success of the finished piece. There are more ways to cast on, work selvedges and bind off than we include here. What follows are the methods we turn to over and over again, and those that we teach in our classes.

Casting On

The goal in choosing a cast on is to use one that gives you the look you want and the desired elasticity. Elasticity may be crucial to usability—if the cast on at the top of a sock is too tight, it won't fit comfortably around the calf.

> **THE CARDINAL RULE OF CASTING ON**
> If you want an elastic edge, cast on with a needle at least two sizes larger than what you'll be knitting with or cast on holding two needles together. Once the stitches are cast on, begin the first row with the needle called for in the pattern.

Elastic Cast Ons

Choose an elastic cast on for the bottoms of sweaters, sleeve cuffs, tops of socks and anywhere else you may need extra stretch.

Long-Tail Cast On

The long-tail cast on is one of the most commonly used cast ons. It is very elastic, and because it puts a knit stitch on the needle, it's a great choice for knitting in the round. If you're working back and forth, when you turn the needle around you'll have purl stitches facing, so the first row should be a wrong-side row; this depends, of course, on what you're knitting.

You'll need a tail long enough to cast on all the stitches. One way to estimate is to wrap the yarn around the needle ten times, measure the amount used and multiply based on the required stitch count. For example, if ten wraps = 5" (12.5cm), and you want to cast on one-hundred stitches, you'll need 50" (127cm).

1 In your left hand, pass the yarn around your thumb and index finger and then place both the tail and the ball yarn in your palm. Hold on to both ends with the other three fingers. With a needle in your right hand, bring the point down behind the strand between the thumb and index finger and then toward you, twisting it clockwise to put a loop on the needle. We use this method for the first stitch in lieu of a slipknot.

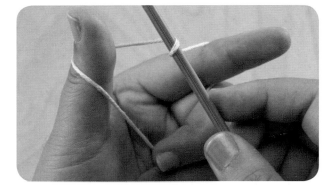

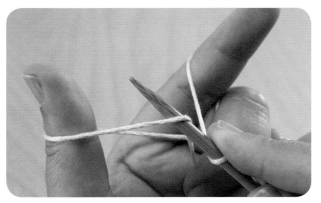

2 *Pass the needle up through the loop of yarn around your thumb, hooking the front strand.

3 Pass behind the strand on your index finger from right to left. Bring the needle and yarn down through the loop on your thumb.

4 Drop the loop from your thumb and gently tug on the strands to tighten the cast-on stitch.

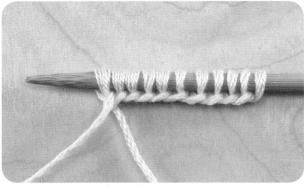

5 Repeat from * to cast on the remaining stitches.

Elastic Cast Ons (continued)

Left-Handed Long-Tail Cast On

This is basically the mirror image of the "regular" long-tail cast on. Because you're casting onto the left needle, you'll have knit stitches facing you for the first row in back-and-forth knitting.

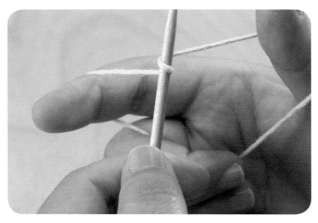

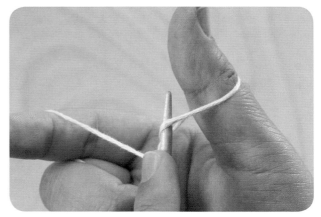

1 In your right hand, pass the yarn around your thumb and index finger and then place both the tail and the ball yarn in your palm. Hold onto both ends with the other three fingers. With a needle in your left hand, bring the point down behind the strand between the thumb and index finger and then away from you, twisting it counterclockwise to put a loop on the needle.

2 *Pass the needle up through the loop of yarn around your thumb, hooking the front strand.

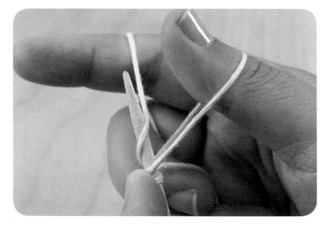

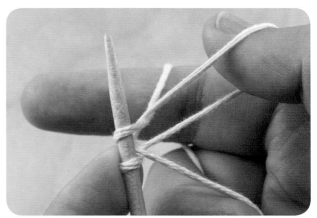

3 Pass behind the front strand on your index finger from left to right.

4 Bring the needle and yarn down through the loop on your thumb.

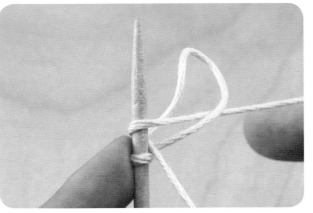

5 Drop the loop from your thumb and gently tug on the strands to tighten the cast-on stitch.

6 Repeat from * to cast on the remaining stitches.

LOCKING IN THE CAST-ON TAIL

If you work with the ball yarn over your thumb and the tail over your index finger, you can lock in the tail so it stays in place and is in perfect position to begin seaming. To lock in the tail of a long-tail cast on, place the tail over the working yarn from back to front before working the first stitch. When you've finished the row or round, pull down on the tail to lock it in place.

Long-tail cast on, not locked

Long-tail cast on, locked

Long-Tail Cast-On Variation

This variation is basically the reverse of the "regular" long-tail cast on. If you turn the work for back-and-forth knitting, you'll have knit stitches facing you for the first row.

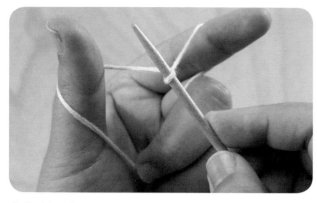

1 Position the yarn as described for the long-tail cast on, making one stitch without a knot.

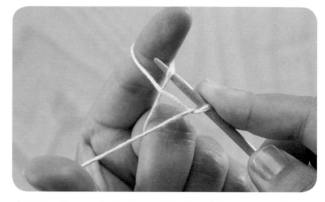

2 *Pass the needle tip through the loop of yarn around your index finger from back to front, hooking the back strand.

3 Pass behind and under the strand on the back of your thumb. Bring the needle and yarn up through the loop on your index finger. This locks the end stitch and the first stitch made and places a horizontal bar under the stitch.

4 Drop the loop from your index finger and gently tug on the strands to tighten the cast-on stitch. Repeat from * to cast on the required number of stitches.

Long-Tail Knit/Purl Cast On

This is a combination of the "regular" long-tail cast on and the variation. Simply alternate the two cast-on methods to put both knit and purl stitches on the needle. Use this to cast on for ribbings or for seed or moss stitch. If the work is turned for flat knitting, stitches cast on the regular way will be purls on the right side, and stitches cast on with the variation will be knits on the right side.

CASTING ON FOR SEAMED EDGES

Leave a Tail for Seaming
Leave a tail long enough to sew an entire seam. Wind this tail into a "butterfly" by wrapping the yarn in a figure-eight pattern around your thumb and index finger. When you have about 4" (10cm) left, wrap the tail around the center of the figure eight and make two half hitches.

Mark the First Seam Stitches
Tie a piece of thin cotton yarn between the first and second stitches and the last and next-to-last stitches. When the time comes to join, you'll know exactly where the starting seam stitch is.

German Twisted Cast On

This cast on has an extra twist at the base and is very elastic.

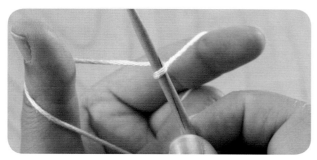

1 Hold the yarn as for a long-tail cast on.

2 *Bring the needle under both strands on the thumb from front to back.

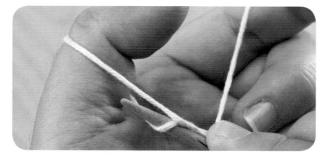

3 Then bring the needle down through the loop on the thumb.

4 Pick up the strand on your index finger—you'll have a figure-eight loop coming off your thumb—and pass straight down through the loop closest to the needle.

5 Drop the loop from your thumb and tighten the stitch. Repeat from * to cast on the required number of stitches.

Tubular Cast On

Use this cast on when you're knitting in the round and beginning with a 1/1 rib. It is very elastic and a great choice for sleeves or sock cuffs.

Rib with ravel and waste yarn

Using waste yarn and your method of choice, cast on half the number of stitches needed and knit two rows. Divide the stitches onto four double-point needles, join for working in the round and knit two more rounds with waste yarn. With a smooth cotton or nylon ravel cord, knit one round. Join the main yarn and proceed as follows.

Round 1: *K1, yo; repeat from * to end of round.
Round 2: *K1, yarn forward, slip 1 purlwise, yarn back; repeat from * to end of round.
Round 3: *Yarn back, slip 1 purlwise, yarn forward, p1; repeat from * to end of round.
Round 4: *K1, p1: repeat from * to end of round.

At this point you can change to 2/2 rib as follows. *Knit one, skip the purl stitch, insert needle through front of second stitch, knit it and leave it on the needle, purl the skipped stitch, drop both stitches from the needle and purl the next stitch; repeat from * to end of round.

If you prefer, you can work this round with a cable needle as follows: *Knit one, place the next purl stitch on a cable needle to the back, knit the next stitch, purl the stitch on the cable needle and the next stitch on the needle. Repeat from * to end of round. When you've completed the rib, wrap the cotton or nylon ravel cord around one finger and pull gently to remove it from the work.

Firm Cast Ons

Choose a firm cast on for edges that don't need to stretch, such as scarves, pillows and afghans.

Knitted Cast On

This cast on, while firm, results in a loose edge of stitches, great for picking up for mitered knitting or for adding a border.

1 Place a slipknot on the left needle. *Insert the right needle into the loop and knit one stitch.

2 Insert the left needle into the front of this stitch and slip it to the left needle. Repeat from * to cast on the remaining stitches. The right side of the work is facing when you finish casting on.

Cable Cast On

This cast on is similar to a knitted cast on but with a tighter edge.

1 Begin as for the knitted cast on so you have two stitches on the left needle. *Insert the right needle between the two stitches and knit one.

2 Insert the left needle into the front of this stitch and slip it to the left needle. Repeat from * to cast on the remaining stitches. The right side of the work is facing you when you cast on.

Provisional Cast Ons

Use a provisional cast on when you want to keep the edge stitches live and return to them later.

For example, if you can't decide what kind of ribbing or border you want on a sweater, you can go back when you've finished and knit the border in the opposite direction. A provisional cast on works well for a turned hem or a neckline if you're working top down—hemming with live stitches is very elastic. You can also use provisional cast ons to create pieces with matching ends such as scarves—cast on provisionally and work one half of the scarf, then go back and put the cast-on stitches on the needles and knit the other half in the opposite direction. Done correctly, the change in direction will be almost invisible.

A very easy method is to simply cast on with waste yarn and begin knitting with the project yarn. Carefully cut the waste yarn out of the stitches to free them for finishing.

Stockinette stitch is provisionally cast on, then the rib is knit in the opposite direction.

Crochet Chain Cast On

You'll need a crochet hook that is larger than the corresponding knitting needle size you'll be using and waste yarn that is the same weight or heavier than your project yarn.

1 Crochet a chain with six to ten more stitches than the required cast-on stitches and fasten the end loosely so it won't unravel. Pick up and knit the required number of stitches through the bumps on the back of the chain, beginning with the last chain made.

2 When picking up the cast-on stitches, you're actually picking up between the stitches, so the new stitches are a half stitch off-center of the original stitches. This means you'll have a half stitch at each end of the original stitches. To maintain the correct stitch count, convert one of these half stitches into a whole stitch. It's easiest to do this at the end of the cast on without the tail. Unravel to expose the live stitches one at a time and place them on a needle, making sure none of them are twisted.

3 At the end of the cast-on stitches, the waste yarn passes through a half stitch below the last full stitch. Simply place this loop on the needle and treat it like a regular stitch.

Crochet Over the Needle Cast On

This cast on will yield the same results as the crochet chain cast on. You'll need a crochet hook and waste yarn.

1 Using waste yarn, chain six to ten stitches. Hold the ball yarn, chain and needle in your left hand and the hook in your right hand. *Bring the waste yarn under the needle. Bring the crochet hook over the needle, wrap the yarn around the crochet hook and draw the yarn through, forming a stitch on the needle.

2 Bring the yarn back under the crochet hook. Repeat from * to cast on the required number of stitches. Chain ten and fasten off loosely.

Work one plain knit or purl row before beginning a pattern. If you get to the end of the stitches and realize you have too few, knit or purl the necessary stitches into the back of the beginning chain as for the crochet chain cast on. When you're ready to use the stitches, unravel the chain and place the stitches on a needle as for the crochet chain cast on, converting one of the half stitches into a regular stitch.

Invisible Provisional Cast On

Unlike the two crochet methods described previously, with this provisional cast on you can work the first row with both knits and purls—there's no need to work a plain knit or purl row first.

1 With the waste yarn and main yarn held together, make a slipknot with an 8" (20.5cm) tail and place it on the needle. With your palm facing downward, the main yarn over your index finger and the waste yarn over your thumb, *bring the needle under the waste yarn from front to back, then pass over the top of the main yarn.

2 Bring the main yarn under the waste yarn from back to front, completing the first stitch.

3 Now bring the needle over and under the main yarn, placing the yarn over the needle from front to back to form the second stitch. Repeat from * to cast on the required number of stitches—do not include the slipknot in the count.

When you return to put the provisional stitches back on a needle for working, you'll note that every other stitch is twisted. You can leave them this way if you're going to work a rib, treating the twisted stitches as purls, or you can knit into the back of the twisted stitches for Stockinette or another stitch pattern. Place the stitches on a needle, undo the slipknot and pull out the waste yarn.

Center-Start Circular Cast Ons

Use these methods to start a toe-up sock or a top-down hat.

. . . .

Cast On and Divide

Many patterns call for casting on eight stitches and dividing onto four double-point needles. If you find this awkward, cast on the eight stitches and slip four stitches to a second needle. Join into a round and knit two onto each of four needles. Knitting them onto the four needles is a bit more stable than dividing them and then knitting. You can also knit the four stitches on each of the two needles and divide them onto four needles on the second round.

. . . .

Crochet Circular Cast On

This method makes a neat beginning with no bulk.

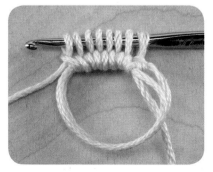

1 Leaving a 4" (10cm) tail to be woven in later, wrap the ball yarn twice loosely around your thumb. Remove the loop from your thumb. Work eight single crochets into the loop, leaving the stitches on the crochet hook.

2 Distribute the stitches onto four double-point needles, two stitches on each needle.

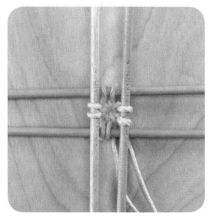

3 Pull up on the tail to snug the stitches into a tight ring.

Decorative Cast Ons

Here are a few cast ons that will add a little something extra to your knitting.

Two-Color Long-Tail Cast On

If you use two colors with the long-tail cast on, the color around your thumb will be the base of the work, providing a thin contrasting border.

Picot Cast On

Use the cable method to cast on five stitches. Bind off two stitches and place the remaining stitch from the right needle onto the left needle. Undo the slipknot at the beginning to neaten up the start. *Use the cable cast-on method (see page 62) to cast on four stitches, bind off two stitches and place the remaining stitch from the right needle to the left needle. Repeat from * for the desired (even) number of stitches on the needle.

Casting On Additional Stitches at the End of a Row

Sometimes you'll need to cast on more stitches at the end of a knitted row; for example, if you're knitting a sweater front or back in one piece, you'll need to cast on for the sleeves. Here are a couple of methods.

Backward-Loop Cast On

This cast on, also known as the e-wrap or single cast on, can be used to begin a project, but because the stitches formed this way are tight and can be difficult to knit into, we usually reserve it for adding stitches to an already knitted row.

Hold the needle with the stitches in your right hand and the working yarn in your left hand. Wrap the yarn around your left index finger from front to back, insert the needle under the yarn on the front of your index finger, remove the loop and tighten up the stitch.

Added Knitted Cast On

After finishing a purl row in Stockinette stitch, turn the work and use the knitted cast on (see page 62).

Added Purled Cast On

After finishing a knit row in Stockinette stitch, turn the work and *insert the needle from back to front in the last stitch, purl and place the resulting stitch on the needle. Repeat from * to cast on the remaining stitches.

Selvedge Edges

One of our favorite knitting questions is "What do you think about slipping the first stitch of every row?" How you work the selvedges largely depends on what will happen with the edges once they're knitted. Will it be the finished edge of a scarf? Will it be sewn together with another edge? Will you be picking up the stitches and knitting off them? Each one of these scenarios calls for a different type of edge.

Finished Selvedges

Choose one of these edges for a scarf or other project that won't be seamed.

Twisted Slip-Stitch Edge
Slipping the first stitch knitwise and purling the last stitch of every row produces a very neat edge with a twisted stitch.

Color Slip-Stitch Edge
This edge looks especially nice when you're working garter stitch in a two-color stripe pattern with two rows of each color.

Selvedges for Seaming

If you're going to work a mattress stitch seam (see Chapter Seven), keep the first and last stitch of every row in Stockinette stitch. This edge stitch may or may not be included in your knitting instructions. If it is, that fact is usually pointed out. If it is not included, add two stitches when you're casting on and work them in addition to the stitches in the instructions.

Selvedges for Picking Up

Choose the Stockinette stitch edge or the chain stitch edge, depending on how you're using the picked-up stitches.

Stockinette-Stitch Edge
If you're going to pick up stitches along the selvedge and knit in a perpendicular direction to add an edging or perhaps the front band of a cardigan, the easiest edge to work with is Stockinette stitch. This gives you one edge stitch for every row, and from this you can easily pick up stitches at any rate (see Picking Up Stitches on page 69).

Chain-Stitch Edge

If you're going to knit an edging in the same direction as the main piece and join it to the selvedge as it is knitted, the best edge to work with has slipped stitches. For this edge, slip the first stitch of every row purlwise. This creates a neat "chain-stitch" edge, wherein you have one edge stitch for every two rows. Cast on for the edging and work the first row, working the last stitch of edging together with the first stitch of the selvedge. Then work the second row of edging away from the main piece and join the last stitch of the third row to the main piece. You're joining the edging at the end of every other row, so a rate of one stitch for two rows works perfectly.

Picking Up Stitches

As noted previously, the best selvedge for picking up to knit in the opposite direction is a one-stitch Stockinette edge, which has one edge stitch per row.

To pick up a stitch, insert a needle through the entire edge stitch, picking up two loops, and then knit it as a normal stitch.

Before picking up an edge, you need to figure out the ratio at which to pick up the stitches. The width of the new knitting must match the length of the previous knitting so everything lies smoothly. The most common pick-up rates are two stitches for three rows and three stitches for four rows. Here's how it works.

Say you're working at a gauge of six stitches and eight rows per inch (2.5cm). When you turn the work on its side, you'll have eight edge stitches in 1" (2.5cm). However, because your stitch gauge is six stitches per inch (2.5cm), you want to pick up only six stitches in those eight rows. A little bit of math dictates that you should pick up three of every four stitches. Pick up three stitches, skip one, pick up three, skip one, etc., until

you've picked up the entire edge to be knitted. But don't skip the last stitch of an edge; if you've just picked up three stitches and one stitch remains on the edge, go ahead and pick it up.

Of course, you'll have to take into account the number of stitches needed for the piece you're knitting onto the edge. If the ratio you've figured out won't give you the exact number of stitches you need, you can do one of two things. You can use the ratio as a guide and pick up a few more or a few less to get the right number, or you can pick up at exactly the ratio and increase or decrease a few stitches in the first row.

What If I Knitted the Wrong Type of Edge?

Preplanning goes a long way, but sometimes we don't know what we'll need when we start knitting, we've changed our mind along the way or we just plain didn't make the right choice. There's usually a way to deal with this.

Add a Finished Edge

If you haven't worked a decorative edge for a scarf or other flat piece of knitting, you could finish the piece with an edging of half double crochet or perhaps a knitted-on I-cord.

Half Double-Crochet Edge

Join the yarn to the beginning stitch by inserting the crochet hook under both loops of the stitch. Yarn over hook, draw through loop; yarn over hook, go back into same beginning stitch, draw loop through (three loops on hook), yarn over and draw through three loops. *Yarn over, insert hook under both loops of the next stitch, yarn over and draw a loop through (three loops on hook), yarn over and draw through three loops. Repeat from * to finish the selvedge edge.

Knitted-On I-Cord Edge

Cast on three stitches onto a double-point needle. Slide the stitches to the other end of the needle and knit two stitches, then knit the third stitch together with the first stitch of the unfinished edge. *Slide the stitches to the other end of the needle, knit two, then knit the third stitch together with the next stitch of the unfinished edge. Repeat from * to finish the selvedge edge.

Choose an Alternate Seaming Method

If you don't have a Stockinette edge stitch, you can simply choose another method of seaming (see Chapter Seven). Or, if you have a slipped-stitch edge and want to work mattress stitch, this will work.

....

Choosing an Alternate Seaming Method

If you've worked a slipped-stitch edge and have one edge stitch for every two rows, you can still pick up for knitting in the opposite direction. The only caution here is minding the pick-up rate (see Picking Up Stitches on page 69).

2/3 Pick Up in Slipped-Stitch Edge
To pick up at a rate of two for three, *pick up one stitch for the first chain, two stitches for the next chain, one stitch for the third chain; repeat from *.

3/4 Pick Up in Slipped-Stitch Edge
To pick up at a rate of three for four, *pick up one stitch for the first chain, two stitches for the next chain; repeat from *.

NOTE: *To pick up two stitches into one chain stitch, knit the first stitch through both loops and knit the second stitch through one loop only of the same chain stitch.*

....

Binding Off

As it is with casting on, so it is with binding off—you want to choose the method that gives both the desired look and the desired elasticity.

....

Elastic Bind Offs

Use these as you would elastic cast ons: for the bottoms of sweaters, tops of socks and anywhere else you may need extra stretch.

Large-Needle Bind Off

Work a regular bind off (see page 73) on a needle two or more sizes larger than the project needle.

Suspended Bind Off

Begin as for a regular bind off (see next page) but when pulling the first stitch over the second, leave the first stitch on the tip of the left needle. Knit the next stitch and then drop both loops from the left needle.

Sewn Bind Off

This bind off is worked much like Kitchener stitch (see Chapter Seven). It works great when binding off in rib but also works with Stockinette and other stitch patterns.

The easiest way to work the bind off for a 1/1 rib is to separate the stitches onto two needles: Place the first stitch on the front needle, the second stitch on the back needle, the third stitch on the front needle, etc. Cut a tail three times the width of the edge to be bound off. Thread the tail onto a tapestry needle. Pass through the first stitch on the front needle from back to front and then through the first stitch on the back needle from front to back. *Pass through the first stitch on the front needle from front to back and drop the stitch from the needle, then pass through the next stitch on the front needle from back to front but leave it on the needle.

Pass through the first stitch on the back needle from back to front and drop it from the needle. Then pass through the next stitch on the back needle from front to back but leave it on the needle. Repeat from * until all stitches have been bound off.

Invisible Bind Off

Draw the yarn through the stitches of the last row. Stretch the edge and let the yarn expand to the stretched width and then fasten off and weave in the end.

Firm Bind Offs

Again, use a firm bind off as you would a firm cast on for things that don't need to stretch such as scarves, pillows and afghans.

. . . .

Regular Bind Off

Knit two stitches and pass the first stitch over the second stitch and off the needle, leaving one stitch on the right needle; *knit one and pass the old stitch on the right needle over the new stitch and off the needle. Repeat from * until all stitches are bound off, pulling the yarn tail through the last stitch.

Three-Needle Bind Off

This is a seam or joining method and is covered in Chapter Seven.

> ### DEALING WITH A LOOSE STITCH
> If you find you tend to get a loose stitch at the end of your bind off, try this: Bind off stitches until there is one stitch remaining on each needle. Slip the last stitch from the left to the right needle and slip the stitch on the right needle over this stitch. Remove the needle, cut the yarn and use a crochet hook or tapestry needle to thread the tail through the stitch toward the edge.

. . . .

K2tog Bind Off

*Knit two stitches together and slip the resulting stitch back to the left needle. Repeat from * until all stitches are bound off, pulling the yarn tail through the last stitch. This is the most rigid bind off we know. We recommend it be used only in projects other than garments.

Crochet Bind Off

This slip-stitch bind off looks like a regular bind off, but you may find that the stitches aren't as tight as knitted stitches. Insert a crochet hook into the first stitch on the needle, draw a loop through and drop the stitch from the needle. *Insert the hook into the next stitch and draw a loop through this stitch and the stitch on the hook, dropping the stitch from the needle. Repeat from * until all stitches are bound off, pulling the yarn tail through the last loop.

Decorative Bind Offs

Use these to add a little spice to your project.

Three-Needle Bind Off

This joining method can be worked on the outside for a decorative effect—see Chapter Seven.

Picot Bind Off

With the stitches to be bound off on the left needle, *use the cable cast on to cast on two stitches. Bind off these two stitches and two or three more stitches. Slip the remaining stitch from the right needle to the left. Repeat from * until all stitches are bound off, pulling the yarn tail through the last stitch. Notice that the bound-off edge is much wider than the knitted piece—keep the splay in mind if you plan to use this bind off.

Provisional Bind Offs

Just kidding. To keep the stitches live, place them on a holder.

BINDING OFF IN PATTERN

When instructed to "bind off in pattern," simply work the next stitch as if you were continuing to work the pattern and then pass the previous stitch over it. For example, when binding off a 1/1 rib, you'd knit the first stitch, purl the second and pass the first over the second.

Seed stitch bound off with knit stitches

Seed stitch bound off in pattern

Special Considerations

Planning for Mattress Stitch for 1/1 Rib

If you plan to sew your seams with mattress stitch (see Chapter Seven), cast on an even number of stitches when you are working a 1/1 ribbing. Work the right-side row as k2, *p1, k1; repeat from * to the last stitch. Work the front and the back the same way. Because mattress stitch consumes one stitch from each edge, you'll be left with a knit stitch on one side of the seam and a purl stitch on the other side. There will be no interruption in the ribbing at the seams. (See the Lisdoonvarna sweater on page 256.)

Planning for Half Mattress Stitch for 1/1 Rib

If you plan to seam with a half mattress stitch (see Chapter Seven), cast on an odd number of stitches when you're working a knit one, purl one ribbing. Work the right-side row as *k1, p1; repeat from * to the last stitch, k1. Work the front and the back the same way. Your work will begin and end with a knit stitch. Because half mattress stitch consumes one half stitch from each edge, you'll be left with half a knit stitch on one side of the seam and half a knit stitch on the other side for a continuous ribbing.

6 Shaping

Here's where things get really interesting. Increases, decreases and short rows are used to add and subtract stitches for both sizing and decorative purposes. There are scores of ways to increase and decrease; as with other techniques, here we present the ones we use most often.

Increases

There are several ways to increase the number of stitches in a row to make the knitted fabric wider. Some are more visible than others. Some lean to the right or left, while others are neutral. The method you choose depends on the desired end result.

Many increases are presented with the option of working them on knit or purl rows. This comes in handy when you're working a pattern that says "Repeat increases every third row." So if you're working in Stockinette stitch, you'll work the knit version on the right side and the purl version on the wrong side of the knitting.

Decorative Open Increases

These increases form a decorative hole in the knitting and are used in lace and eyelet patterns.

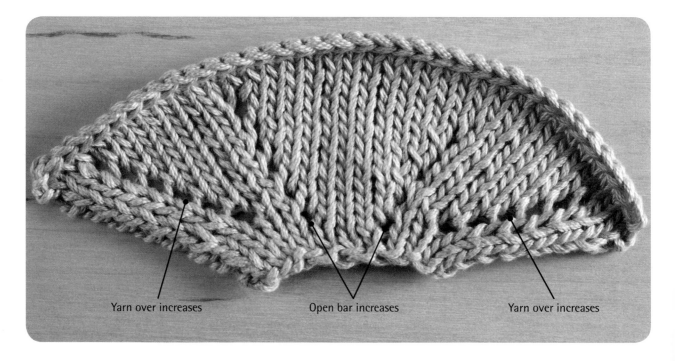

Yarn over increases   Open bar increases   Yarn over increases

Open Yarn Over (yo) Increase
This yarn over can be worked on both right- and wrong-side rows.

Knit Rows
Bring the yarn forward between the needles and then over the top of the right needle to the back (yo)—the new stitch is on the right needle. On the following row, knit or purl the yo.

Purl Rows
Bring the yarn over the top of the right needle to the back and then forward between the needles (yo)—the new stitch is on the right needle. Continue to work to the end of the row. On the following row, knit or purl the yo.

Open Bar Increase
This increase can be worked on both right- and wrong-side rows.

Knit Rows
Insert the right needle under the bar (running thread) between the left and right needles from front to back and work a knit stitch.

Purl Rows
Insert the right needle under the bar between the left and right needles from back to front and work a purl stitch.

Closed Vertical Increases

These increases are somewhat invisible and form a new vertical stitch on the needle. Any closed vertical increase can be used when a pattern says something such as "Increase X number of stitches evenly spaced."

Worked on purl rows   Worked on knit rows

Closed Yarn Over (yo) Increase

This increase can be worked on both right- and wrong-side rows.

Knit Rows
Work as for the Open Yarn Over Increase on knit rows. On the following row, knit or purl into the back of the yo. This twists the stitch, closing up the space created by the yo.

Purl Rows
Work as for the Open Yarn Over Increase on purl rows. On the following row, knit or purl into the back of the yo. This twists the stitch, closing up the space created by the yo.

Knit into the Front and Back of the Same Stitch (kfb)

This increase, abbreviated kfb, is worked on knit rows. It forms a small bump to the left of the stitch being increased.

pfb   kfb

1 Knit into the front of the stitch but leave it on the needle.

2 Knit into the back of the same stitch.

Purl into the Front and Back of the Same Stitch (pfb)

This increase, abbreviated pfb, is worked on purl rows. It will look like the kfb on the right side except that the bump will be to the right of the increased stitch.

1 Purl into the front of the stitch but leave it on the needle.

2 Purl into the back of the same stitch.

Backward Loop Increase

This increase makes a vertical stitch, but the bar at the base of the stitch leans to the right when worked on the right side and to the left when worked on the wrong side.

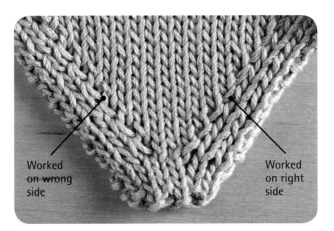

Worked on wrong side

Worked on right side

Right Side
Make a loop so the working yarn comes out of the front of the loop and then place it on the right needle. On the following row, purl the stitch.

Wrong Side
Make a loop so the working yarn comes out of the back of the loop and then place it on the right needle. On the following row, knit the stitch.

Left- and Right-Leaning Closed Increases

Left- and right-leaning increases can be paired to create a mirror image in the knitting. For example, if you're instructed to "increase one stitch at the beginning and end of the next row," you'd use a right-leaning increasing inside the edge stitches at the beginning of the row and its left-leaning companion at the end of the row or vice versa.

....

Make One (m1) Increases

M1 increases are worked with the bar or running thread between the left and right needles. They can be worked as knit or purl stitches and made to lean to the left or to the right.

M1L   M1R

M1 Right Knit
Insert the left needle into the bar between the left and right needles from back to front. Knit the stitch through the front.

M1 Right Purl
Insert the left needle into the bar between the left and right needles from back to front. Purl the stitch through the front.

M1 Left Knit
Insert the left needle into the bar between the left and right needles from front to back. Knit the stitch through the back.

M1 Left Purl
Insert the left needle into the bar between the left and right needles from front to back. Purl the stitch through the back.

Lifted Stitch Increase

These increases are worked into stitches from previous rows and are the most invisible of all.

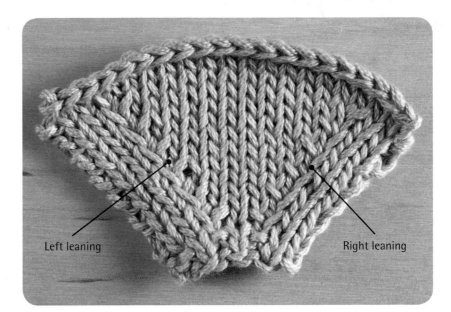

Left leaning

Right leaning

Right Leaning
Insert the right needle from back to front into the stitch one row below the next stitch and lift it onto the left needle. Insert the needle into the front of the stitch and knit it.

Left Leaning
Insert the left needle from back to front into the top of the stitch two rows below the last stitch on the right needle. Knit the lifted stitch on the left needle.

Multiple Stitch Increases

The increases described thus far each make one new stitch. But you can also make two to six new stitches from a single stitch; making more than two new stitches from one is usually done to make decorative bumps or bobbles.

Knit, Purl, Knit into Same Stitch

Knitting, purling and knitting into one stitch results in two stitches increased.

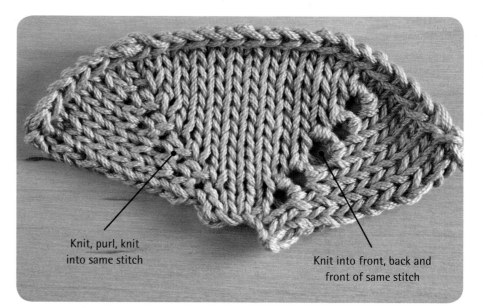

Knit, purl, knit into same stitch

Knit into front, back and front of same stitch

1 Knit the stitch and leave it on the needle.

2 Bring the yarn forward, purl into the same stitch and leave it on the needle.

3 Bring the yarn back, knit into the same stitch and then drop it from the needle. To increase more stitches, repeat the purl, then the knit, etc.

Knit into the Front, Back and Front of Same Stitch

This is similar to the knit, purl, knit increase except that you knit all stitches. Knit into the front of the stitch, then into the back of the stitch, then into the front of the stitch again.

Yarn Over (yo) Increases

You can use yarn overs to increase an even number of stitches into one stitch.

Yarn over increase, four stitches

Yarn over increase, two stitches

1 To increase two stitches, knit the stitch and leave it on the needle.

2 Yo and then knit into the same stitch and drop it from the needle. To increase four stitches, knit, yo, knit, yo, knit into the same stitch.

Centered Double Increases

A centered double increase is made by increasing on both sides of one stitch. When repeated over several rows, these can be used to shape raglan sleeves, thumb gussets and motifs such as hearts and stars. They can be open or closed, but they're always decorative—simply choose the look you want for your project.

Open Double Increases

Open Bar Double Increase
Work an open bar increase, knit one, work an open bar increase.

Yarn Over Double Increase
Yo, knit one, yo.

Closed Double Increases

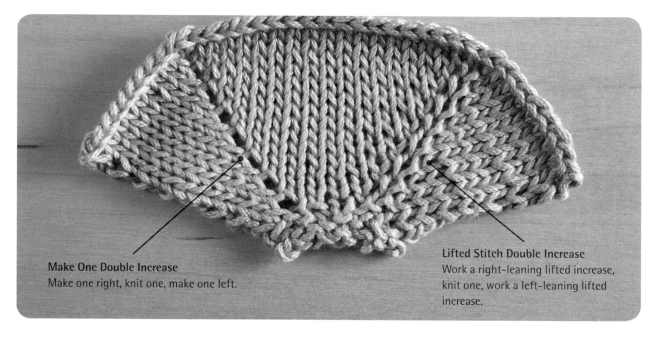

Make One Double Increase
Make one right, knit one, make one left.

Lifted Stitch Double Increase
Work a right-leaning lifted increase, knit one, work a left-leaning lifted increase.

Decreases

Decreasing options abound, and, just as with increases, the method you choose depends on the desired end result. Single decreases lean to the right or to the left, and you can use this feature to create mirror-image lines on either side of a garment. It's up to you to choose which way to slant the stitches, but most commonly you'd want to follow the line of the garment. For example, if you're decreasing at the beginning and the end of the rows so the fabric gets smaller in a triangular fashion, you'd usually choose a left-leaning decrease at the beginning of the row and a right-leaning decrease at the end of the row. Double decreases can be centered or lean to the right or to the left.

Single Decreases

A single decrease makes one stitch from two and it can lean to the right or to the left. The most commonly used pair is ssk and k2tog, but there are other options.

Pair I: Ssk and K2tog

k2tog

ssk

Left Leaning: Slip, Slip, Knit (ssk)

1 Slip the first stitch knitwise and then slip the next stitch knitwise.

2 Insert the left needle into the front of the two stitches and then knit them together through the back loops. It's important to slip the stitches knitwise—stitches slipped purlwise present a stitch crossed at the base, which doesn't mirror the k2tog.

Right Leaning: Knit Two Together (k2tog)

1 Insert the right needle into two stitches on the left needle.

2 Knit them together.

There may be times you'll want to decrease at the beginning and end of every third row. In this case, you'd use Pair I on the right-side rows and Pair II on the wrong-side rows.

Pair II: Ssp and P2tog, Worked on the Wrong Side

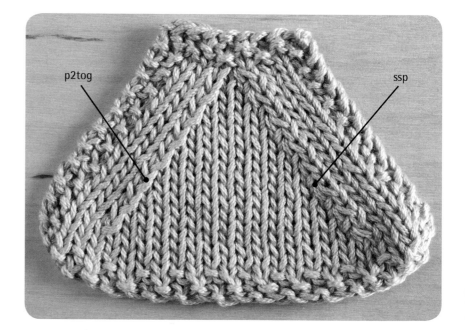

Left Leaning: Slip, Slip, Purl (ssp)

Use this to decrease on wrong-side rows. The resulting stitch will lean to the left on the right side and look like an ssk.

1 Slip the first stitch purlwise and then slip the next stitch knitwise.

2 Slip the two stitches back to the left needle and then purl them together through the back loops.

Right Leaning: Purl Two Together (p2tog)

Use this to decrease on wrong-side rows. The resulting stitch will lean to the right on the right side and look like a k2tog.

Insert the right needle into two stitches on the left needle from right to left and purl the two stitches together.

Pair III: Skp and Ksp

Left Leaning: Slip, Knit, Pass the Slipped Stitch Over (skp)

1 Slip one stitch knitwise.

2 Knit one.

3 Pass the slipped stitch over the knit stitch and off the needle. Be careful not to stretch the slipped stitch when you are passing it over the knit stitch.

Right Leaning: Knit, Slip, Pass the Next Stitch Over (ksp)
This decrease is a mirror image of skp.

1 Knit the first stitch knitwise and then slip it back to the left needle without twisting it.

2 Pass the second stitch on the left needle over the first stitch and off the needle.

3 Slip the first stitch back to the right needle purlwise.

Multiple Decreases

A double decrease is most often used as a central decrease in a pattern panel. Some patterns call for working a double decrease at the beginning and end of a right-side row. We would prefer to work single decreases at the beginning and end of both the right- and wrong-side rows (see Single Decreases, Pairs I and II, beginning on page 85) because double decreases tend to be bulky. However, if you really want to use them, here are two options.

Pair I: K3tog and S3k

Here's another pair of right- and left-leaning decreases worked on the right side.

Right Leaning: Knit Three Stitches Together (k3tog)
Insert the needle into three stitches instead of one and then knit them together.

Left Leaning: Slip, Slip, Slip, Knit (s3k)
Slip the first stitch knitwise, slip the next two stitches purlwise one at a time and then insert the left needle into the front of the three stitches. Knit them together through the back loops.

Pair II: K2sp and Sk2p

Right Leaning: Knit Two Together and Pass One Over (k2sp)
Knit two stitches together and slip the resulting stitch back to the left needle without twisting it, pass the next stitch over the decreased stitches and then slip the resulting stitch to the right needle purlwise.

Left Leaning: Slip One, Knit Two Together, Pass the Slipped Stitch Over (sk2p)
Slip one knitwise, knit two together through the back loops and then pass the slipped stitch over the k2tog.

k2sp

sk2p

Centered Double Decrease
The left-leaning sk2p described above is often used in lace knitting and as the final decrease in leaf and other decorative motifs. Use this centered decrease when you want a vertical result.

Slip two together knitwise, knit one and then pass the two slipped stitches over the knit stitch (s2kp). The result is a centered vertical stitch on top of two decreased stitches, one from each side.

Short-Row Shaping

Short-row shaping is used to add shaping to a specific part of a knitted piece without affecting the surrounding areas, such as for darts in sweater fronts or for sock heels. Short rows allow you to invisibly make the back of a sweater slightly longer than the front to keep it from riding up, or to make the front slightly longer than the back to accommodate a few extra pounds carried up front. Short rows can also be used instead of binding off to shape shoulders, and they can be used to balance stitch patterns with different row gauges within the same fabric. They also make fabulous ruffles, visors and other custom shapes.

Short rows can be worked on the right or wrong side, in Stockinette or garter stitch, and they can be worked in flat or circular knitting.

How to Work Short Rows

Short-row shaping is done by stopping before the end of the row, wrapping a stitch and working back in the other direction. This is often abbreviated as WT (wrap and turn).

Stockinette Stitch, Knit Rows

1 Knit to the place you want to begin shaping. With the yarn in back, slip the next stitch purlwise from the left needle to the right needle and bring the yarn to the front between the needles.

2 Slip the last stitch on the right needle back to the left needle and bring the yarn to the back. You've just wrapped the yarn around that stitch. Turn the work and purl to the other end of the shaping section or to the end of the row.

Stockinette Stitch, Purl Rows

1 Purl to the place you want to begin shaping. With the yarn in front, slip the next stitch purlwise from the left needle to the right needle and then bring the yarn to the back between the needles.

2 Slip the last stitch on the right needle back to the left needle. Turn the work, and with the yarn in position to knit the next stitch, work to the other end of the shaping section or to the end of the row.

Hiding the Wraps

Wrapping a stitch places a horizontal bar at its base.
Here's how to make that unsightly bar disappear.

Right Side

To hide the wraps on the right (knit) side, work to one stitch
before the wrapped stitch. Insert the right needle knitwise
under the wrap and then into the wrapped stitch and knit them
together. Continue to the end of the row, knitting all the wraps
together with the stitches they wrap.

Wrong Side

To hide the wraps on the wrong (purl) side, work to one stitch
before the wrapped stitch. Insert the right needle purlwise into
the back loop of the wrap and lift it onto the left needle, then
purl it together with the wrapped stitch that's on the needle.
Continue to the end of the row, purling all wraps together with
the stitches they wrap.

Garter-Stitch Short Rows

When knitting in garter stitch, you can work short rows
the same as for knitting in Stockinette stitch, except
there is no need to work a final row to hide the wraps.

The small bumps formed by the wraps will blend into the
garter-stitch bumps.

Short-Row Variation

Here's an alternate way to work short
rows without wrapping the stitches. It's
a little more difficult to work, but the
results are nearly invisible.

Stockinette Stitch, Right Side

1 Knit to the place you want to begin shaping. Turn the work, slip one stitch purlwise and purl back. When working the whole row on the right side, knit the slipped stitch, and with the left needle, go behind the work and pick up the second bar down between the first and second stitches on the right needle. Knit this stitch together with the next stitch.

2 The blue thread marks the stitch that you pick up with the left needle to knit together with the following stitch.

NOTE: *There are two bars close together at this point; be sure to pick up the one that's farthest behind.*

Stockinette Stitch, Wrong Side

1 Purl to the place you want to begin shaping. Turn the work, slip one purlwise, knit back. When working the whole row on the wrong side, purl the slipped stitch and slip the next stitch to the right needle knitwise; pick up the bar between the first and second stitches on the right needle (don't count the slipped stitch), return the slipped stitch to the left needle and purl it together with the picked-up stitch.

In this example, the short-row stitch has been purled, the next was slipped to the right needle knitwise and the bar below the first and second stitches on the right needle is picked up with the left needle.

2 The blue thread marks the stitch that gets picked up.

How to Use Short Rows

Bustline Shaping in the Front of a Sweater

Short rows are great for adding fullness to the bustline of a sweater front.

To begin, measure the wearer. Measure the length of the back from the shoulder to the waist. Measure the length of the front from the shoulder to the waist. The difference in inches multiplied by the row gauge is the number of rows that must be added to the front (if the number is not even, add one). Now measure the wearer's side from the underarm to below the bust. Multiply that measurement by the row gauge. This is the number of rows into which you will work the additional short rows. Again, use an even number of rows.

For example, let's say you want to add 2" (5cm) to the front in a 4" (10cm) space (this is the measurement from underarm to underbust), and your row gauge is eight rows per inch (2.5cm). You need to add sixteen front short rows to a side length of thirty-two rows. Work the wrap and turn at least three stitches from the edge. This leaves one stitch for seaming and one plain stitch between the seam and the wrap. Here are the row-by-row instructions for this example:

Row 1: Knit to the last 3 sts, WT.
Row 2: Purl to the last 3 sts, WT.
Row 3: Knit to the end of the row, working the wrap together with the wrapped stitch.
Row 4: Purl to the end of the row, purling the wrap together with the wrapped stitch.
Repeat Rows 1–4 seven more times.

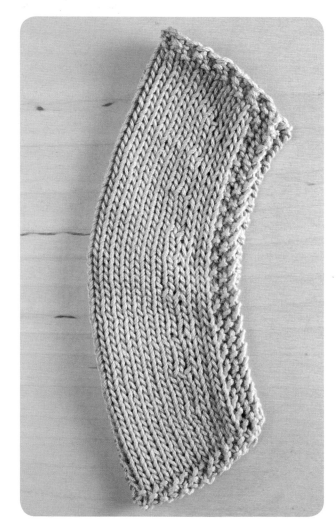

> ### ELONGATING THE FRONT OR BACK
> If you need to add length to the front of a sweater to accommodate a little extra shape or to the back to accommodate a spinal curve, work the same as for bustline shaping, determining how much added length is needed, where the length is needed and over how many rows it will be added.

Shape Shoulders

Sweater shoulders look best when they're slightly sloped up from the side to the neck. Many patterns tell you to bind off a certain number of stitches at the beginning of right-side rows for the left shoulder and the beginning of wrong-side rows for the right shoulder. This shaping method produces a stair-step effect along the seam line that is difficult to disguise. If you instead use short rows, you have live stitches at the end of the shaping you can join with a three-needle bind off or with Kitchener stitch.

Let's say you're working on a sweater back and your pattern says "Bind off twelve stitches each side three times and place remaining stitches on a holder."

Here's how to convert this shaping to short rows.

Row 1: Knit to 12 sts before end of needle, WT.
Row 2: Purl to 12 sts before end of needle, WT.
Row 3: Knit to 11 sts before the wrapped st, WT.
Row 4: Purl to 11 sts before the wrapped st, WT.

Rows 5 and 6: Repeat Rows 3 and 4.
Row 7: Knit, working wrapped sts together with their wraps.
Row 8: Purl, working remaining wrapped sts together with their wraps.

Now you can either bind off thirty-six stitches for each shoulder and place the neck stitches on a holder, or you can place each set of shoulder stitches and the neck stitches on separate holders and later join the back and front shoulder stitches together with three-needle bind off or Kitchener stitch.

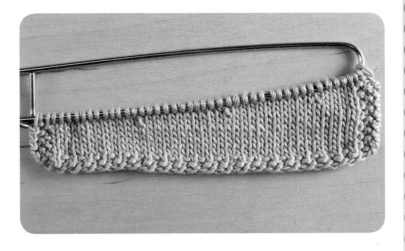

Short-Row Neck Shaping

You can also use short rows to shape a neckline, leaving live stitches to be worked for the finishing. If your pattern says to bind off two stitches at the neck edge five times, you could use short rows as follows. This example describes the left front—the neck edge is at the end of the row, and we begin with thirty-five stitches on the needle.

Row 1: Knit 33, WT.
Rows 2, 4, 6 and 8: Purl.
Row 3: Knit 31, WT.
Row 5: Knit 29, WT.
Row 7: Knit 27, WT.
Row 9: Knit 25, WT.
Row 10: Purl.

You now have ten unworked stitches at the neck edge and twenty-five shoulder stitches. Place the neck stitches on a holder. When setting up for the neck finishing, you'll place these stitches on the needles and work the wrapped stitches together with their wraps on the first row.

Short-Row Heels

Here are two methods of using short rows to shape a heel. The first is a true short-row heel, where all the shaping is done by knitting short rows and wrapping and turning stitches. The second method shapes the heel at the bottom of a heel flap and is a modified short row without wrapping.

True Short-Row Heel

This is a true short-row shaping in that it doesn't involve any change in stitch count. For the first half of the heel you increase the bulk by working from the sides to the center; on the second half of the heel you decrease the bulk by working from the center back out to the sides. For example, let's say your sock has forty-eight stitches. Place twenty-four stitches on hold for the instep and work the heel on the remaining twenty-four stitches.

First half of the heel (RS): Knit to the last stitch (in this case, knit 23), WT, then purl to the last stitch (purl 22), WT. Now knit to the last stitch before the wrapped stitch (knit 21), WT, then purl to the last stitch before the wrapped stitch (purl 20), WT. Continue until you have 7 wrapped stitches on each side of 10 unwrapped center stitches.

Second half of heel (RS): Knit the 10 center stitches, knit the next wrapped stitch together with its wrap, WT (this stitch will have two wraps). Purl to the next wrapped stitch (purl 11), purl the wrapped stitch together with its wrap, WT (this stitch will have two wraps). Knit to the double wrapped stitch, knit the stitch together with its wraps, WT. Purl to the double-wrapped stitch, purl the stitch together with its wraps, WT. Continue until you have worked all 24 heel stitches.

Modified Short Rows with a Heel Flap

Let's say your heel flap has twenty-four stitches. You'll isolate the center ten stitches and decrease on each side of these until twelve stitches remain. When working this heel, it isn't necessary to wrap a stitch before turning—instead, you work the two stitches before the turn together and slip the resulting stitch after turning. There are seven stitches on each side of the ten center stitches. Begin on the right side by working to the end of the center stitches, which in this case is seventeen (seven "side" stitches and ten center stitches), and work a single decrease. Turn the work and slip the first stitch, purl the ten center stitches and work a single decrease. Turn again and slip the first stitch, work the ten center stitches and decrease again. Repeat these rows until you have twelve stitches left.

When working this type of heel, you'll then need to knit a gusset to complete the shaping and rejoin to the instep stitches.

Using Short Rows to Balance Patterns

Row gauge from one pattern to another can be radically different. For example, when working with the same yarn and needles, you may get a Stockinette gauge of eight rows per inch (2.5cm) and a garter stitch row gauge of twelve rows per inch (2.5cm). To use the two patterns side-by-side without puckering, you'd need to elongate the garter stitch portion; to be exact, you'll need to add four extra rows of garter stitch to every eight rows of Stockinette stitch. Here's how you'd work a panel of six garter stitches and six Stockinette stitches.

Row 1: Knit.
Row 2: P6, k6.

Row 3: K6, WT.

Row 4: K6.

Row 5: K6, knit the wrapped stitch together with its wrap, k5.

Row 6: P6, k6.

Row 7: Knit.

Row 8: P6, k6.

Row 9: K6, WT.

Row 10: K6.

Row 11: K6, knit the wrapped stitch together with its wrap, k5.

Row 12: P6, k6.

Ruffles

There are several ways to make ruffles. Short rows is the method to choose if you want to put ruffles on the side of a flat piece as you work the piece. For example, you may want a ruffle up the center front of a sweater piece or on both sides of a flat spine for a two-ruffle scarf. Calculate the number of short rows needed based on the desired fullness.

Let's say you want a four-to-one ruffle (meaning that the ruffle is four times fuller than the flat piece) that is 3" (7.5cm) deep on the left edge of a piece. Your gauge is six

stitches per inch (2.5cm). You want a 3" (7.5cm) ruffle, which requires eighteen stitches. Cast on the number of stitches needed for the flat piece, plus eighteen. For a four-to-one fullness, you'll need four rows in the ruffle for every one row in the flat piece. The ruffle will have graduated fullness, with the fullest part at the outside edge. Because the number of ruffle stitches is divisible by three, let's make the short rows in three groups of six stitches. Here's how to work a garter-stitch piece.

Row 1 (RS): Knit.

Row 2: K6, WT.

Row 3: Knit.

Row 4: K12, WT.

Row 5: Knit.

Row 6: K18, WT.

Row 7: Knit.

Row 8 (WS): Knit to the end of the flat piece.
You now have 2 rows in the flat piece and 8 rows in the ruffle.

You could also use the same proportions but add a little extra fullness at the very edge. Work as outlined above, but add an extra short row of three stitches between each of the graduated short rows.

Other Custom Shapes

Short rows can be used to make all kinds of custom shapes. Once you figure out the width and length of the shaping, simply reduce the number of stitches for the width over the number of rows you'll be adding for the length; to reverse any shaping, increase the same number of stitches over the same number of rows.

7 Flat and Circular Knitting

The shape of some projects more or less dictates whether you'll work back and forth in rows (flat) or in the round (circular). For example, most rectangular scarves will be knit flat, and most socks will be knit circularly. Choosing whether to knit a sweater in the round or flat is largely a matter of personal preference, but there are times when one way will work better than another. For example, some knitted patterns, especially when worked in the round, can make the fabric bias when worked over large areas. It's possible to remedy this by using fake seams at the sides, but it might be better to knit the garment flat and sew the pieces together. Alternatively, if you're working a multicolored pattern, it's usually best to knit circularly, mostly so you can always see the pattern on the right side and have less of a chance for making errors, but also because knitting all the stitches will help you produce a fabric with even tension. We also know knitters who dislike seaming so much they'll figure out how to knit almost anything in the round.

Flat Knitting

Odd as it may seem, one of the first things you need to think about before beginning to knit your sweater is how you will finish it. For most sweaters you'll have side seams, shoulder seams, armhole seams and underarm seams. If you choose your seaming method before you knit, you can knit with the selvedge edges that will work best for that method.

Seaming Rows to Rows

These methods are used when joining rows to rows, such as for a sweater side seam.

Mattress Stitch

This is hands-down our favorite way to join side and underarm seams. It results in a straightforward, strong and invisible seam. If you plan to seam with mattress stitch, the two seams to be joined should be knit with a Stockinette selvedge-edge stitch. You should have a tail long enough to sew the seam, and the two edge stitches should be marked (see Chapter Five).

1 Thread the long tail remaining from the cast-on edge onto a tapestry needle. Bring the needle up through the space between the first and second edge stitches on the piece without the tail (this would be the marked stitch discussed in Chapter Five and on the right in this example) and down through the corresponding stitch on the side with the tail (on the left in this example). Bring the needle up through the same space on the right side again.

2 Pick up one bar between the edge stitch and the next stitch on the left side.

3 Pick up two bars on the right piece.

4 From here on, pick up two bars from one side and then two from the other, drawing the thread through gently but firmly.

Mattress Stitch for Striped Knitting

Begin as for regular mattress stitch. If you started correctly and stayed on track, when you get to the first stripe you'll be picking up two bars of the old color on one side and then one bar of the old color and one bar of the new color on the other side. Depending on how many rows there are in the stripes, you'll then work two bars of the new color on both sides until you get to the end of the stripe, then you'll end with two bars of the new color on one side and one bar of the new color and one bar of the old color on the other side. When everything is tightened up, the stripes will exactly align.

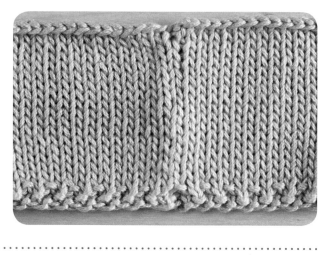

Mattress Stitch Without an Edge Stitch (Half Mattress Stitch)

If you forgot to include an edge stitch at the selvedge, fear not—you can seam using a half stitch from each side.

1 Thread the tail onto a yarn needle. Bring the needle up through the center of the first edge stitch on the piece without the tail and then up through the corresponding stitch on the side with the tail.

2 Bring the needle up through the same space on the opposite side again. Proceed as for regular mattress stitch, working into the center of the two edge stitches.

Mattress Stitch on a Slip-Stitch Edge

If you have a slip-stitch edge and want to work mattress stitch, you can work the seam as follows.

1 Notice that behind each chain stitch there are two loops. Begin by passing through the lower loop on the first edge (left in this example). On the right edge, pass under both loops of the chain stitch.

2 Pass under the two loops behind the first chain stitch on the left—these are the two loops above the first loop passed through in Step 1.

3 On the right edge, pass through the upper loop behind the same chain and the lower loop on the next chain. Continue in this manner.

Crocheting Seams Together
This is another method of joining
seams with a Stockinette edge stitch.

1 With wrong sides facing, insert a
crochet hook through the first knot
of the first piece and then through the
loop of the second piece.

2 Yarn over the hook and draw the
yarn through both stitches. Hold the
two pieces with right sides together.

3 Continue along the seam line,
working knot to loop, to the end of
the seam. Draw the yarn through the last
loop and weave in.

Seaming Garter-Stitch Rows
There is no invisible way to join garter stitch to garter stitch. Here are three methods of seaming garter-stitch edges,
each with a different result.

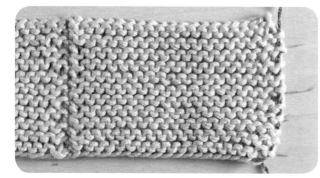 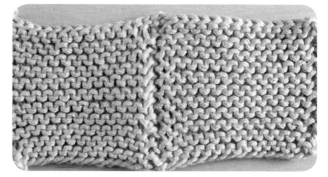

Herringbone Garter Join
Sew the edges with a tapestry needle in a herringbone pattern;
come up through the knot on one edge and down through the
knot on the other edge. (The pink thread shows which stitches
to pick up.)

Regular Mattress Stitch on Garter Join
Work a Stockinette-stitch edge on both pieces to be joined and
sew a regular mattress stitch seam. This method is neat but it
elongates the seam.

Slip-Stitch Mattress Stitch on Garter Join

For the best results, work your garter-stitch pieces with a slip-stitch edge and join with mattress stitch for slip-stitch edges.

Seaming Stitches to Stitches

Use these techniques to join stitches to stitches, such as shoulder seams.

· ·

Three-Needle Bind Off

This is a tidy method for joining two sets of live stitches.

Three-needle bind off with right sides held together

Three-needle bind off with wrong sides held together

1 Place the two needles holding the stitches with right sides together in your left hand. Insert a third needle into the stitch on the front needle and then into the stitch on the back needle, and knit the two stitches together.

2 *Knit the next stitch on the front needle together with the next stitch on the back needle, then slip the first stitch on the right needle over this stitch. Repeat from * until all stitches are joined.

Kitchener Stitch for Stockinette Joins

Also called grafting, this is an invisible method of
joining two sets of live stitches.

1 Hold the two needles holding stitches together with wrong
sides together. To set up, insert a threaded tapestry needle
into the first stitch on the front needle purlwise and leave the
stitch on the needle.

2 Insert the needle into the first stitch on the back needle
knitwise and leave it on the needle.

3 *Insert a threaded tapestry needle into the first stitch on
the front needle knitwise and slip the stitch off the needle.
Then insert the tapestry needle into the second stitch on the
front needle purlwise and leave the stitch on the needle.

4 Insert the tapestry needle into the first stitch on the back
needle purlwise and slip the stitch off the needle. Insert
the tapestry needle into the second stitch on the back needle
knitwise and leave the stitch on the needle. Repeat from * until
all stitches are joined.

Kitchener Stitch for Reverse Stockinette Stitch Joins

You can work this join from the inside, as for Stockinette stitch as described on the previous page, or you can reverse the knitwise/purlwise direction of the joining stitches.

*Insert a threaded tapestry needle into the first stitch on the front needle purlwise and slip the stitch off the needle, then insert the tapestry needle into the second stitch on the front needle knitwise and leave the stitch on the needle. Insert the tapestry needle into the first stitch on the back needle knitwise and slip the stitch off the needle, then insert the tapestry needle into the second stitch on the back needle purlwise and leave the stitch on the needle. Repeat from * until all stitches are joined.

KEEPING PATTERN WITH KITCHENER STITCH JOIN

The Kitchener stitch essentially adds another row of knitting between the pieces being joined. To make an invisible seam when working something other than Stockinette or reverse Stockinette stitch, you'll need to stop the pattern short on at least one of the pieces being joined. For example, if you're working a pattern that has two knit rows between patterned rows, if you end having worked one knit row on one of the pieces and the patterned row on the other, when you join with a Stockinette Kitchener stitch you'll have two knit rows between the last patterned rows.

Kitchener Stitch for Knit and Purl Combos

When working the knit stitches, work as for the Stockinette join, and when working the purl stitches work as for the reverse Stockinette join. If the stitches to be joined have come together from opposite directions, the same thing happens here as with provisional cast ons—you'll be a half stitch off (see Chapter Five). The resulting graft won't be as seamless as a Stockinette-stitch graft, but it's a lot less visible than joining with other methods. If the stitches to be joined are going in the same direction, i.e., you're joining the provisionally cast-on edge to the live ending stitches, you can make a seamless join, but it's not as easy as it should be. When working the knits to knits and purls to purls, you'll find that on the cast-on edge a purl stitch following a knit stitch is hidden behind the knit stitch. Pay careful attention to the thread path and don't overlook those demure purls.

2/2 rib graft, opposite directions

2/2 rib graft, same direction

Seaming Stitches to Rows

There are times when you'll need to seam a vertical piece to a horizontal piece, perhaps to join a sweater front to a shoulder saddle. It's best to keep the stitches on the vertical piece live. First, you need to know the stitch-to-row gauge (see Chapter Five). For this example we'll suppose a gauge of six stitches and eight rows per inch (2.5cm).

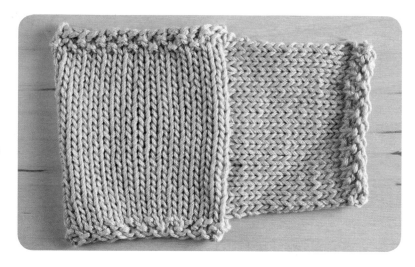

1 Position the two pieces on a flat surface, perpendicular to each other, with the stitches below the rows. Insert a threaded tapestry needle into the first live stitch from back to front and then pass under the bar of the corresponding horizontal stitch.

2 Pass through the first stitch again from front to back and drop it from the needle. Then pass through the next live stitch from back to front. Repeat this once more.

3 When you get to the third live stitch, pass under the bars of the next two horizontal stitches. Continue in this manner, joining three live stitches to four rows, until you reach the end of the seam.

Seaming Live Stitches to Bound-Off Stitches

We use this method when joining shoulder seams on vests. It has the advantage of a bound-off edge for stability yet is nearly invisible. Work the back and bind off the shoulder stitches. Work the front and leave the shoulder stitches live.

Align the live stitches on a needle with the bound-off stitches with right sides facing. Insert a threaded tapestry needle into the first stitch on the needle from back to front, pass under both loops of the corresponding bound-off stitch from right to left and then pass back through the same live stitch from front to back. Bring the needle through the next live stitch from back to front and repeat the process until all stitches are bound off.

Setting in Sleeves

The cap of a set-in sleeve is usually about 2" (5cm) wide. Align the cap to the shoulder seam so there is 1" (2.5cm) on either side of the seam. Use a stitches-to-stitches seaming method at the underarm, a row-to-row method along the sides of the seam and the armhole, and the stitches-to-rows method at the cap. (See the Ambrosia sweater on page 246.)

Counting and Marking Rows

The best way to ensure that your knitted pieces match in length, i.e., the front and back of a sweater or the two sleeves, is to count rows rather than use a tape measure. And the best way to count rows is to mark them as you go.

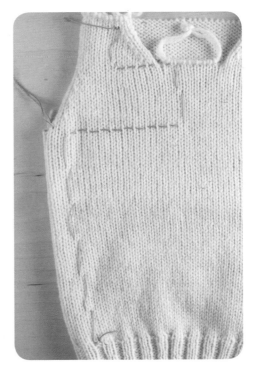

Thread a 24" (61cm) length of contrasting color cotton thread onto a tapestry needle. Anchor one end of the thread in the row where you want to start counting, about 2" (5cm) from the edge. As you knit, mark every tenth row by passing the needle under both sides of a stitch. Continue marking until you've reached the desired length to the underarm. Mark the last row even if it is not a tenth row. When you work the corresponding piece, you'll know exactly how many rows to knit. If you're knitting a sweater and have just reached the underarm, stitch toward the center, picking up every third stitch about ten times. Continue marking in tens to the neck or shoulder bind off.

Circular Knitting

With circular knitting you have no garment seams, a godsend to many of us! Circular knitting is the technique to use for socks, gloves and some sweaters.

If your piece has a circumference of 16" (40.5cm) or more, you can work on a circular needle; for smaller pieces, you'll need double-point needles. This last statement used to be true until the birth of the 8" (20cm) circular needle and before knitters started knitting socks on two circular needles or on one long circular needle with the magic loop method. But here we'll focus on the traditional methods.

Choosing Needles

Your project will determine the length of needle to use, whether it's a circular or double point—it's most comfortable to use a circular that is only slightly smaller than the piece, and it's least cumbersome to use double points that are only slightly longer than the line of stitches each will hold. (See Chapter Two for more needle information.) When using double points, stitch count or pattern repeat will determine whether you use a set of four or five (with stitches on three or four needles)—if the number of stitches is divisible by three, use a set of four; if divisible by four use a set of five.

Joining the Round

Most patterns set up for circular knitting begin with a similar statement: "Cast on X number of stitches and join into a round, being careful not to twist the stitches." If all the stitches are not oriented the same way on the needle, you'll end up with a Möbius loop instead of a tube.

There are several ways to join the first and last stitches together to begin the round. One way is to

Twisted stitches

Beginning of Möbius loop

simply start knitting the first cast-on stitch with the yarn attached to the last cast-on stitch. Give the yarn a little tug before knitting the next stitch to tighten things up a bit. You may still have a gap between the last and first stitches; when weaving in the tail, use it to close the gap.

It is also possible to join in the round without a gap.

Joining in the Round Without a Gap

1 Cast on one extra stitch. Slip the first cast-on stitch to the right needle.

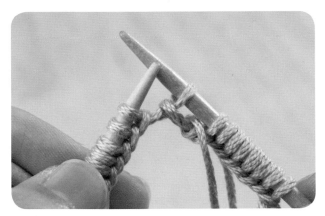

2 Bring the last cast-on stitch over it and off the needle. Then slip the stitch back to the left needle and begin knitting. Tug on the yarn tail after knitting the first stitch.

Working the Rounds

When using a circular needle, place a marker on the needle between the first and last stitches to mark the end of the round. Follow your pattern, and when you reach the marker, you've completed one round.

On double-point needles, if the end of the round is also at the end of a needle, place a marker in the last stitch and move it up as you work. Or skip the marker and check where the cast-on tail is—it marks the end of the round.

Fake Seams

There are times when you may want to add "fake seams" up the sides of a circularly knit item. Some stitch patterns, including Stockinette stitch, may have a tendency to bias when worked in long rounds. Adding a line of single purl stitches or a line of three seed stitches at each side can help control this. If you're working a fitted piece that will be shaped at the sides, it's helpful to have a center "seam" on which you can increase or decrease on either side. This is especially important if you need to make several increases before the added stitches can be incorporated into the pattern. (See the Ambrosia sweater on page 246.)

Steeks

When working a sweater in the round, you have to accommodate openings in the knitted tube for armholes and a neckline; if you're planning a cardigan, you also need to accommodate a center front opening. This is done with a bridge of extra stitches called a steek. When you've completed the body of the garment, you'll machine sew a row or two of stitching on each side of the center steek stitch and cut through the center of the steek. Then you can pick up stitches along the front to work a button band, around the neck to work a neck finishing and around the armholes for an armhole band or a sleeve.

Let's say you're working a two-colored V-neck vest that uses both colors in every round. Cast on and join into a round. Place markers for the sides and the center front and work circularly until you reach the armhole depth. Knit to the first side marker, slip the marker, cast on three total stitches using the backward loop method and place another marker. Rejoin the round and repeat at the second side marker. When you come to the armhole steeks, alternate the colors on every row: use A, B, A on the first row and B, A, B on the second row. When you get to the beginning of the V-neck shaping, do the same thing: Slip the marker, cast on three stitches to create the steek and place another marker.

Multicolored steek

Neck stitches on hold with steek cast on above it

If you're working a cardigan, you'll need to begin with a center steek in the first round. There are two ways to do this, depending on what you plan for the rib and the button band. If you're planning a button band that will be knit perpendicularly to the fronts, cast on the number of stitches for the bottom of the sweater and then cast on a three-stitch steek at the center front. If you want a band that is worked parallel to the fronts, work the bottom ribbing or border flat to the desired depth, place the number of stitches needed for the button bands on hold and then cast on for the steek and proceed. See Chapter Sixteen for more information about button bands.

For sleeves, you'll leave a certain number of armhole stitches on hold at the underarm, but the number depends on the type of sleeve: For a drop shoulder you may only need two to four stitches, for a set-in sleeve or perhaps a vest, you may need twelve or more. Place the stitches hold, then cast on stitches for the steek.

For a crew-neck pullover, you'll leave a certain number of center front stitches on hold and proceed as for sleeves. If you're working a crew-neck cardigan, when you get to the depth to begin the shaping, place the front steek and an equal number of stitches from each side of the steek on hold. Break

the yarns and attach them to the other side of the neck opening. Knit to the beginning of the held stitches, cast on for the steek, rejoin and continue knitting, working neck shaping decreases at both neck edges.

Stitching and Cutting

Using a fine zigzag setting on a sewing machine, sew one or two rows along the stitches on each side of the center steek stitch. When you're sure everything's secure, cut through the column of center steek stitches. You can now pick up along the stitches closest to the steek and knit bands or sleeves from there.

Troubleshooting and Special Considerations

Loose Stitches with Double Points

When knitting with double-point needles, the last stitch on the previous needle is often loose. If you're working a rib, beginning each needle with a knit stitch and ending with a purl can prevent this. If you're working Stockinette stitch, work one or two stitches from the next needle onto the current needle every two or three rounds. Be sure you mark the beginning of the round so you can return to it for any pattern changes or shaping.

Reverse Mattress Stitch

If you somehow end up with purl stitches on the edges, you can put the seams to the outside and make them decorative. Work as for regular mattress stitch, but work from the inside—the purl stitches will roll to the outside.

To Bind Off or Not to Bind Off

While joining live stitches by grafting offers seamless finishing, sometimes you'll want to bind off to add some stability to a join. You don't need any extra strength at the underarms of a sweater, so you can keep the underarm stitches live and graft them to the sleeves. However, if you're going to add a collar or a hood to a neckline, it's usually best to loosely bind off the stitches and then pick up along the bound-off edge. This will keep the neck edge from stretching due to the weight of the collar or hood.

Part III
Decorative Knitting

At last, we get to the fun stuff! There are many ways to incorporate color into your knitting, and **Chapter Eight presents eight of them** (how's that for balance?) including stranding, intarsia, mosaic knitting, mitered knitting, double knitting, working with multicolored yarn, adding color with duplicate and cross-stitches, and even working two-color braids. Once you know how to use these techniques, you can really let yourself go wild!

Although the Aran knitting we recognize as fisherman knit sweaters is relatively new to the knitting world (that world that started sometime during the thirteenth century), most of us think of it as "traditional," and most of us love it. **Chapter Nine discusses the basics of cable crossings, traveling stitches, allover and panel designs, bobbles and backgrounds.** These techniques can, of course, be applied to all types of designs, from sweaters fit for old salts to sweaters ready for the runway.

Scarves, bridal accessories, tablecloths, shawls, baby clothing, evening wear—all these items are a great way to showcase knitted lace. All you need to know here is how to decrease and how to work a yarn over. Yeah, we know: There's a little more to it than that, and **Chapter Ten covers special decreases, scalloped versus straight edges, changing the look with needle size, blocking and fixing mistakes.** And if you prefer following row-by-row instructions to working from a chart, we hope to convert you here.

Just in case you don't think the decorative techniques presented thus far offer enough options for dressing up your knitting, **in Chapter Eleven you'll learn how to bead it up**. Beads can be incorporated into everything from purses to pullovers, and presented are five different methods for adding the SBOs (shiny bright objects) to your knitting.

⑧ Color Knitting

E ven those of us who don black and gray clothing most days have to admit we
get excited when we walk into a well-organized yarn shop with zillions of colors
everywhere we look. Here are several techniques for working with more than one
color at a time; we also give a nod to multicolored and self-patterning yarns.

Fair Isle Knitting (Or Not)

An entire book would be needed to adequately cover
the subject of Fair Isle knitting, and fortunately for
us there are a couple of excellent sources out there.
Here we'll cover some of the basics, beginning with
the fact that most "Fair Isle" knitting isn't. No, that's
not a typo. What we've come to call Fair Isle knitting

is any multicolored patterned knitting that uses the
technique of stranding. True Fair Isle knitting uses only
two colors per round to create multicolored motifs that
originated in knitting from Fair Isle, which is part of the
Shetland Islands. So let's call our multicolored knitting
"stranded" knitting.

Circular versus Flat Stranded Knitting

If you're planning an allover multicolored stranding
project, it's possible to work back and forth, but it's
probably best to work in the round. There are several
reasons for this, the first one being that you will always
see your pattern on the right side and won't have to
knit blind on the wrong side of the work. Secondly,
most of us work with a slightly different tension when
purling versus knitting, and this is more apparent in
multicolored designs. That said, if you're a steek-phobe
(see Chapter Seven) and must work flat, follow these
same rules for circular knitting regarding color changes,
floats and tension.

Background yarn stranded under pattern yarn

Background yarn stranded over pattern yarn

Changing Colors

To maintain consistency in both tension and design, you need to be consistent about which color goes over the other and which goes under the other. Generally, when changing colors the background color will go over the other strand, and the pattern color will go under the other strand. The result is that the pattern strand will stand out from the background, making the design more distinct. This consistency is most easily achieved if you work in the round and can manage to work with one color of yarn in your right hand and the other color in your left.

For a simple two-color design in which a dark color is the background and a light color forms the pattern, you'd hold the background color in your right hand and the pattern color in your left. Some knitters work with both colors in either their right or left hands. This is fine, as long as you pay attention to the orientation of the strands as you change color. For the swatch shown on the previous page, the teal was stranded over the cream at the bottom of the swatch, which makes the cream motif stand out from the background. When the stranding is reversed and cream goes over teal, the motifs become smaller and recede into the background.

Stranding holding background color in right hand, pattern color in left hand

Pattern color goes under the background color

Background color goes over pattern color

Floats

Strands formed on the back of the work by the yarn not in use are called floats. In general, you don't want the unused yarn to float over more than four or five stitches, and most charts made for knitting take this into account. If you do need to carry a yarn over more than five stitches, you should catch it in the working yarn every five or fewer stitches. To do this, simply bring the yarn not in use up and over the working yarn before knitting the next stitch.

Some knitters like to work the yarn not in use together with the one in use on every stitch. They do this by weaving the idle yarn over the first stitch and under the next. Not only do we find this method tedious, it produces a fabric that's a bit too thick and stiff for our taste—for all the bother, we'd rather just buy Kevlar.

Catching floats on the back of the work

Tension

When stranding, it's also important to leave plenty of room for the stitches to lie flat. After you've worked two or more stitches of one color and are ready to change colors, spread the just-knit stitches out on the right needle, bring the new yarn loosely across the back of those stitches and knit the next stitch. If you pull the new color too tightly, you'll end up with an uneven and too-small eyesore.

> ### EVEN TENSION IN FLAT STRANDED KNITTING
> If you have a tension problem with purl rows, go have a cup of tea or take a deep breath. Then try this. Usually our purl stitches are larger than our knit stitches, so try working the wrong-side rows on a needle one size smaller than the one used on knit rows. Try this in a gauge swatch first to be sure you're happy with the result.

Spread out the stitches before using the next color

Swatch with tight floats

Swatch with evenly tensioned floats

Swatching for Multicolored Stranding

It's extremely important to do a gauge swatch in the multicolored pattern of your garment. The tension you get from a single-yarn swatch will be very different from that of a multi-yarn swatch, even when using the same yarn. The importance of gauge is discussed in detail in Chapter Twelve; here's how to make your multicolored gauge swatch.

If you'll be knitting flat, simply work a 4" (10cm) square swatch in pattern. If you'll be knitting in the round, we cannot stress enough how important it is to work your swatch exactly as you'll be knitting it, i.e. with all knit stitches and no purl stitches. There are a couple of ways to do this.

Knitting a Circular Swatch

Isolate a motif or part of your chart to swatch. You should do a swatch that will be at about 10" (25cm) around and 5" (12.5cm) high so that when you're finished you can lay it flat and easily measure an area that's 4" (10cm) square. Knit the swatch in the round, following the chart.

If you don't want to do such a large swatch, cast on the number of stitches needed for a 4" (10cm) square charted area and then cast on twenty more stitches. Divide onto three needles so you have ten stitches on Needles 1 and 3 and the motif stitches on Needle 2. Work a couple of rows with the main color. Now work alternating main color and contrasting color stitches on the first and last eight stitches on Needles 1 and 3, two main color stitches before and after the motif and the charted motif over the center stitches on Needle 2. Cut the swatch up the back, lay it flat and measure for stitches per inch (2.5cm).

Knitting a Swatch and Cutting the Yarn at the End of Every Row

If you don't want to swatch in the round, another option is to swatch on two double-point needles, working knit rows only. At the end of the row, cut the yarn, leaving a short tail, slide the stitches to the other end of the needle and begin again at the start of the next knit row, again leaving a short tail. You should add four to six extra stitches on each side of the charted knitting and anchor both colors in these stitches. This method actually takes us just as long as adding the extra twenty stitches for circular swatch knitting, but it's your choice.

Knitting a Swatch with Loose Strands at Back

We've had students who are extremely reluctant to waste even 6" (15cm) of yarn on a swatch. If you're one of them, try this method. Using two double-point needles, work as for the swatch with the cut ends, but at the end of the row pull out enough yarn to strand loosely behind the work and knit the next row. Once you've measured for gauge, go ahead and unravel it and knit with this yarn.

Intarsia

Intarsia is the method to use if you want to work motifs of different colors without carrying multiple strands along the back of the work. Rather than working the yarns directly from the ball or skein, you'll work with bobbins or long strands of different colors. The most important thing to remember about intarsia is that you need to twist the yarns together when changing colors.

Changing Colors

1 If you're knitting a block of green and you want to knit the last stitch of the block with cream, twist the yarns by bringing cream under the green, then knit the stitch with cream.

2 If you're knitting a block of cream and want to knit the first stitch of the next block with cream, just knit the stitch with cream; to work the next green stitch, bring the green up over the cream and continue.

3 If you're purling a block of green and want to purl the last stitch of the block with cream, bring the cream under the green, then purl the stitch with cream.

4 On the other side, if you're purling a block of cream and want to purl the first stitch of the next block with cream, just purl the stitch with cream and then pick up green over the cream and continue. The photo shows the cream stitch purled and the green going over the cream to continue.

Preparing Yarn and Following a Chart

The easiest way to talk about this is through example, in this case a two-color tulip on a plain cream background. If this lone tulip is to appear on the front of a cardigan, you'll work with separate balls of background color on each side of the motif and strands of green, blue and cream (background) within the motif.

   Because you're not going to carry yarns along the back, each section of the motif will need its own strand of yarn. To calculate the length of each piece, count the number of stitches in the area to cover. Wrap the yarn around the needle once for each stitch and add about 8" (20cm).

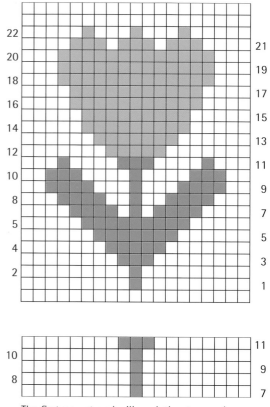

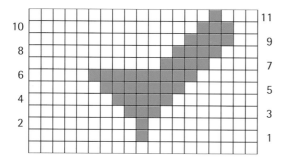

You'll need three strands of green. The first strand will be used for the first six rows of pattern, which is forty-one stitches. On Row 7 you'll introduce two new strands. The original strand will work the remaining stitches of the right leaf.

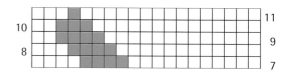

The first new strand will work the stem and sepal, seven stitches.

The second new strand will work the remaining stitches of the left leaf, sixteen stitches. For the blue you need only one length long enough to work 103 stitches.

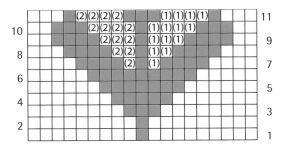

For the cream you'll begin using two separate lengths of the body yarn, one on each side of the motif, plus two additional strands to fill in between the leaves, each one long enough to knit fourteen stitches.

To begin Row 1 of the chart, work with the background color to the center stitch of the chart, knit one stitch with green and then continue with the background color to the end of the row. Work Row 2 on the wrong side the same way. Because Rows 1 and 2 have only one green stitch in the center, it's okay to continue with one background yarn and introduce the second one on Row 3.

On Row 3, knit with cream to the green stitch, knit three green, join a new ball of cream and knit to the end of the row. On Row 4, purl with cream to the green stitch, purl five green, then purl to the end of the row with the other ball of cream. Continue in this manner through Row 6. Be sure to twist the colors as described on page 119.

On Row 7, knit to the green stitch with cream, knit four green, attach a new cream strand and knit one cream, attach the shortest green strand and knit

one green, attach second cream strand and knit one cream, attach the longer green strand and knit four green, and then finish the row with the other ball of cream. Now you're set up with one strand of green for each leaf, one for the stem and one strand of cream for each area between the leaves.

When you've finished Row 11, cut all the green strands and the two short cream strands to a length just long enough for weaving in. Beginning with Row 12, work the background with the two balls of cream and use the one long strand of blue for the flower.

By the time you get to Row 21, you'll probably have no interest in joining any new strands of cream to work the top of the tulip. That's okay—we didn't either. We worked the final two rows by stranding the background and flower colors, dropping one ball of cream and continuing with the other.

Right side

Wrong side

Mosaic Knitting

Mosaic knitting is an easy way to work with two colors of yarn. You end up with an interesting two-color pattern, but you work with only one yarn at a time. The first two rows are knitted with one color, the next two rows are worked with the other color, etc.

The technique was developed by Barbara Walker, and her book *Mosaic Knitting* is loaded with charts for motifs and bands. The designs can be worked in garter stitch, Stockinette stitch or a combination of the two. Mosaic patterns can be written out, but they are most commonly presented in chart form, which is much easier to follow. You need to know only three things to follow a mosaic pattern:

1. The color of the first stitch of an odd-numbered (right side) row is the color you'll work for that row and the next (wrong-side) row.
2. On a dark row, you knit all the dark stitches and slip all the light stitches. On a light row, you knit the light stitches and slip the dark stitches.
3. On right-side rows, slip stitches with yarn held in back (to the wrong side). On wrong-side rows, slip stitches with yarn held in front (also to the wrong side).

Reading Mosaic Charts

Here is a chart for a Greek-key type of pattern. The first and last stitches are edge stitches. If you want to work multiple repeats, work the first stitch, the twelve-stitch repeat as many times as desired and then the last two stitches.

Because the first stitch in Row 1 is white, you will work Row 1 and Row 2 with white. However, you can see that there are two blue stitches in these rows—this means you will have to cast on with blue or work the row before beginning the chart with blue.

The first four rows written out would look like this:

Row 1 (RS, white): K1, *sl 1 wyb, k11; repeat from * to last 2 sts, sl 1 wyb, k1.
Row 2 (WS, white): K1, *sl 1 wyf, k11; repeat from * to last 2 sts, sl 1 wyf, k1.
Row 3 (RS, blue): K1, *k1, sl 1 wyb, k3, sl 1 wyb, k1, sl 1 wyb, k3, sl 1 wyb; repeat from * to last 2 sts, k2.
Row 4 (WS, blue): K1, *k1, sl 1 wyf, k3, sl 1 wyf, k1, sl 1 wyf, k3, sl 1 wyf; repeat from * to last 2 sts, k2.

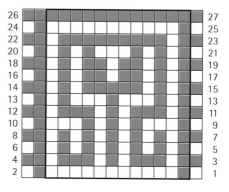

We hope you agree that it is much easier to follow a chart than row-by-row text—it's certainly a lot easier to present! On the next page is the motif worked four different ways. In the first sample, all the stitches are knit; in the second sample, all the cream stitches are knit, but the green stitches are purled on wrong-side rows; in the third sample, all green stitches are knit, but the cream stitches are purled on wrong-side rows; and in the final sample, all stitches are knit on the right side and purled on the wrong side.

Garter stitch mosaic

Combination mosaic with green garter stitch and cream
Stockinette stitch

Combination mosaic with cream garter stitch and green
Stockinette stitch

Stockinette stitch mosaic

Designing Mosaics

Once you get the hang of this technique, you may want to create your own motifs. The most important thing to know is that you shouldn't slip more than three stitches in a row, or the work will pucker. The only other rule is that in order to have a stitch of the color you're not currently working with, that stitch must have been worked in that color in the previous row.

Square designs lend themselves to mosaics better than those that have a lot of curves. However, it is possible to work designs with a little bit of curve, such as a heart. Note that single stitches of the dark color are added to the background as necessary to satisfy the "don't slip more than three stitches" rule.

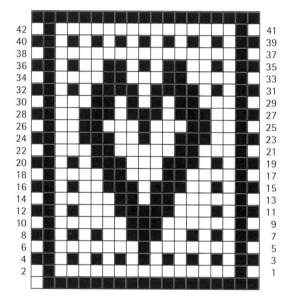

Mitered Knitting

Mitered knitting, also known as domino knitting, is really more of a shaping technique than it is a colorwork technique, but it looks so great when worked with several colors we couldn't help but include the basics here. Begin by making one square and then add more squares above the first one to form a strip. Subsequent strips are then added to the original strip until the fabric is the desired size. The result is a sort of patchwork, but you don't have to sew the patches together—they're connected as they're knit. You also weave in most of the ends as you go, so the finishing is not nearly as tedious as you might expect.

The Technique

Here are the methods you'll use to make a mitered square. Because you'll be working on a limited number of stitches for each square, choose short needles to knit with. We use our double points here, and you can add a stopper to one end of each needle if you're worried about the stitches falling off the other end.

Casting On
Mitered squares begin with an odd number of stitches. Cast on using the knitted-on or cable method (see Chapter Five) leaving a short (3" [7.5cm] or less) tail. Don't use the long-tail cast on here, because in order to weave in the tail, it needs to be on the opposite end of the working yarn after the cast on.

Weaving in the tail

Edge Stitches
With the exception of the first stitch of the first row, you'll slip the first stitch of every row knitwise and purl the last stitch of every row.

Forming the Miter
On right-side rows, you'll knit to the center three stitches, work a double decrease and work to the end of the row. All wrong-side rows are worked even. Continue in this manner until you have only one stitch left.

Joining Colors and Weaving in Ends
You'll always join a new color on a right-side row. To start a new color on Row 2, you'll slip the first stitch and simply knit the next with the new color, leaving a short (3" [7.5cm] or less) tail. When knitting the third stitch, bring the cast-on tail over the working yarn and then knit the stitch. Repeat this for several stitches until the tail is woven into the back of the work. When you work Row 4, weave in the tail of the second color in the same manner. All tails should be woven in with the first stitches of the right-side row after they are introduced.

There are no rules regarding how many colors you may use or how to use them, except that each wrong-side row is worked in the same color as the previous row. Limiting each square to two colors keeps things manageable, but this is not a hard rule; you should feel free to experiment and do your own thing.

The Basic Garter Square

Here's a basic two-color square. Color A is cream, and Color B is teal.

Cast on an odd number of stitches; seventeen are shown here, with A.

Row 1: (WS) With A, k16, p1.
Row 2: With B, sl 1, k6, sl 1, k2tog, psso, k6, p1.
Row 3: With B, sl 1, k to last st, p1.
Row 4: With A, sl 1, k5, sl 1, k2tog, psso, k5, p1.
Row 5: With A, sl 1, k to last st, p1.

Continue in this manner, changing colors every other row and working one fewer stitch before and after the center decrease on right-side rows until you have three stitches left and then work a double decrease on these stitches so you have one remaining stitch. Regardless of which color you used for the last row, work the remaining three stitches together with Color A so it will be in position to pick up stitches for the next square.

That's it—your first two-colored mitered square! If you're finished, cut the yarn, thread the tail through the last stitch and pull up taut. If you'll be adding another square to form a strip, keep the stitch live and on the needle.

Variations

Mitered squares can also be knit in Stockinette stitch or a combination of garter and Stockinette stitches. The same rules apply to edge stitches as noted previously. With the exception of the first stitch of the first row, slip the first stitch of every row knitwise and purl the last stitch of every row.

Stockinette stitch basic square

Combination basic square

> **MARKING THE CENTER STITCH**
> If you don't want to count stitches as you're working a square, put a pin-type marker on the right side in the center stitch—this will be the center of the three-stitch double decrease, so stop one stitch short of this one and work the decrease. Move the marker up after every right-side row.

Knitting the First Strip of Squares

To make the second square of the first strip, begin with the live stitch from the first square on the needle and continue with A to pick up and knit seven stitches along the top of the square. When you get to the corner, go slightly around the corner to pick up the last stitch of the outside edge—this will be the center stitch. Cast on eight more stitches. Now you can work the second square the same as the first, using the same or a different contrast color. Continue making squares like this to the desired height.

Knitting Subsequent Strips of Squares

To begin the second strip, cast on eight stitches and then pick up and knit the last stitch on the bottom edge of the square in the first strip—this will be the center stitch. Pick up and knit eight stitches along the side edge of the square in the first strip. Now you can work the square as usual. For the next square, pick up eight stitches along the top of the just-completed square, pick up one in the corner and then pick up eight stitches along the side of the next square of the first strip. Continue making squares for this and subsequent strips in this fashion.

LOOSEN UP
When you change colors and slip the first stitch of a right-side row, it's easy to pull the edge stitches too tight. After slipping the first stitch, knit the next stitch loosely, loosening the edge stitch by inserting a needle if necessary.

Knitting in Multiple Directions

Here's where things get really interesting. Working with multiple colors and in multiple directions creates distinctive, organic compositions. The sample shown here has two strips of two squares of alternating colors each knitted in one direction. The next set of four strips begins along the bottom of the first square, the one after that begins diagonally opposite the first square and the last set begins along the left side of the first square. You could also create some interesting op-art effects with crisp yarns in black and white.

Knitting Triangles

You can use triangles to shape your mitered pieces into something other than a square, or you can use them as a filler between squares to make a piece that shows on the diagonal. Here's an example of the latter.

Filler Triangles

Knit two basic squares and place them next to each other with the right side facing and the last stitch of each square at the top. Beginning at the top stitch of the right square, pick up and knit along the edge of this square. When you reach the corner, pick up through the corresponding corner of the other square, picking up one stitch through two corner loops. Now pick up and knit along the edge of the second square. From here you work as for a square, but knit one fewer stitch at the end of each row. When you've worked the final decrease, you'll have the original number of stitches plus one, divided by two.

Here's the row-by-row for joining squares that begin with seventeen stitches. Pick up and knit eight stitches along the side of the first square, pick up the corner stitches as described above, then pick up and knit eight stitches along the side of the second square.

Row 1: K16, p1.
Row 2: Sl 1, k6, sl 1, k2tog, psso, k5, p1, turn.
Row 3: Sl 1, k11, p1, turn.
Row 4: Sl 1, k4, sl 1, k2tog, psso, k3, p1, turn.
Row 5: Sl 1, k7, p1, turn.
Row 6: Sl 1, k2, sl 1, k2tog, psso, k1, p1, turn.
Row 7: Sl 1, k3, p1, turn.
Row 8: Sl 2, k2tog, psso.

You'll end with nine stitches (17 + 1 = 18, 18 ÷ 2 = 9). Place the stitches on hold. Work the same filler triangle on the bottom of the piece.

Diagonal miters

Beginning and Ending Triangles

Beginning and ending triangles fill in the small triangular voids in each corner to create a square or rectangular piece of knitting. Our sample shows these knitted with teal.

Left Triangle

With right side facing, pick up and knit nine stitches along the edge of the square.

Row 1: K8, p1.
Row 2: Sl 1, k6, p2tog.
Row 3: Sl 1, k5, p1, turn.
Row 4: Sl 1, k4, p2tog.
Row 5: Sl 1, k3, p1, turn.
Row 6: Sl 1, k2, p2tog.
Row 7: Sl 1, k1, p1, turn.
Row 8: Sl 1, p2tog.

Place the remaining five stitches on a holder with the top held stitches.

Right Triangle

With right side facing, pick up and knit nine stitches along the edge of the square.

Row 1: K8, p1.
Row 2: Sl 1, k6, p1, turn.
Row 3: Sl 1, k5, p2tog.
Row 4: Sl 1, k4, p1, turn.
Row 5: Sl 1, k3, p2tog.
Row 6: Sl 1, k2, p1, turn.
Row 7: Sl 1, k1, p2tog.
Row 8: Sl 1, p1, turn.
Row 9: P2tog.

Place the remaining five stitches on a holder with the top held stitches.

Now you can knit a few rows and bind off or continue for a larger piece. Repeat on the bottom of the diagonals.

Double Knitting

Double knitting is exactly what the name implies: You knit two rows at the same time. The resulting fabric is double the thickness of regular knitting. You're knitting two right-side rows at once: One will be the front of the piece, and the other will be the back. Worked in a two-color design, the design will be the same on both sides, but the colors will be reversed. Double knitting can be worked in Stockinette stitch, ribbing or in any textured stitch, for that matter. However, you'll need to be very comfortable with a stitch pattern (or have a gymnastic brain) in order to work both right- and wrong-side rows of a textured stitch at the same time.

Casting On

There are a couple of ways to cast on for double knitting.

Cast-On Method 1

Use the cast-on method of your choice with the two yarns held together (Color A and Color B). Each cast-on stitch will actually be two stitches (one of each color). Cast on the number of stitches needed for the project. For example, if you want a scarf that's forty stitches wide, cast on forty stitches with the two yarns held together. This will result in eighty stitches on the needle, and every other stitch will be a different color; one color will be worked for the side of the fabric facing you, and the other will be worked for the opposite side. You will probably have to manipulate the stitches so that Color A is always to the right of Color B.

Cast-On Method 2

You can also cast on using only one color. With only one yarn, the edge is less bulky and a bit neater. Use the method of your choice to cast on the required number of stitches for the project with Color A. To set up for double knitting, join B and proceed as follows: *Knit one with A and leave the stitch on the needle; bring both yarns forward, purl the same stitch with B and slide both stitches off the needle; repeat from *. You now have twice as many stitches as you started with, and every other stitch is a different color.

The Edges

Neat edges for double knitting are difficult to achieve; covering them with crochet or I-cord is a good option. However, if you don't want to take that extra step, here are a few ways to work the edges.

Do-Nothing Edges

Knit the first stitch and purl the second stitch of every row, which will result in regular Stockinette-stitch edges that roll in slightly. The two pieces of fabric will not be joined together at the edges. This is how the lower section of the plain Stockinette swatch was done.

Twist and Knit

Twist the strands together at the beginning of each row and then proceed as usual. The plain Stockinette-stitch edges will be sealed. This is how the midsection of the plain Stockinette swatch was done.

Knit with Two Strands

Knit the first and last stitches of every row with both strands held together for an edge of two-color garter stitch. This is how the upper section of the plain Stockinette swatch was done.

Slip-Stitch Edges

For this edge, slip the first stitch (A) with both yarns in front and slip the second stitch (B) with both yarns in back. This will seal the edges and create a chain-stitch edge, the same as in one-color knitting. This is how the two-color design swatch was done.

Plain Stockinette Stitch

Let's start off with the easiest stitch: Stockinette. We'll also start without a design—we'll simply have one color on the front and the other on the back. The stitches are cast on with the regular long-tail method with Color A (teal).

For the first row, join B, then knit with A and purl with B as follows:

Row 1: *With both yarns in back, k1A; with both yarns in front, p1B; repeat from * to the end of the row.

Row 2: *With both yarns in back, k1B; with both yarns in front, p1A; repeat from * to the end of the row.

Repeat Rows 1 and 2 to make a two-faced fabric. If you don't twist the two yarns together at the end of each row, you'll end up with two pieces of Stockinette stitch that can be separated—the swatch was knit this way at the bottom.

Two-Color Designs

Any two-color chart can be used for double knitting, but you'll need to be an ambidextrous visualizer. Every square on the chart is one stitch, but it represents a stitch of one color on the facing side and the other color on the back side. For this chart, Color A is cream and B is teal. This swatch was cast on with A and a regular long-tail cast on, and the first two stitches of each row are slipped.

Cast on twenty stitches with Color A. Work Row 1 as for regular Stockinette-stitch double knitting: *With both yarns in back, k1A; with both yarns in front, p1B; repeat from * to the end of the row. Work Row 2 as for Row 1, but knit the B stitches with B and purl the A stitches with A. The first patterned row of the chart is Row 3, which you read from right to left. Work the first seven stitches of the chart as established, knitting seven with A and purling seven with B. For the color change, knit the next stitch with B and purl the corresponding stitch on the back with A. You'll see that on the needle you now have two B stitches followed by one A stitch. Work the next four stitches by knitting with A and purling with B and then knit one with B and purl one with A. Complete the row by knitting with A and purling with B. Now for Row 4, you'll need to imagine that all the white stitches on the chart are blue and knit with B, and the blue stitches are white and knit with A.

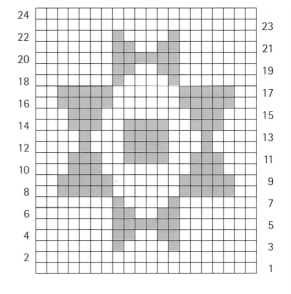

Knit/Purl Combinations

Here's a sample of two-color, 2/2, double-knit rib—knit that ten times fast! As with any two-color knitting, if you change colors with knit stitches, you won't see two-color purl bumps on the right side. Begin by casting on a multiple of four plus two stitches (the swatch shows eighteen stitches) in Color A (cream). Join Color B.

> **Row 1:** *(With both yarns back, k1A and leave stitch on needle, bring both yarns forward and p1B in the same stitch) twice; (with both yarns back, k1B and leave stitch on needle, bring both yarns forward and p1A in the same stitch) twice; repeat from * to last 2 stitches, (with both yarns back, k1A and leave stitch on needle, bring both yarns forward and p1B in the same stitch) twice.
>
> **Row 2:** *(With both yarns back, k1B; with both yarns forward, p1A) twice; (with A forward and B back, p1A; k1B) twice; repeat from * to last 4 stitches, (with both yarns back, k1B; with both yarns forward p1A) twice.
>
> **Row 3:** *(With both yarns back, k1A; with both yarns forward, p1B) twice; (with B forward and A back, p1B; k1A) twice; repeat from * to last 4 stitches, (with both yarns back, k1A; with both yarns forward, p1B) twice.

To transition to the main piece where A will be the background on one side and B will be the background on the other, begin plain Stockinette double knitting as described above. If A is the first stitch on the needle, begin with both yarns back and knit with A. If B is the first stitch on the needle, begin with both yarns back and knit with B.

Binding Off

There are several methods for binding off, some more visible than others.

Bind-Off Method 1

This is the fastest method and can be used on a piece that began with Cast-On Method 1 (see page 130). With Color A, knit two together (one A stitch and one B stitch) twice and then *pass the first stitch on the right needle over the second stitch and off the needle as for a regular bind off. Knit the next pair together. Repeat from * until all stitches are bound off. This same method can be used holding the two yarns together.

Bind-Off Method 2

Separate the knits and purls onto two separate needles. With A, join the two sides with a sewn bind off (see Chapter Five).

Bind-Off Method 3

Work one row of plain Stockinette double knitting as for the transition from ribbing as described above. With A, knit one, purl one, knit one; pass the first stitch over the next two; *purl one and pass the first stitch over the next two; knit one and pass the first stitch over the next two; repeat from * until all stitches are bound off.

Increasing in Double Knit

Increase Method 1

This method is the same as the m1 increase (see Chapter Six) and is the easiest one to work with double knitting. Lift the running thread between two stitches on the facing fabric and knit it to make one right or left, as you like. Then lift the running stitch between two purl stitches from the other side and purl it to make one left or right, again as you like. Resume double knitting as established.

Increase Method 2

This method is the same as the lifted stitch increase (see Chapter Six). You'll have to do a bit of extra maneuvering to keep the stitches in the correct order, but the increase is nearly invisible. Using the same color yarn as the next stitch, and with both yarns back, work a lifted increase and then knit the next stitch. Slip the last stitch worked onto a cable needle and hold it in front. Bring both yarns forward and, with the other color, work a lifted increase purlwise and then purl the next stitch. Slip the last stitch onto a cable needle and hold it in back. Place the stitch on the front cable needle onto the right needle and then place the stitch on the back cable needle onto the right needle.

Decreasing in Double Knit

You can work knit two together or slip, slip, knit on the facing fabric and purl two together or slip, slip, purl on the other side (see Chapter Six). To decrease on the facing (knit) side, slip one knit stitch purlwise to the right needle, slip the next purl stitch onto a cable needle and hold in back, slip the knit stitch back to the left needle and work the next two stitches together with both yarns back. Now place the purl stitch on the left needle and work the next two purls together with both yarns in front.

Fixing Mistakes

The methods for fixing an incorrectly knit stitch are the same as with single knitting. If you've worked a purl that should have been a knit or a Color B stitch that should have been a Color A stitch, undo the column of stitches to the mistake, correct the stitch and use a crochet hook to work back up to the needle. For more information about fixing mistakes, see Chapter Four.

Working with Hand-Painted and Variegated Yarns

It's happened to us all: We've been awestruck by the beauty of a multicolored hand-painted yarn and borrowed from the grocery money to buy it. We excitedly wound the yarn, did a gauge swatch (you did do a gauge swatch, didn't you?) and cast on for a new pair of socks. Barely halfway down the leg (or the foot), we're crushed by the sight of stripes or blotchy pools of color in the fabric. This is not at all what we envisioned when we saw the yarn in the skein. The good news is that many of these yarns have improved greatly over their years of popularity, and the results are more even and satisfying. Let's take a brief look at the anatomy of multicolored yarn.

small gauge swatch you are happy with has nothing to do with the fabric you'll get when casting on for a sweater. The only way to accurately predict the look of the knitted yarn is to do a life-size sample.

Hand-painted yarns don't have repeats that are as precise as those found in variegated yarn, but the colors do repeat regularly. The same thing holds true for these yarns: You need to do a life-size swatch to see what you're going to get from it. A small swatch can change character depending on where you started in the color repeat.

Repeats

Machine-produced variegated yarn has a measurable length of each color that consistently repeats throughout the skein. As a result, this yarn will look very different when knitted in a narrow strip than it will when knitted in a wider piece. That's why a

Adding Texture

By simply knitting these yarns in a textured stitch, either by following a stitch pattern or by randomly inserting purl stitches, a colorway can take on a whole new life. As always, the best way to choose a stitch for your yarn is to experiment with different options. For our sample, we worked Stockinette stitch for all shades of green and changed to reverse Stockinette stitch for the golds and browns.

Self-Patterning Yarn

Thanks to the advent of self-patterning yarns, we can now knit intricately patterned socks and other small items without too much brainwork. For those of us with type-A personalities who need to take charge, we can also calculate and cut lengths of the color repeats to make larger patterns; the pillow shown here was done that way, starting from the center and knitting out to the edges.

Self-patterning sock yarn

Here, the same yarn is used in measured lengths of solid and pattern.

Multicolored Motifs

Hand-painted or variegated yarns can be used to great effect as a substitute for several individual contrasting colors. Following a chart for colored knitting, use a solid color for the main color and a multicolored yarn for all contrasting color stitches.

Multicolored Ribbing

Multicolored, or corrugated, ribbings are often used on traditional Fair Isle sweaters, but they can also be used in any of your multicolored projects.

Your ribbing can be 1/1, 2/2 or whatever you like. However, because you'll be stranding the yarns, the ribbing will not have the accordion characteristics of a one-color ribbing.

The cast on can be done in one or two colors. When casting on with two colors, one color will be the base, and the other will form the stitches on the needle (see Chapter Five). A one-color cast on is just as effective—it's simply a matter of choice.

To prevent the ribbing from having any contrasting purl bumps showing on the right side of the piece, work Row 1 as all knit stitches. For a 1/1 rib, *knit one in the main color, knit one in the contrast color; repeat from * to the end of the row or round; for a 2/2 rib, *knit two in the main color, knit two in the contrast color; repeat from * to the end of the row or round. This puts the bumps from the color change on the wrong side of the rib. Now you can knit the main color stitches and purl the contrast-color stitches for the rib. If you're introducing a second (or third or fourth) contrasting color, do so on the right side and work the first row of

these stitches in knit. Of course, you could also opt to purl the main-color stitches and knit the contrast-color stitches.

Two-Color Braids

Braids look great for cuffs, pocket tops, bottoms of hats, tops of socks and other borders. They can be used right at the cast-on edge, anywhere in your knitting or just before a bound-off edge.

From top to bottom:
Simple two-row braid, variation braids running in both directions, three-row braids running in both directions

. . . .

Simple Two-Row Braid

Work this braid, which is shown at the top of the sampler swatch, after having worked a round or row with Color A.

Worked in the Round (even number of stitches)

Round 1: *Knit 1 B, knit 1 A; repeat from * to end of round.

Round 2: With both yarns forward, *purl 1 A, drop A, bring B under A, purl 1 B, drop B, bring A under B; repeat from * to end of round.

Worked Flat (even number of stitches)

Row 1: *Knit 1 B, knit 1 A; repeat from * to end of row.

Row 2: With both yarns to back (RS of work), *knit 1 B, drop B and bring A over B, knit 1 A, drop A and bring B over A; repeat from * to end of row.

When you've finished Round or Row 2, your yarns will seem hopelessly entangled. They are. But if you're going to continue with A only, simply cut B and pull it free. If you want to continue in a two-color pattern, you'll have to untwist the yarns.

Row 1 of braid worked flat

Row 2 of braid worked flat

Continue with A only.

Three-Row Braid

To work a three-row braid at the cast-on edge, work a two-color long-tail cast on (see Chapter Five) and then begin with Row 1. To work this braid at any point in your knitting or just before the bind off, end after having worked one row of A, then begin with Row 1. The two bottom braids on the sampler were worked this way.

Worked Flat
Row 1: *Knit 1 A, knit 1 B; repeat from * to end of row.
Row 2: With both yarns to back, *knit 1 B, drop B, bring A over B, knit 1 A, drop A, bring B over A; repeat from * to end of row.
Row 3: *Purl 1 A, drop A, bring B over A, purl 1 B, drop B, bring A over B; repeat from * to end of row.

To work the braid in the opposite direction, work Rows 2 and 3, bringing the yarns under rather than over.

Worked in the Round
Round 1: *Knit 1 A, knit 1 B; repeat from * to end of round.
Round 2: With both yarns forward, *purl 1 A, drop A, bring B over A, purl 1 B, drop B, bring A over B; repeat from * to end of round.
Round 3: With both yarns forward, *purl 1 A, drop A, bring B under A, purl 1 B, drop B, bring A under B; repeat from * to end of round.

When you've finished Round 2, your two yarns will seem hopelessly entangled. Don't worry—when you work Round 3, they'll untangle.

To work a braid that faces in the opposite direction, work Round 1, Round 3 and then Round 2. You can also work Round 1 with Color A only for a more subtle effect.

Variation Braid

This braid looks similar to the three-row braid but is worked over two rows. The third and fourth braids from the bottom of the sampler were worked with this method. Note that the V of the braid is not connected like it is in the three-row braid.

Worked Flat
Row 1 (RS): *Purl 1 A, drop A, bring B over A, purl 1 B, drop B, bring A over B; repeat from * to end of row.
Row 2: *Knit 1 B, drop B, bring A over B, knit 1 A, drop A, bring B over A; repeat from * to end of row.

To work this braid in the opposite direction, bring the yarns under before working the next stitch.

Worked in the Round
Round 1: *Purl 1 A, drop A, bring B over A, purl 1 B, drop B, bring A over B; repeat from * to end of round.
Round 2: *Purl 1 A, drop A, bring B under A, purl 1 B, drop B, bring A under B; repeat from * to end of round.

To work the braid in the opposite direction, work Round 2 and then Round 1.

Duplicate Stitch

Duplicate stitch can be used to simulate two-color knitting in small areas. The process literally duplicates a knit stitch in a new color. In this example we've duplicate stitched the tulip used for the intarsia example.

1 Thread a strand of yarn onto a tapestry needle. Bring the yarn from back to front at the base of the stitch (below the V).

2 Bring the needle from right to left under both loops of the stitch in the row above and pull the yarn through. Bring the needle from front to back at the original exit point and then up at the base of the next stitch to be covered.

> **REDUCING BULK**
> When duplicate stitching, split your plies and use only half the original yarn. This will cover the stitch without adding bulk.

Cross-Stitch

For cross-stitching, make an X over two vertical stitches. String the Xs together to create a pattern. Use the whole strand of yarn to add dimension.

Embroidery

Anything goes here—crack open your old (or new) needlework texts and use any patterns you find there or make up your own. Use half the ply of your yarn to make lazy-daisy stitches, French knots, stem stitches or whatever else you like.

Knitting Stripes in the Round

We've all seen them—otherwise-adorable baby hats, almost-handsome scarves, could-have-been-great sweaters. What makes these striped garments also-rans is the unsightly stair step that interrupts the stripes at the beginning/end of the color-change rounds.

There are several ways to deal with this problem. One way is to knit the first color and then join the second color and knit one round. When you get back to the join, slip the first stitch of the second color and then continue knitting in that color until it's time to change again. The lower three joins on the swatch (at right) were done this way.

Another way to minimize the join is to begin as described above, but when you get to the first stitch of the new color, lift the stitch below it onto the left needle and knit the two stitches together. We think this works better, and the center three joins on the swatch were done this way.

The top of the swatch shows what happens if you do nothing at all.

If you're going to be knitting deep stripes with more than a few rounds, cut the old color at the end of the repeat. Each time you begin a new color, slip about ten stitches from the left needle to the right needle to change the place where the colors are joined. Begin knitting with the new color. When you get to the tail of the old color, weave the tail of the old color over, under, over and under the new color for three or four stitches. When you're three or four stitches in front of the tail of the new color, bring that tail over the working yarn and knit the stitch. Now you have something that looks like a float on the back of the work. When you work the remaining stitches of the round, work this "float" under, over and under the working yarn. When you've finished the stripes, gently tug on what's left of the tails and finish weaving them into the back of the work.

Deep stripes

⑨ Cables

Whether used in traditional Aran sweaters or as freelance agents in modern compositions, cables add deep and rich texture to your knitting. As with other subjects addressed in this book, this is not meant to be a complete guide to the subject but rather an overview of the types of cables and accents you can use, along with a few tips for excellent results. For details on working crossings with a cable needle, see Chapter Four.

Types of Cables

There is a lot of variety within each of the categories that follow. Cables can change direction, have more or fewer stitches, have longer or shorter repeats and comprise only knit stitches or a combination of knits and purls.

Simple Cables

The simplest form of cable is one that crosses two sets of stitches over each other in one direction and at set intervals. The most common of these are 2/2, 3/3 and 4/4 cables, where you pass two stitches over two, three stitches over three or four stitches over four. Simple math will give us the crossing intervals: Add the two sides together for the total number of stitches in the cable to get the number of the crossing row. For example, 3 + 3 = 6. Cross a 3/3 cable every six rows. This is not absolute, but the minimum number of rows you'll want to have between crossings unless you want a very tight and very dense cable. Feel free to add as many rows as you want between crossings.

Cables can cross to the right or to the left. To cross a cable to the right, wherein the left stitches cross on top of the right stitches, place half the cable stitches on a cable needle and hold them in back of the work, knit the other half of the cable stitches from the left needle and then knit the stitches from the cable needle. To cross a cable to the left, place half the cable stitches on a cable needle and hold them in front of the work, knit the other half of the cable stitches from the left needle and then knit the stitches from the cable needle.

The first sample shown here begins with two 3/3 or six-stitch cables. The cable on the right features a left crossing cable every six rows, and the cable on the left crosses to the right every six rows. About halfway up, each cable was increased two stitches to become 4/4 or eight-stitch cables, which are turned every eight rows.

Double Cables

Double cables have both a right and left crossing on the same row and grow from a center stem. Our sample shows two twelve-stitch double cables. The one on the right appears to climb upward—it's worked with a 3/3 right cross, followed by a 3/3 left cross, and the crossings are done at eight-row intervals. The cable on the left climbs downward. It's worked the same as the other cable except that the order of the cable crossings is reversed—the first is a left cross, and the second is a right cross.

Plaited Cables

Plaited cables, like simple cables, usually comprise two sets of the same number of stitches crossing each other, but unlike simple cables, they have additional stitches and the crossings are staggered. For example, a six-stitch plait, shown at right in our sample swatch, has a 2/2 left crossing plus two knit stitches on Row 3 and then two knit stitches plus a 2/2 right crossing on Row 7. The nine-stitch plait, also shown in the swatch, has a 3/3 left crossing plus three stitches on Row 3 and then three stitches and a 3/3 right crossing on Row 9 (see an example of plaited cables in the Lisdoonvarna Aran on page 256).

Double-Crossing Cables

Don't worry—these cables are straightforward and honest! Double-crossing cables often require the use of two cable needles and involve both right and left crossings with the same group of stitches. The resulting cables have a lot of dimension, and we love to place beads in the center (see the Beady Cable Gloves on page 218). The cable on the right half of the sample uses the same cable as the gloves—one stitch crosses to the left over three stitches, and one stitch crosses to the right over the same three stitches. The other cable involves three sets of three stitches—the third set crosses the second set from left to right and then the first set crosses the other two from right to left.

Traveling Stitches

Although not technically a cable, patterns made with traveling stitches are frequently used in cable designs as well as in many other stitch patterns—they often appear as stems for leaf patterns.

A traveling stitch is usually a knit stitch that moves upward from right to left and/or left to right on a background of reverse Stockinette stitch. To move a stitch to the left, put the stitch onto a cable needle and hold in front, work the next stitch and then knit the stitch from the cable needle through the back loop. To move a stitch to the right, work to the stitch before the traveling stitch, put this stitch onto a cable needle and hold in back, knit the traveling stitch through the back loop and then work the stitch from the cable needle. Traveling stitches can also cross each other. To make a right cross, hold the first stitch in back and knit the second stitch through the back loop and then knit the first stitch through the back loop. To make a left cross, hold the first stitch in front, work the second stitch and then work the first. Whether the traveling stitches are crossing or moving straight up, they are always knit through the back loop.

Accents

There are various ways to dress up and accent your cables. Here are a few ideas.

Two-Color Cables

These are best worked with three separate strands of yarn. Our sample starts with a blue strand for the stitches before the cable and half the cable stitches, a white strand for half the cable, and another blue strand for the stitches after the cable. When working the cable crossing, use the first strand of blue for the stitches before the cable, the white strand for half the cable, and the second blue strand for the other half of the cable and the stitches after the cable. When changing colors, use the twisting technique employed in intarsia (see Chapter Eight).

Twisted Stitches

Twisted stitches are described and shown in Chapter Four. Columns of twisted stitches on both sides of a cable add a defining touch.

Bobbles

Bobbles can be added in a staggered fashion on both sides of a cable. They can also be placed inside a large diamond cable or even in the center of a double-crossing cable. Bobbles are formed by increasing one stitch to three or five stitches, working a few rows and then decreasing back to one stitch. Our sample shows bobbles worked in Stockinette stitch at the bottom and bobbles of seed stitch at the top.

Panels

Traditional Aran sweaters usually feature panels alternating with cables and background stitches. Some panels showcase a distinctive motif, such as a diamond cable, while others feature allover designs.

Diamond Cables

In Irish folklore, diamonds represent wealth. Diamond cables can be short or long, wide or narrow. They look best on a reverse Stockinette-stitch background and can be filled in with a seed, double seed or garter stitch. Often used as a center panel, they can stand alone or have one or more partners. The part of the diamond that moves, or the cable part, can be one, two, three or more stitches, and they can be flanked by twisted stitches and/or bobbles.

Woven Trellis and Basket Stitches

There are several variations of these cable stitches that form an allover design that mimics woven baskets. The patterns can be dense, with a four-row crossing interval like our sample, or more open. They can have purl stitches between the cables or not. Our sample grows nicely from a 2/2 rib.

Honeycomb Cables

Honeycomb is one of the most aptly named cable patterns—you can almost taste the nectar. In Irish folklore, the honeycomb represents hard work. But it's really not difficult. This pattern has lots of depth and would be a good candidate for holding beads.

Trinity Stitch

One of the best-known stitches among Aran sweater knitters, the trinity stitch is simple to work and offers great texture while remaining somewhat open between the bobbles.

Cabled Ribs

Because cables by nature are somewhat accordionlike, they make great ribs. Shown here are a rib of simple two-stitch right-crossing cables separated by two purl stitches and a rib of four-stitch left-crossing cables separated by an eyelet stitch.

Baby cable rib

Cable and eyelet rib

Background Stitches

Cables need a fairly plain background against which they can strut their stuff. Popular choices shown in our sample are (in ascending order) reverse Stockinette stitch, seed stitch, double seed stitch and moss stitch. These allover designs are handy to use at the sides of the body and on the undersides of sleeves.

Planning Cable Designs

There are several things to consider when planning a cabled garment, especially when mixing different cables and patterns. Here are a few things to ponder at the drawing board.

Balancing Patterns

If you want to use cables that have varying crossing intervals (or total rows in the repeat), you'll be happiest if you choose cables that play well together. Cables that get along the best are those that divide evenly into the cable with the longest repeat (don't worry—we'll go easy on the math). For example, if you choose a twenty-four-row cable, you can use four-row, six-row, eight-row and twelve-row cables, which will all catch up with each other at regular intervals. In the space of twenty-four rows, you'll have six four-row cables, four six-row cables, three eight-row cables, two twelve-row cables and one twenty-four-row cable. (See the Lisdoonvarna Aran on page 256 for a real-life example.)

Calculating Cable Take Up

All the moving and crossing of stitches in cables causes the fabric to draw in significantly. If you're going to transition from a rib at the bottom of a sweater and then to a shoulder seam, you'll need to do some increasing and decreasing to keep the garment shape consistent. The absolutely best way to figure out how much your cable pulls in is by swatching.

If you're knitting a sweater that begins with a rib, knit a ribbed swatch that has the same number of stitches as your cable pattern. Measure the swatch and calculate the number of stitches per inch (2.5cm). Now knit the cable pattern on that number of stitches and compare the gauge of the two swatches. The difference will be the number of stitches you'll need to increase at the end of the rib, before you begin the cable pattern.

However, there are other considerations to factor in, too. This method would result in a cabled fabric that's the same width as the rib. If you want the rib to be a bit smaller than the body, to pull the sweater in at the bottom, you'll need to increase more stitches before beginning the cable pattern. A good way to figure this out is to knit a Stockinette-stitch swatch that has the same number of stitches as your cable pattern. Compare the gauge of the cable swatch to the Stockinette swatch and increase above the ribbing accordingly. When you get to the neckline and shoulder seams, decrease the cables at the same rate. The same would apply to the tops of sleeves. See the Lisdoonvarna Aran on page 256 for another method of calculation.

If you're knitting a scarf or another non-fitted item, you can begin and end with the same number of stitches as the cable pattern and show off the splay at each end as a design feature.

Increasing and Decreasing Cables

We've addressed the reason for increasing and decreasing to compensate for cable take up and shaping; here's how it works. If we're ending a rib and starting a cable pattern, and we want a six-stitch cable, we'll do a set-up row with four stitches for that cable. To increase, slip two stitches to the cable needle and hold in back or front, knit one, increase one, knit one; then do the same with the stitches from the cable needle. We use the lifted increase here.

To decrease at the top of a cable panel—say, for a shoulder seam—return the six-stitch cable to four stitches. For a left-crossing cable, the most invisible way is to k2tog (the first two stitches of the cable), k1, ssk (the fourth and fifth stitches), k1. For a right-crossing cable, k2tog, k1, ssk, k1.

TRANSITIONS
If you really want to show your knitting know-how, you'll plan the transition from a ribbing to a cable pattern so the ribs flow seamlessly into the cable design. Every case will be different, but the Lisdoonvarna Aran (see page 256) shows several examples.

Increasing and Decreasing in the Body or Sleeves

When shaping a cabled sweater, a great place to hide increases and decreases is on either side of a cable panel. For example, sleeve shaping is usually done at the beginning and end of right-side rows. But we prefer to shape the sleeve on both sides of a center cable panel. Not only will the shaping be nearly invisible, you'll have a straight seam to join at the underarm, increasing your chances of reaching knitting perfection. The example shown here has a six-stitch cable with two purl stitches on each side that are then flanked with seed stitch. The increases are made at the junction of the seed stitch and the purl stitches. We use the lifted stitch increase method (see Chapter Six) and make a right-leaning increase before the panel and a left-leaning increase after the panel. Use the same theory for decreasing, choosing your favorite mirrored pair.

Fixing Mistakes

Even the most diligent knitter may occasionally turn a cable in the wrong direction. If this happens to you, we hope you don't carry on for too long without noticing—you should stop often and admire your work. However, if you notice an incorrect cable crossing several rows back, you can still fix this without ripping out the rest of your work.

1 Locate the stitches that were incorrectly crossed—for this six-stitch cable, these would be the three stitches that crossed to the right but should have crossed to the left.

2 Trace these three stitches up to the needle and unravel them down to the error. Place the stitches on a short double-point needle or a small stitch holder and push them through to the front on the other side of the cable.

3 Begin picking up and knitting them as you would any Stockinette stitches.

4 Weave them under and over the other side of the cable at the appropriate interval as you work your way up. You could also make this correction with a crochet hook, picking up one stitch at a time and bringing all three to the next crossing.

⑩ Lace

According to the lace knitterati, lace knitting and knitted lace are two different things. Lace knitting qualifies as such only if every row of the knitting is patterned, i.e., has a variety of stitches that add to the overall pattern of the lace. If you get to take a vacation in the form of plain knitting or purling on every other row, you're making knitted lace. In our humble opinion, the terminology doesn't matter. We'd rather focus on the intricate, delicate and beautiful results you can achieve with strategically placed yarn overs and decreases.

Special Decreases

When working with lace patterns, you may encounter decreases you don't normally use with other knitting techniques. The first sample shown here is patterned on every row. It has a double decrease that is worked at the same place on both right- and wrong-side rows. Other than lacework, we can't think of another instance when you'd want to work this doubled-up double decrease, but it makes perfect sense here. The decreases are worked as follows.

S2kp
Slip two stitches together knitwise, knit one, pass the two slipped stitches over the knit one and off the needle.

S2pp

1 Slip two stitches together purlwise as if you were going to purl them together through the back loops.

2 Purl one and pass the two slipped stitches over the purl one and off the needle.

Would You Like Scallops With That?

Notice that the double decreases create a scalloped edge at the cast-on end of the swatch. If you want a straight edge, work six or more rows in Stockinette stitch, garter stitch, seed stitch or another stitch of your choice before beginning the lace pattern.

Size Matters

This second sample is knit with a plain purl row for all wrong-side rows. As in the first sample, the double decreases—in this case, p3togs—create a scalloped edge at the cast-on end.

The swatch is knitted with needles appropriate to the type of yarn; i.e., we used a US 6 (4mm) needle with a sport yarn.

Many knitters like to use larger-than-normal needles when knitting lace to accentuate the airiness of the pattern. Here's the same swatch knitted on US 13 (8mm) needles. Yes, this is a bit extreme, but there's nothing we won't do to prove a point!

The Magic of Blocking

Blocking is an essential part of most knitting, but never more so than with lace. What comes off your needles bears little resemblance to what you'll see once the piece has been blocked and all those eyelets are fully open. If you're using lace in a shaped garment such as a sweater or hat, it is essential that you wash and block your gauge swatch before beginning. The size change can be drastic. Of course, if you're knitting a scarf or shawl, the finished size doesn't matter as much.

Unblocked feather lace swatch

Blocked feather lace swatch

Fixing Mistakes in Lace

Because you've deliberately put holes in your knitting and used an overabundance of decreases going in different directions, it's nearly impossible to drop down a few rows to fix mistakes.

If you're working a pattern that has a plain knit or purl row for all wrong-side rows, you can rip back to the plain row just below the mistake and place the stitches of the plain row back on the needle. Use a needle to unknit the row with the error, one stitch at a time, resulting in all knit or all purl stitches on the needle.

If you're working a lace that has patterning on every row, you can protect yourself in the event of a mistake by using a lifeline. Decide on a regular interval for the lifeline, such as every ten rows on a narrow piece or perhaps every four rows on a wider piece. Once you've completed the designated row, thread a yarn needle with a sufficiently long piece of smooth cotton thread or yarn and string the thread through the stitches on the needle. Work to the next designated row and lay another line. When you get to the third designated row, check your work carefully to be sure there are no errors and then pull out the first line and use it in this row.

Missed Yarn Overs

If you discover in the middle of a row that you neglected to make a yarn over in the previous row, don't fret—it's an easy fix.

1 In this example, we've discovered that we've missed a yarn over in the previous row.

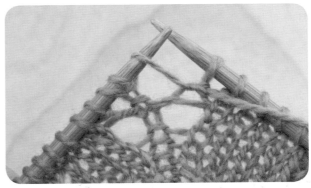

2 Pick up the thread that's between the stitch on your right needle and the next stitch and place it on the left needle. Work the stitch according to the pattern.

If your wrong-side row is plain and you don't notice the missed yarn over until the next patterned row, you can still recover without ripping.

1 In this example, we've discovered that we've missed a yarn over two rows ago.

2 Pick up two strands between the needles. Lift the lower strand over the upper strand and off the needle.

3 Transfer the resulting stitch to the left needle and proceed according to plan.

To Chart or Not to Chart

Make no mistake about it: Given the option of working from a charted pattern or a row-by-row text pattern, we would both choose the chart. This is true no matter what we're knitting, but especially for lace. We'll make an example of the Little Parachute lace used to illustrate special decreases that were explained on page 148.

Little Parachute (multiple of 14 + 2)

Row 1: K1 *yo, k2, sl 2, k1, p2sso, k2, yo, k7; repeat from * to last st, k1.

Row 2: P1, *p8, yo, p1, sl 2, p1, p2sso, p1, yo, p1; repeat from * to last st, p1.

Row 3: K1, *k2, yo, sl 2, k1, p2sso, yo, k9; repeat from * to last st, k1.

Row 4: P1, *yo, p2, sl 2, p1, p2sso, p2, yo, p7; repeat from * to last st, p1.

Row 5: K1, *k8, yo, k1, sl 2, k1, p2sso, k1, yo, k1; repeat from * to last st, k1.

Row 6: P1, *p2, yo, sl 2, p1, p2sso, yo, p9; repeat from * to last st, p1.

Repeat Rows 1–6 for pattern.

Each row is written for sixteen stitches per row. You can glean from the way the rows are written that the first and last stitch of each row is an edge stitch because the first stitch comes before the asterisk indicating a section to repeat, and the last stitch comes after the group of stitches has been repeated. But that's about all you can tell at first glance.

When the pattern is charted, you can immediately see that there are two edge stitches and that the fourteen-stitch repeat is actually two distinct seven-stitch patterns. Having all that information up front allows us to get into the rhythm of the pattern from the beginning.

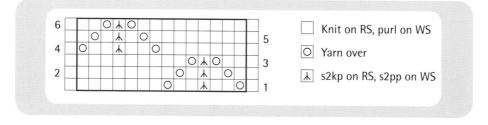

☐   Knit on RS, purl on WS

Ⓞ   Yarn over

人   s2kp on RS, s2pp on WS

What Does "No Stitch" Mean?

The example used above to advocate for charts is a very simple lace, wherein every row has the same number of stitches. When you get into more complex designs, the stitch count may fluctuate from row to row. A lace repeat will always begin and end with the same number of stitches, but anything goes in between. This phenomenon spawned the use of the plain dark symbol in a chart that stands for "no stitch."

Let's analyze the chart for a design called Falling Leaves. The pattern is a multiple of twelve plus one, and the chart shows two repeats. To begin this pattern, you'll need to cast on twelve stitches for each repeat. However, beginning with Row 5, yarn overs add to the stitch count, and when we complete Row 9 we have twelve stitches for each repeat. So, to chart this, we use the handy "no stitch" symbol in columns below the yarn overs so we'll have enough squares in the grid to chart all twenty-four stitches for Row 9.

Beginning with Row 11, we start decreasing stitches, so we again add the "no stitch" symbol to indicate changes in stitch count. After Row 21 is completed we're back to the fullest repeat of twelve stitches, and by decreasing in Rows 23, 25 and 27, Row 28 has a repeat of twelve stitches and we're ready to begin again at Row 5.

Although the stitch count changes many times within the repeat, it does so in a way that is easy to organize into a chart. With more complicated charts, there is no apparent pattern for the "no stitch" conundrum, and these patterns are extremely difficult, bordering on impossible, to chart.

Falling Leaves

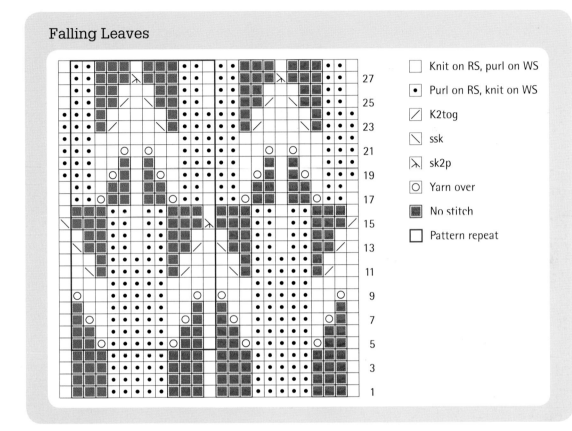

☐	Knit on RS, purl on WS
•	Purl on RS, knit on WS
╱	K2tog
╲	ssk
⋏	sk2p
○	Yarn over
▦	No stitch
☐	Pattern repeat

How to Proof a Lace Pattern or Chart

If (or should we say "when" because it happens to everyone) you get to the end of a row and realize your stitch count is not what it should be, the first thing to do is check for a mistake in your knitting. If you don't see anything obvious, check the pattern or chart for an error. First, look at the pattern row before the one you're working on and check the completed stitch count. For example, let's say you run into a problem on Row 13 of Falling Leaves. The ending stitch count in the repeat on Row 11 is twenty stitches (the k2togs and ssks are one

stitch each once they're worked). Now look at Row 13 to determine how many stitches are necessary to work the row; this is different from the number of stitches you'll have once you've completed the row, but you need to know how many stitches to begin with. So, in this row, each k2tog and ssk counts as two stitches because that's how many you need to work them. The beginning stitch count for Row 13 is twenty stitches. In this case, we're sorry to say that the error is yours, and you need to go back to the knitting and find where you went astray.

Lace Edgings

If you're knitting a shawl or scarf, you can add a whole new dimension to your project with a knitted-on edging. Most edgings are knitted separately once the main piece is finished and joined to the main piece as they're worked. If you know you're going to add a border, you'll be very happy to have worked chain-stitch edges by slipping the first stitch of every row (see Chapter Five). Ideally, you'll also have knitted your scarf with a number of stitches and rows that synchronizes with the number of rows in your chosen edging. For example, your scarf has 220 rows of fifty stitches, and your edging has a ten-row repeat.

Getting Started

The first thing you need to do is pick up stitches around all the edges of the main piece (see Chapter Five). You'll need to pick up a number of stitches that will accommodate the row repeat of the edging, and you'll need to work with one or two circular needles, depending on how many stitches you have.

Simple Sample

Our sample has a center square that has a fifteen-stitch repeat and two edge stitches on each side for a total of nineteen stitches. We worked the four-row pattern nine times, slipping the first stitch of every row, for a total of eighteen chain stitches on each side. We chose a simple four-row edging. The edging will be attached to the main piece on every other row, so any multiple of two stitches is needed on each of the four sides of the main piece.

After working the last row of the square, knit one row, decreasing one stitch; pick up eighteen chain stitches along the first side; remove the provisional cast on (if you didn't do one, just pick up into the cast-on stitches) and decrease one stitch; then pick up eighteen chain stitches along the second side. The result is that we have eighteen stitches on each side of the square, ready to attach the lace to. Because we'll need to do extra rows at the four corners to make the right angles, we'll delegate the end stitches of each section to being corner stitches. We now think of our stitches as sixteen edge stitches on each side and two stitches in each corner.

Cast on the number of stitches indicated for the edging onto a double-point needle. If you use a provisional cast on, you'll be able to graft the ends together for a nearly invisible join. Our edging begins with a wrong-side row. On the second row, we worked to the last stitch and then knit the last stitch of the edging together with the first held stitch of the main piece, a stitch right after a corner stitch. We worked Row 3, slipping the first stitch, and then on Row 4 we knit the last stitch of the edging together with the next stitch of the main piece. If your edging is worked in the opposite direction, i.e., the rows that go from the outer to the inner edge are wrong-side rows, you'll need to join the edging to the main piece on the wrong side.

Continue along the edge until you reach the first corner. The number of rows you'll need to turn the corner will vary depending on what you're knitting. For our simple sample, each corner has two four-row repeats. When the first corner stitch is reached, we worked Rows 1 through 3 without attaching them to the main piece, and then we attached Row 4. We repeated this with the second corner stitch. We completed three more sides and corners and then grafted the first row to the last row to finish the piece.

Real-Life Situations

Our little sample is neat and tidy with a small number of stitches and row repeats. If you're actually knitting something life-size, you can be sure things won't always fall so neatly into place. It's best if you plan the main piece to exactly fit your edging, but you'll most likely have to adjust the pick-up rate along the sides to accommodate the number of rows in a pattern repeat. Simply pick up a few more or fewer stitches along the edge as needed. To pick up an extra chain stitch, knit under only one loop of the last chain stitch knitted.

11 Knitting with Beads

As if having endless types of fiber, infinite forms of yarn in countless colors and boundless combinations of patterns wasn't enough, someone out there had the brilliant idea to spice it up with beads. Yes, you can have your knit and bead it, too.

Beads for Knitting

Most bead knitting projects use seed beads, which can be round or cylindrical in shape. These beads come in several sizes, most commonly 15°, 13°, 11°, 8° and 6°—the larger the number, the smaller the bead. The most important consideration is finding a bead with a hole large enough to accommodate the yarn you'll be stringing or hooking them onto. In general, choose the following bead sizes according to yarn weight.

Yarn Weight	Bead Size
Lace	11° or 13° (for super-fine yarn)
Fingering	8°
DK or sport	6°

SHOPPING FOR BEADS
Bring a piece of yarn and a stringing needle with you to the bead shop to check your chosen beads. In addition to making sure the beads will slide easily over the yarn, you'll want to be sure the holes are smooth—if the beads have a lining that is uneven, it could snag the yarn and cause damage.

Stringing Beads

Most methods of knitting with beads require that you string the beads onto the working yarn before beginning. This can be accomplished with a big eye beading needle, which is actually two very thin pieces of metal joined together at each end, making most of the needle the eye. Another option is a dental-floss threader. In both cases, thread the yarn through the eye or the loop, pick up beads with the needle or plastic strand and slide them down onto the yarn. As you knit you'll push beads farther down on the yarn to free up enough to knit with and pull up a bead or beads as you need them.

STRINGING LOTS OF BEADS
If you're going to be stringing lots of beads, take the time to rewind your yarn before you begin, even if it comes in a ready-to-knit ball or skein. This gives you an opportunity to search for knots and divide the yarn into separate balls if necessary. There are few things more frustrating than moving 200 beads down the yarn only to be stopped by a knot before you've finished your first row.

Bead Knitting

With this method, a bead is knit or purled into a stitch as it is worked. You can create an allover beaded piece by working a bead into every stitch, or you can form a pattern of beads on a plain yarn background.

Beads All Over

If you're planning to work a bead into every stitch, you'll need to do a little fancy stitching to keep the fabric from biasing. Because a bead will lie on only the right half of the stitch, knitting and purling beaded stitches with regular stitches will pull the fabric to the right. This is evident in our first sample swatch, which was worked back and forth by knitting with beads on the right side and purling with beads on the wrong side. Notice how the beads all lean in the same direction.

Biased bead knitting

Beaded Knit Stitch

1 Push a bead up about ½" (1cm) from the needle.

2 Work the stitch as usual, carrying the bead on the yarn that goes around the needle. Pull the bead through the stitch so it lies on the front of the work.

Beaded Purl Stitch

1 Push a bead up about ½" (1cm) from the needle and work the stitch as usual, carrying the bead on the yarn that goes around the needle.

2 Push the bead through the stitch so it lies on the front of the work.

Stop the Bias

To keep the fabric from biasing, you can twist the stitches of every other row. This produces a fabric that looks quite different from the first sample, because the beads of every other row lean in the opposite direction. There are two ways to twist a stitch. The first way is to work a regular beaded knit stitch but work through the back loop. The second way is to work through the back loop and bring the yarn with the bead up over the top of the needle, rather than under the needle as for a regular stitch. We find this to be the most effective method.

Unbiased bead knitting

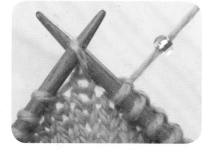

1 Insert the needle as if to knit through the back loop.

2 Bring the yarn with the bead over the top of the needle and knit the stitch, pulling the bead through the stitch.

If you're working in the round, alternate regular and twisted rounds. If you're working back and forth, work twisted knit stitches and regular purls. The second swatch shows this method.

Working with Charts

If you're doing an allover pictorial design, you'll have to string your beads following a chart of your design. Begin reading the chart from the top left and then string row by row to the bottom so the last bead strung is the first bead knit. Be sure you have no distractions while you're stringing—if you get it all right, you don't have to think about the pattern as you're knitting. It will just come to life all on its own!

You can also follow a chart where the background color will be plain knit stitches without beads. You'll string by starting at the top and ending at the bottom as for an allover chart. However, you'll also have to follow the chart while you're knitting so you'll know which stitches are plain and which ones are beaded. Because the beads are not on every stitch, you can use either the regular or the twisted method without worrying about bias. Our swatch shows the twisted method.

Beaded Knitting

Strange as it sounds, there is a difference between bead knitting, described on page 157, and beaded knitting. With beaded knitting, a bead (or beads) lies on the thread between two stitches. A bead lying between two knit stitches will show on the back of the work, and a bead lying between two purl stitches will show on the front of the work. This is a very easy method to master.

If you have a stitch pattern that has two purl stitches together, purl the first stitch and slide up a bead. Purl the second stitch. The bead sits between the two purl stitches.

You can also shape your knitting with this method by adding more or fewer beads between the stitches. This is the method used in many of the beaded purses that were fashionable in the early twentieth century. If you're going to work a shaped piece, you'll need to work in garter stitch and add beads to every row. Our sample shows an undulating design.

If you want to cast on with multiple beads between the stitches, you'll need to use the backward loop method (see Chapter Five).

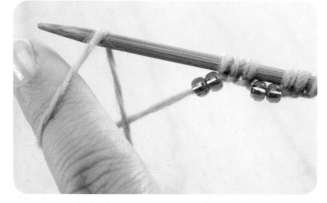

1 Cast on three stitches, *push two beads up to the needle, cast on three stitches.

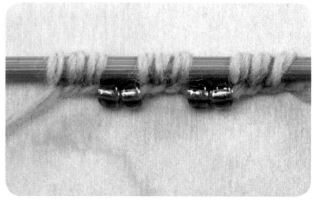

2 Repeat from * for desired number of stitches and beads.

To bind off at the other end to mirror the cast on, cut the yarn leaving a tail long enough to bind off with. Bind off three stitches, *string two beads and push them up to the needle, bind off three stitches; repeat from * to bind off all stitches.

Slip-Stitch Bead Knitting

This is another easy method to use, and with it you can place a bead anywhere in the pattern you can slip a stitch.

It's best to place beads over knit stitches rather than purl stitches; a knit stitch is flat, and the bead will lie flat. If you place a bead over a purl bump, it may lean left, right, up or down. Our swatch shows beads that were all slipped on the right side on fields of Stockinette stitch between borders of seed stitch.

Right-Side Rows

1 Bring the yarn forward and slip a stitch.

2 Slide up a bead, bring the yarn back, leaving the bead in front of the slipped stitch, and work the next stitch.

Wrong-Side Rows

1 Bring the yarn to the back (which is the right side of the work) and slip a stitch.

2 Slide up a bead, bring the yarn forward and work the next stitch, leaving the bead in front of the slipped stitch on the right side.

Hooked Bead Knitting

This method, in which you pull a whole stitch through a bead with a crochet hook, is the one preferred by many knitters, mostly because you don't have to string all those beads onto your yarn before starting. However, if you're going to add a lot of beads, keep in mind that you'll have to pick up a hook and a bead, place the bead and put the hook down again for every bead you want to place. On the plus side, this method saves wear and tear on your yarn, and we use it often with delicate lace yarn.

1 You can hook a bead from the right or wrong side of the knitting. Pick up a bead with a crochet hook, hook the stitch and take it off the needle.

2 Holding everything under tension with the hook straight up and down, slide the bead from the hook onto the stitch.

3 Replace the stitch onto the left needle. Slip the stitch or knit it.

Our first hooked swatch has beads added to a honeycomb pattern. Because the honeycombs have two center stitches, we opted to bead both of them so the beads would sit in the center of the pattern and not off to one side or the other.

The second swatch has beads following the diagonal lines of a pattern. The diagonals are formed on right-side rows with k2togs and ssks. Beads are hooked onto these stitches on wrong-side rows.

Beaded honeycomb

Diagonal beads

Carry-Along Bead Knitting

Another way to add beads to your knitting is to carry them along on a separate strand of yarn. This allows you to incorporate beads that are too small to slide over your main yarn.

For example, you can add size 11° beads to a sport-weight project if you string the beads onto a lace-weight yarn and carry the beaded yarn along with the main yarn. You can either knit the carry-along yarn together with the main yarn or simply weave it from front to back as you knit with the main yarn only. In either case, when you want to place a bead or beads, bring the carry-along yarn to the front, work a stitch or stitches with the main yarn only, slide beads up on the carry-along yarn and then either bring the carry-along to the back or begin to knit it with the main yarn again.

Our swatch uses a sport-weight yarn for the main yarn, and we have beads strung on a fingering-weight yarn. The two yarns are knitted together on the first and last stitches only to anchor the carry-along and then woven from front to back over sets of two stitches. Because the knitting is back and forth, once we've finished a right-side row we need to get the yarn back to the other side for the next right-side row. You could do this by stranding it along the back, catching it into every fifth stitch (see stranding techniques in Chapter Eight) or weaving it from front to back again, with or without beads.

Beaded Cast On

If you want to add beads to the edge of a ruffle or other piece, you can add beads to the long tail method.

Cast on one stitch, *push a bead up to the needle, cast on one stitch; repeat from * for desired number of stitches and beads. Be careful not to allow the beads to go through the cast on stitches. They should rest between the stitches.

Part IV

Garment Planning

Now that you know a lot of what there is to know about yarn, tools and techniques, it's time to put this knowledge to use by knitting garments. This section is by no means a comprehensive guide to designing your own garments, but it will help you do just that. You can also use these methods to customize patterns from other sources.

Chapter Twelve includes the all-important discussion of gauge, and we hope it convinces you that there is always time to do a gauge swatch. Guidelines for taking measurements, planning for ease and choosing knitting direction (bottom-up, top-down or side-to-side) are also covered.
Sleeves take center stage in Chapter Thirteen, and we've laid out a simple and understandable way of planning the shape and size of several styles. Math is a necessary evil here for those of us who are arithmetic-phobes, but, again, we strove to make the calculation process as painless as possible. Chapter Fourteen moves on up to the neckline, and we've included several neckline shapes with easy-to-understand instructions for adding a variety of collars.
Pockets can be both utilitarian and decorative, and Chapter Fifteen tells you how to plan and add several varieties, including how to knit a built-in pocket as an afterthought. We begin to button things up with Chapter Sixteen, which covers button bands and buttonholes, zippers, and frogs. And finally, Chapter Seventeen covers blocking, cleaning and storage of your fabulous and thoughtfully knitted items.

⑫ Planning Projects

With your arsenal now full of stitching know-how, it's time to look at what you need to know before casting on for a project. Some of the information is intended to help you design your own garments, but it can also be used to alter or improve someone else's design, customizing it for your personal use.

....

Why Gauge Matters

Here it is: the all-important discussion of gauge and how it affects the success or failure of a project, especially a garment. In the knitting world, gauge refers to the number of stitches and rows in a specific square of knitted fabric, usually 4 square inches (10 square centimeters). As discussed in Chapter One, yarns are categorized by manufacturers into certain weight groups, and each group encompasses a particular gauge. In addition to using the weight of yarn called for in a project, it is essential that you achieve the specified gauge when following a pattern, or the garment will not fit.

Let's say you're knitting a sweater with a finished chest circumference of 38" (96.5cm). If you're knitting the garment back and forth, this means that the front and back pieces will each measure 19" (48.5cm). The specified gauge is twenty stitches over 4" (10cm), or five stitches per inch (2.5cm). The main part of the front and back will be worked over ninety-five stitches: 19" (48cm) × 5 stitches per inch (2.5cm) = 95.

If the pattern requires a specific number of stitches for a repeat, this number may be rounded up or down by a few stitches. As long as it's close to ninety-five stitches, the result will be very close to 19" (48.5cm).

However, if your yarn and needle combination does not result in exactly five stitches per inch (2.5cm), you're going to have a problem. Let's say your swatch has twenty-two stitches in 4" (10cm) instead of twenty. This is an inch gauge of five and a half stitches per inch (2.5cm). If you cast on the specified ninety-five stitches, your resulting front or back of the piece will be only 17¼" (44cm). If the front and the back are 17¼" (44cm) wide, your garment will have a finished circumference of 34½" (87.5cm), not the desired 38" (96.5cm). Alternatively, if your knitting yields a gauge of four and a half stitches per inch (2.5cm) and you use the specified ninety-five stitches, each half of the garment will measure 21" (53cm), for a total chest circumference of 42" (106.5cm), not the desired 38" (96.5cm).

Making the Gauge Swatch

Begin by using the needle size specified in the pattern. You'll need to cast on the number of stitches necessary to make a 4" (10cm) swatch. If the gauge is twenty stitches in 4" (10cm), you'll cast on twenty stitches. It's a good idea to cast on one or two edge stitches, but don't include these stitches when you measure. Work the swatch in the main pattern of the sweater, whether it's Stockinette stitch, seed stitch or any other stitch pattern, until the piece measures about 4" (10cm) in length. We recommend that you remove the swatch from the needles for accurate measuring. You can either bind off (if you like to hoard swatches) or simply slide the stitches off the needle–then you can unravel the swatch and reuse the yarn.

Now measure the twenty stitches between the edge stitches. If this measurement is exactly 4" (10cm), you're ready to roll. However, if the twenty stitches measure less than 4" (10cm), you'll need to try again on a larger needle; if the twenty stitches measure more than 4" (10cm), you'll need to try again on a smaller needle. Continue to adjust the needle size until you get exactly twenty stitches in the 4" (10cm) swatch.

SWATCHING IN THE ROUND

If you're going to work a project in the round, it is essential that you swatch in the round. See Chapter Eight for details.

Row Gauge

Many patterns also include a row gauge, which is the number of rows within 4" (10cm) of knitting. Usually if you get the correct stitch gauge, you'll also get the correct row gauge. But in knitting, as in all aspects of life, there are no guarantees. As discussed on the previous page, it is crucial that you work with the correct stitch gauge to ensure a proper fit. If the row gauge is not exactly accurate, you can usually work a few more or fewer rows to get the required length. However, if you're working a cable or other repeating pattern that has a specified number of rows, you'll have to accept the fact that you may be slightly off in the length measurements.

Measuring Body Parts

In order for anything to fit properly, it's important to measure the wearer accurately. Correct measuring is the cornerstone of any project, and this is especially true for garments.

Measuring for Sweaters

WHAT YOU'LL NEED FOR MEASURING

- Tape measure
- Measuring chart (see next page)
- Pencil with eraser
- Three pieces of bias tape, each 1½ yards (1.5m) long. You'll use one piece of tape around the chest, one around the waist and one around the hips.

If you often knit for yourself, members of your family or friends, keep a file with a measurement sheet for each. It's a good idea to check and update measurements from year to year or project to project to accommodate any changes. Don't try to take your own measurements—have a close friend or a tailor take them for you.

Ideally, the person being measured should wear a close-fitting T-shirt. Position one tape around the body, 2" (5cm) below the armholes (red line on diagram), and tie it or pin it so it stays in place. Place the second tape around the waist (blue line on diagram) and the third around the hip or where the lower edge of the garment will hit (green line on diagram). Make sure the tapes are snug enough that they won't shift and that they're at the same levels on the front and the back of the body. These tapes will be used to determine the lengths of various parts of the body.

With your body taped up and ready, let the measuring begin. Each measurement is important and pertinent to the others. Take your time, measure carefully and enter each measurement in the appropriate box of the chart.

These are the basic measurements necessary to construct almost any type of garment. If you're not knitting a tailored or fitted garment, you can ignore the last three measurements: M, N and O. This chart will work for men, women and children of all sizes.

A: Chest/bust circumference
Measure the bust or chest at the fullest part and record under A.

B: Chest to front neck
Measure straight up from the upper tape to the bottom of the U-shaped notch in the throat and record under B.

C: Upper arm
Measure the upper arm at the fullest part and record under C.

D: Shoulder
Measure from the edge of the neck to the shoulder joint. In fact, measure both shoulders. Many times there is a difference between the two due to when someone is predominately right- or left- handed. Record the longer measurement under D.

E: Wrist
Measure around the wrist and record under E.

F: Hip (or lower garment edge)
Measure around the lowest tape you placed on the body and record under F.

G: Back shoulder-to-shoulder
Measure straight across the back from shoulder joint to shoulder joint and record under G.

H: Chest to back neck
Measure straight up from upper tape to the prominent bump at the top of the spine. If the head is tilted slightly forward, this bump becomes very evident. Record this measurement under H.

J: Overall length
Measure from the back neck (the prominent bump at the top of the spine) to the lowest tape and

record under J. This is the overall length and should be equal to the total of H (see previous page) plus K (see below).

K: Underarm to hip
Measure the distance between the upper and lower tapes at the side of the body and record under K.

L: Underarm to wrist
With the arm extended slightly from the body, measure from the upper tape to the wrist and record under L.

M: Waist
Measure around the middle tape and record under M.

N: Waist to underarm
Measure from the upper tape to the waist tape and record under N.

O: Waist to hip (or lower garment edge)
Measure from the middle tape to the lower tape and record under O.

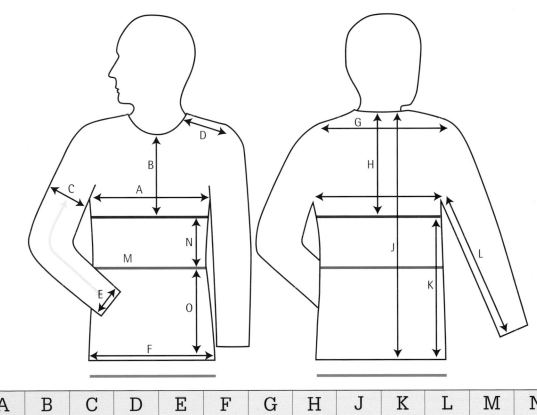

A	B	C	D	E	F	G	H	J	K	L	M	N	O
Chest/Bust Circumference	Chest to Front Neck	Upper Arm	Shoulder	Wrist	Hip	Shoulder-to-Shoulder Back	Chest to Back Neck	Overall Length	Underarm to Hip	Underarm to Wrist	Waist	Waist to Underarm	Waist to Hip

Measuring for Hats

Place one end of the tape measure on the forehead and then wrap it around the head at the widest point; this is the head circumference. With the tape still in place, use a second tape to measure across the top of the head; divide this measurement by two for the height of the crown.

Measuring for Gloves and Mittens

Well-fitting gloves and mittens will see a lot of use, and careful measurements will help you produce these for you and yours.

A: Measure the width of the palm on the dominant hand just above the thumb extension.
B: Measure the length of the palm from the wrist to the base of the middle finger.
C: Measure the length from the wrist to the tip of the middle finger.
D: Measure the circumference of the wrist.
E: Measure the circumference of the forearm (this is relevant if you're knitting a glove with an extra long cuff).

Measuring for Socks

The most important measurement for a sock is the ankle circumference; this is the measurement that will be used as the basis for the foot and leg. Take all the following measurements into account when planning socks.

A: Ankle circumference
B: Leg length
C: Foot length

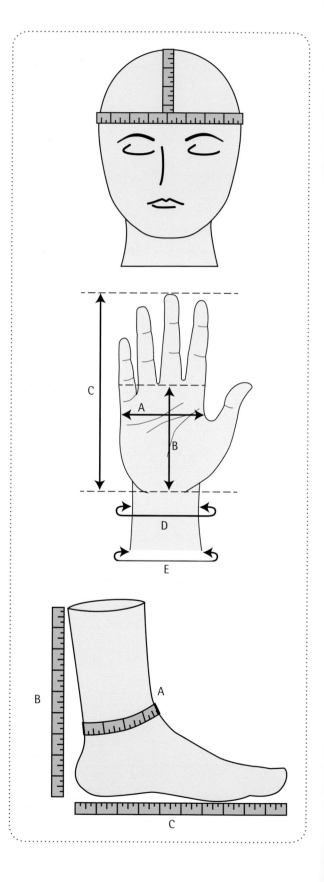

Planning for Sweater Ease

When it comes to knitted sweaters, there are five categories of fit.

* **Very close-fitting sweaters** are knitted to the actual chest/bust circumference or less.
* **Close-fitting sweaters** will be 1" to 2" (2.5cm to 5cm) larger than the actual chest/bust circumference.
* **Standard-fitting sweaters** will be 2" to 4" (5cm to 10cm) larger than the actual chest/bust circumference.
* **Loose-fitting sweaters** will be 4" to 6" (10cm to 15cm) larger than the actual chest/bust circumference. This is the ease to choose for outerwear.
* **Oversize sweaters** will be 6" (15cm) or more larger than the actual chest/bust circumference.

Negative Ease

The best-fitting hats, socks and mittens fit a little snugly, helping them to stay on the body.

If you put a 22" (56cm) hat on a 22" (56cm) head, the first gust of winter wind is going to take it away. And if you put a 10" (25.5cm) sock on a foot/leg with a 10" (25.5cm) circumference, the sock will sag. Generally speaking, you'll want to plan 10 to 20 percent negative ease. So for that 22" (56cm) head, a 17$\frac{1}{2}$" to 20" (44.5cm to 51cm) hat will fit well. If you're knitting with a stitch pattern that has some stretch to it, choose the smaller measurement; if your stitch pattern is dense with little elasticity, choose the larger measurement. The same goes for socks and mittens.

Sweater Shapes

Sweater shapes can range from basic squares to curved, body-fitting forms. They can be straight up and down, snug at the waist, have a raised or empire waist, or they can flare down from the shoulders in swing style.

If you know how to construct garments, consider your body measurements with desired ease and sketch the parts out on graph paper. You can then figure the stitch requirements based on your gauge. If you, like most people, don't have a clue how to draft a pattern, consider using sewing patterns as a basis for knitting patterns. Choose a style, stitch up a down-and-dirty version in a jersey fabric and try it on to see if you like the style. With the help of a friend you can use pins to alter the fit of this jersey version. Make sure all the alterations will stay in place, mark the "seam lines" and take the pieces apart. Now you can lay out and trace the custom pieces onto full-size graph paper and figure out stitch counts based on your gauge.

If this sounds simplistic, it is. Lessons on custom design would fill a book of its own and are too lengthy to include here. We just want to let you know what can be done. Sweaters can also have different sleeve shapes, necklines, collars, closures and pockets. These details are covered in future chapters.

Balancing and Centering Patterns

The different parts of garments align with parts of the body. For example, side seams are at the sides of your body, zippers and buttons are usually at the center front or the center back, hats have a front and a back, and mittens have a palm and a back. Everything works with the symmetry of the body, and you'll usually want to center a color or texture pattern to complement this symmetry.

Centering and balancing motifs on a knitted garment takes some planning, but working out the technical details is well rewarded when you can knit away, knowing you'll be pleased with the results.

Getting Started

The first thing you'll need is a schematic for your garment that has all the pertinent numbers for your desired measurements. You don't need to have the gauge figured out yet—you just need the desired measurements.

Next, you'll need a chart of the motif, which tells you the number of stitches in each repeat. Our example has a fourteen-stitch, fourteen-row repeat. Because the first stitch and first row of the repeat are also the last stitch and last row of the pattern, you need to add one stitch and one row to the final repeat for balance. Most designs have an "up" point, marked A on the chart, and a "down" point, marked B. One of these points will be placed at the center front of your garment.

The next step is to make a pattern swatch with your chosen yarn. Wash and dry the patterned swatch as you will the finished garment. Then measure for the number of stitches and rows per inch (2.5cm). For this exercise, we'll assume a gauge of six stitches and eight rows per square inch (2.5 square centimeters).

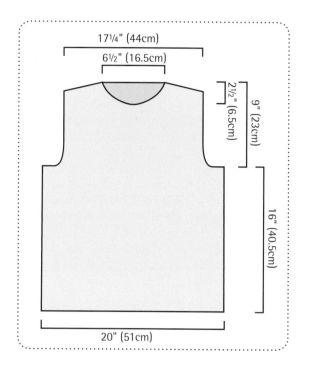

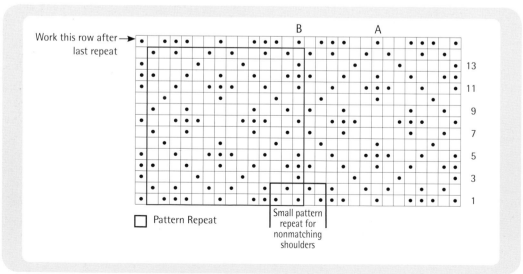

[172]

Centering a Pattern Horizontally

The desired finished chest/bust circumference is 40" (101.5cm). Divide the 40" (101.5cm) circumference by two to get a 20" (51cm) width each for the front and the back. Multiply this width by the stitch gauge to get the number of stitches needed: 20" (51cm) × 6 stitches to the inch (2.5cm) = 120 stitches. If you're knitting back and forth in two pieces, add two edge stitches for the seams but do not include them in the stitch count for patterning.

To determine how many pattern repeats you'll have, divide the total number of stitches by the number of stitches in one repeat: 120 stitches ÷ 14 stitches = 8½ pattern repeats, plus one balance stitch. While this works out neatly to 120 stitches, it does involve a partial repeat. To center the patterns, you'll need to choose one of the following options:

* If you place a down point (B) at the center front, you'll have four and one-fourth motifs on each side of the center. When you join the seams, you'll be joining two one-fourth motifs. You could go with this and hope no one notices.

* You could work the pattern in the round on 238 stitches, giving you seventeen pattern repeats. If you work in the round, you won't need extra balancing stitches. Because you have an odd number of repeats, the center front or back will have an up point, and the opposite side will have a down point. You could do this when working flat, placing an up point at center front and a down point at center back. However, whether worked circularly or flat, this solution will cause a problem at the shoulders—the patterns will not match but be half a motif off.

* Adjust the number of stitches to work only with whole repeats. By recalculating for a 42" (106.5cm) finished garment, your numbers for the back or the front would look like this: 21" (53cm) × 6 stitches per inch (2.5cm) = 126 stitches. Divide 126 stitches by 14 stitches per pattern repeat, and you get 9 pattern repeats. So, you'd cast on 129 stitches total: 126 stitches for 9 repeats + 1 stitch for balance + 2 edge stitches. Of course, if this is too big, you could change your needle size for a tighter gauge (see the gauge discussion on page 166 and Altering Patterns on page 176).

Depending on how the garment is seamed, the balance stitch can be omitted and the two pieces joined to look like one continuous piece. Because you'll be working with an even number of stitches, the pattern at the center front and back will be off by one stitch, but this will hardly be noticeable. The shoulders will also be off by one stitch but you can line these up before joining. One way to do this is to decrease one stitch at the neck edge of the front and one stitch at the shoulder edge of the back, bringing the patterns back into alignment.

If you want absolute balance and need the center neck stitch at the front and back to be the same and the shoulder to align exactly, you can bind off an even number of stitches at one underarm and an odd number of stitches at the other underarm on both the front and the back. You'll need to shape the sleeves to match these armholes, being sure to bind off the even/odd number of stitches to align to the corresponding part of the armhole. Worked this way, the sleeve underarms will match the body, and the top-center sleeve stitch will align with the shoulder seam.

Centering a Pattern Vertically

It's important that the body and sleeves end on the same pattern row at the underarm. The best way to ensure this is to first work the sleeves to the desired length, ending with Rows 1 or 8 of the pattern. To determine which pattern row to begin the body with, lay the sleeve flat and measure down from the underarm to the desired body length minus the ribbing. If this measurement falls on Rows 1 or 8 of the pattern, no adjustment is necessary—simply knit the rib and then begin the pattern on Rows 1 or 8. However, if this measurement falls on, for example, Row 5 of the pattern, you'll need to knit four fewer or three more rows of ribbing to get the exact length and begin and end with Row 1 or 8 of the pattern repeat. We realize the difference here is relatively minor. However, if your repeat covers a larger number of rows, you'll be happy to have figured out this balance.

Balancing for Shoulder Seams

If you're working with an even number of repeats and end the back shoulder edge on Rows 14 or 7 and the front shoulder edge on Rows 1 or 8, you'll have a perfect pattern match when knitting, sewing or weaving the shoulders together.

If you're working with an odd number of pattern repeats (like the seventeen in the example on centering a pattern horizontally), your shoulder stitches will not match. Here are a few remedies.

* When you've reached the shoulders, work a small two- or three-row pattern picked out of the main pattern (see the small red box on the chart), finishing both the front and back shoulders with these rows.
* Work a few rows of garter stitch at the shoulder edges before binding off or joining.
* With wrong sides together, bind off with a decorative braid or cord.
* With wrong sides together, work a single crochet bind off (see Chapter Five).

Special Considerations for Fair Isle

If there are multiple patterns in the garment, they should all share a common center point and ease out to the seams. When working Fair Isle patterns, you will generally have large patterns separated by small patterns called peeries. Many times the multiples of the large patterns—on which the garment size is based—do not match the multiples of the smaller peeries. Do the math and then either increase or decrease stitches to the next nearest peerie-pattern repeat. Revert to the original stitch count to knit the next large pattern. Because these few increases and decreases are worked over 200 to 300 stitches, they are imperceptible.

Planning Aran Patterns

Traditional Aran or Irish fisherman sweaters typically combine several different cable and allover patterns and feature a center panel.

We've included one in the project section (see the Lisdoonvarna Aran on page 256) and explain the planning and knitting process along the way. But here's a tip that can help you in the initial concept phase: Choose the patterns you'd like to include and knit a long swatch comprising all of them, at least a few inches (approximately 5cm) of each. Photocopy the swatch and cut the copy into pattern sections. Lay down the pattern for the center panel and move the remaining patterns around on the right or the left of the center until you have a combination you like.

Knitting in Different Directions

Sweaters can be knitted in three directions: from the bottom up, from the top down or from side to side. The method you choose is a matter of personal preference, but here are a few things to consider when making that choice.

Knitting from the Top Down

Top-down devotees prefer this method to facilitate trying on the garment, ensuring that the measurement from the neck to the underarm is correct. A top-down pullover that's knit in the round begins with the neck stitches (the smallest circumference) to the largest (the chest). With raglan-sleeve shaping, the tops of the sleeves are included in the widest circumference, so there is very little calculating to do. You can try the sweater on as you go, and if it's not increasing fast enough, you simply increase more. The sleeves are separated from the body at the underarm, and this is the only place you'll have to do any finishing once the garment is knit. If you cast on with a provisional method, you can decide what type of ribbing or other border to use when the rest of the sweater is done. Also, if you happened to cast on too many stitches when you started and the neck is too big, you can decrease them and work a tight ribbing to finish.

Another advantage to knitting from the top down is that you can make a sweater for growing children last a bit longer. Children usually grow faster in length than in width, and it's easy to undo the lower edge of the body and the sleeves and add length for another year or so of wearing. Provided, of course, that you have enough yarn and there isn't another munchkin waiting in line for the sweater. Ganseys were traditionally worked in the top-down style so the sleeves and lower body of the sweaters could be reknit when damaged or worn out by seamen or sailors.

One more plus to knitting from the top down is that if you don't have quite enough yarn, you can make your sweater slightly shorter than planned. If you've knit from the bottom up and run out of yarn before you've reached the shoulder, there's little you can do about it.

Knitting from the Bottom Up

Most sweaters are worked in this direction, and because you start with the widest measurement, you'll need to be disciplined about preplanning. Once you've determined the number of stitches required and knit up to the armholes, there's nothing you can do to alter the width but rip out and start over. But that's why you've taken the time and effort to learn all you can about gauge and measurements, right?

Sweater bodies knit from the bottom up can be worked in the round, back and forth in one piece for a cardigan, back and forth in two pieces (front and back) for a pullover, or back and forth in three pieces for a cardigan. You can also work ribbing back and forth and then steek and knit the rest of the body in the round (see Chapter Seven). Sleeves for these sweaters are also usually knit from the bottom up and sewn to the body. However, if you're working in a pattern that doesn't look too different when viewed from the bottom up or the top down, you can put the body together, pick up stitches around the armholes and knit the sleeves from the top down. This allows you to check sleeve length as you go and make adjustments as desired.

If you don't know what kind or depth of ribbing or border you want at the bottom, you can cast on with a provisional method and knit the border from the body down when the rest of the sweater is finished (see Chapter Five). This allows you a little more freedom.

Knitting Side to Side

You can also choose to knit garments horizontally, from side to side. For a cardigan, begin at the center front and work around to the other side of the center front. Or, if you're working a distinct pattern you want to show in mirror image from the center out, begin at the center back with a provisional cast on and work to one side of the center front, then pick up the cast-on stitches and work to the other side of the center front. If you're working a garment in two pieces (front and back), you'll cast on at one side and work to the other.

It's important to keep in mind that fabric worked horizontally will not have the same drape as fabric knit vertically. In fact, it will have more drape, which is why this method is chosen for some specialty designs. Examine a piece of knitted fabric. If you hold it vertically with one hand on each side and pull, the space between the stitches will increase, and the piece will stretch. Now hold that same knitting horizontally and pull—you'll see that the space between the rows won't increase, and the piece will have very little stretch. This can be an advantage or a disadvantage; it's just something you need to keep in mind.

Altering Patterns

Let's face it: Most of us do not fit neatly into the standard sizes offered by clothing manufacturers, and therefore our body measurement won't be exactly the same as those offered in most knitting patterns. We may have arms that are shorter or longer than "standard" or a waist that is higher or lower than most. Or we may be perfectly proportioned but want a finished garment that's slightly larger or smaller than the sizes offered. With a little knitting know-how, you can alter just about any pattern to your own measurements.

Adjusting Length

Length is probably the easiest measurement to alter. If a pattern gives a finished measurement from hip to underarm that's longer or shorter than your desired length, or if the pattern calls for sleeves that are longer or shorter than your arms, simply work to your measured length and start the armhole shaping.

If you're working a stitch pattern that has more than a four-row repeat, the adjustment in length will be tied to the number of rows in a repeat. For example, if you're working a cable pattern that has a twelve-row repeat, any length adjustment will have to be a multiple of twelve rows. If you're working a standard worsted gauge of eighteen stitches and twenty-four rows in 4" (10cm), you can adjust the length by 2" (5cm) by adding or subtracting one twelve-row repeat.

Things can get a little more complicated if you have to factor shaping into the piece you're altering. Let's say you're working on a fitted sweater, and your custom measurement from waist to underarm is 1½" (4cm) less than what's specified in the pattern but all other measurements are fine. First, determine how many stitches are increased between the waist and the underarm. These will have been spread over the pattern's measurement from waist to underarm, but you'll have to incorporate these into 1½" (4cm) worth of fewer rows. Here is one scenario.

The pattern specifies the following:

* Row gauge is eight rows per inch (2.5cm).
* Waist-to-underarm measurement is 6" (15cm).
* Number of stitches increased on each side from waist to underarm is twelve.
* There are forty-eight rows from waist to underarm (6" [15cm] × 8 rows per inch [2.5cm] = 48).

To work the twelve increases on each side evenly, increase at the beginning and end of every fourth row, but because your waist-to-underarm measurement is only 4½" (11.5cm), you'll work your increases over thirty-six rows (4½" [11.5cm] × 8 rows per inch [2.5cm] = 36). To work the twelve increases on each side evenly, you'll increase at the beginning and end of every third row.

Adjusting Width

Making small adjustments to the width of a pattern can be a little trickier than lengthening or shortening a piece, but this doesn't mean you can't do it! The body width presented in knitting patterns is based on the gauge and the number of stitches. If your sweater is worked in a simple Stockinette or seed stitch, you can add any number of stitches necessary to obtain your desired width.

The pattern specifies the following:

* Stitch gauge is six stitches per inch (2.5cm).
* Chest measurement is 38" (96.5cm).
* Number of stitches to cast on for the back is 116 (19" [48cm] × 6 stitches per inch [2.5cm] = 114, plus 2 edge stitches).

Your desired chest measurement is 41" (104cm), so you'll need 125 stitches (20½" [52cm] × 6 stitches per inch [2.5cm] = 123, plus 2 edge stitches). Because the pattern is written for an even number of stitches, you should round the 125 up or down one stitch, so let's use 124 stitches.

Because you're working with eight stitches more than the pattern calls for, you'll also need to make some adjustments to the rest of the pattern, i.e., you'll have to account for those extra eight stitches when working the armhole, shoulder and neck shaping. You could come up with several ways of doing this.

Here's one solution:

* Bind off one extra stitch at the underarm on each side.
* Include two more stitches into each shoulder than stated in the pattern.
* Include two more stitches in the neck than stated in the pattern.

The number of stitches to cast on for a sweater is determined by the gauge as well as the number of stitches in a pattern repeat. This is why not all patterns are written for chest/bust measurement increasing in 2" (5cm) increments. Let's examine the following scenario.

The pattern specifies the following:

* Stitch gauge is five and a half stitches per inch (2.5cm).
* Pattern repeat is sixteen stitches.
* Sweater is knit back and forth with full pattern repeats on both front and back.

In this example, each pattern repeat is about 3" (7.5cm) wide (16 stitches in pattern repeat ÷ 5.5 stitches per inch [2.5cm] = 2.9). If only full pattern repeats are used on the front and back, this sweater will only be sized in chest/bust circumference increments of 5" to 6" (13cm to 15cm). (Many designers are too clever to offer a pattern like this—we present this for example only.)

Finished bust/chest measurements:

* 35" (89cm) (6 pattern repeats: 6 repeats × 16 stitches in a repeat = 96 stitches ÷ 5.5 = 17.45 × 2 = 34.9" [88.5cm], rounded up to 35" [89cm])
* 40³/₄" (103.5cm) (7 pattern repeats: 7 repeats × 16 stitches in a repeat = 112 stitches ÷ 5.5 = 20.36 × 2 = 40.72" [103.5, rounded up to 40³/₄" [103.5cm])
* 46¹/₂" (118cm) (8 pattern repeats: 8 repeats × 16 stitches in a repeat = 128 stitches ÷ 5.5 = 23.27 × 2 = 46.54" [118cm], rounded down to 46¹/₂" [118cm])

You decide you want a sweater that's between the first and second sizes. The first size has six repeats on both the back and front and the next size has seven repeats on both the back and front. To knit a size in the middle, you'd have to add half a repeat to both the back and the front. This would require placing one-quarter of a repeat at the beginning and one-quarter of a repeat at the end of both the back and the front. When the side seams are joined, you'd have half a repeat at each side. This would look really dumb, which is why this option is not presented with the pattern.

However, you can customize the size in a couple of ways. If the sixteen-stitch repeat is one that is worked in distinct columns, you could add stitches between the repeats. These stitches can be in garter, seed or reverse Stockinette stitch, or just about any pattern you want; check the gauge and add the appropriate number of stitches between the repeats. If the repeats don't present in columns that are easy to add stitches between, simply add the extra stitches before and after the repeats, forming a different pattern at the sides of the sweater.

Adjusting with Gauge

Now that you understand gauge and why it's so important that you get it right before beginning a project, consider this twist: To alter a pattern so it's larger or smaller than a given size, knit it at a different gauge. That's right—you can intentionally knit a garment in a gauge that is different from the stated gauge to get the size you want. If a pattern is sized for a finished bust/chest measurement of 36" (91.5cm), 40" (101.5cm), 44" (112cm), etc. and what you really want is 38" (96.5cm), you can follow the pattern for either the 36" (91.5cm) with a gauge that has fewer stitches per inch (2.5cm) or the 40" (101.5cm) with a gauge that has more stitches per inch (2.5cm).

The pattern specifies the following:

* Pattern gauge is five stitches per inch (2.5cm).
* The back of the size 36" (91.5cm) is worked on 90 stitches (18" [46cm] × 5 stitches per inch [2.5cm] = 90).

If you follow the instructions for the size 36" (91.5cm) and work at a gauge of 4.75 stitches per inch (2.5cm), your finished sweater will be 38" (96.5cm) (90 stitches ÷ 19" [48cm] finished = 4.74).

⑬ Sleeves

Sleeve types are named for the way they are shaped at the top, and the way they're shaped dictates how they are attached to the body. The four most common sleeve shapes are drop shoulder, modified drop shoulder, raglan and set-in. Any of these sleeves can be full length, three-quarter length or short. They can begin with a close-fitting rib, a not-so-close-fitting cuff or even a bell-bottom. The bottom of the sleeve doesn't affect any other part of the garment, so anything goes there. It's the shape at the top that distinguishes the sleeve.

· ·

Drop Shoulder Sleeves

These are the simplest sleeves to work.

They usually begin at the bottom and increase to a prescribed width. This prescribed width is reached on or very close to the last row of the sleeve. The sleeves are worked straight across the top, bound off and then sewn to the garment. However, you could also opt to sew the side seams of your garment to the edge of the armhole and then pick up stitches around the armhole and decrease the sleeve down to the cuff. The garment body is worked straight—there is no armhole shaping on the body. Here are some general guidelines for sizing a drop shoulder sleeve.

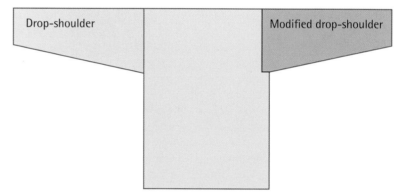

Drop-shoulder   Modified drop-shoulder

Modified Drop Shoulder Sleeves

* Armhole depth equals one-fourth of the chest circumference. In other words, if your sweater has a finished chest measurement of 38" (96.5cm), the distance from the shoulder to the underarm is 9½" (24cm).
* Width at the top of the sleeve equals twice the armhole depth. If your armhole measures 9½" (24cm) from shoulder to underarm, your sleeve must be 18" (45.5cm) at the top to fill the entire armhole.

Modified drop shoulder sleeves are very similar to drop shoulder sleeves but are attached a bit closer to the body. This gives them a slightly more tailored look. The armhole depth and the width at the top of the sleeve are calculated the same as for drop shoulder sleeves. The difference is that the top width is reached 1" to 2" (2.5cm to 5cm) below the top of the sleeve, and the sleeve is worked even for the last 1" or 2" (2.5cm or 5cm). On the body, 1" to 2" (2.5cm to 5cm) are bound off at the bottom of the armhole, bringing the armhole edge that much closer to the center of the garment.

Raglan Sleeves

These sleeves join the body of a sweater on a straight diagonal from the underarm to the neckline, and the stitches at the top of the sleeve become part of that neckline.

Working Raglans

Along with the Body

A pullover worked in the round or a cardigan worked back and forth in one piece can be worked from the top down or the bottom up. If you're working from the top down, begin with the number of stitches needed for the neckline, which includes some stitches for the top of the sleeve. Increase on each side of the "line" from neckline to underarm, front and back. Here's where using perfectly paired increases (see Chapter Six) will really demonstrate your pro status. It's your choice whether you want the increases to slant toward the shaping line or away from it; either way works, but slanting toward the line is more common.

If you're working a pullover in the round or a cardigan back and forth from the bottom up, work the body to the underarm and set the piece aside. Then work the sleeves from the cuff to the underarm length and width. At this point the sleeves are joined to the body and worked together up to the neck shaping. The diagonal line from the underarm to the neck is formed by decreasing on each side of the line of stitches,

thereby decreasing both the body and sleeve stitch counts. Again, perfectly paired decreases (see Chapter Six) make a huge difference here.

Separately from the Body

Of course, you can also work a raglan sweater in separate pieces—a front, a back and two sleeves—and sew them together. The shaping calculations are the same as those for working in one piece.

Determining Raglan Decreases

You'll need to know all the usual body measurements and desired ease (see Chapter Twelve) to calculate the number of stitches in the full width (finished chest measurement) of the sweater. All other measurements are based on the finished chest measurement.

With raglan shaping, it is very important to make sure you have the right number of rows between the underarm and the neck in which to increase (if working from the top down) or decrease (if working from the bottom up) the needed number of stitches. Multiply the underarm-to-back-of-neck measurement (see Chapter Twelve) by the row gauge—that's the number of rows you have available for the raglan shaping.

The top of the sleeve is included in the neck stitches, and the width of the sleeve top can vary from 1" to 4" (2.5cm to 10cm). The width of the sleeve at the upper arm, which is the widest part of the sleeve, is one-third of the body plus 1" to 2" (2.5cm to 5cm). So, if your finished chest measurement is 38" (96.5cm), the widest part of your sleeve will be about 14" (35.5cm) (38" [96.5cm] ÷ 3 = 12.66" [32cm], rounded to 12½" [32cm] plus 1½" [4cm] = 14" [35.5cm]).

For our example, we'll assume a sweater worked in the round from the bottom up at five stitches per inch (2.5cm).

Once the body and the sleeves have been worked to the underarm, join the sleeves to the body and continue

working in the round and decreasing to the neckline. Leave about 20 percent of the sleeve stitches at the center of the underarm on hold to be grafted to the body later, and leave the same number of body stitches at the underarm on hold. In this case, you'd leave about 3" (7.5cm) or fourteen stitches from each piece on hold.

* Sleeve stitches = 70 (14" [35.5cm] × 5 stitches per inch [2.5cm] = 70)
* Stitches to hold = 14 (70 stitches × 20 percent = 14)

Now knit the remaining sleeve stitches and the body together into one round. Work even for 1½" to 2" (4cm to 5cm) and then begin decreasing. Depending on the number of rounds in which you have to decrease and how many stitches you need to decrease, you'll decrease one stitch on each side of the four joining points every fourth round three or four times and then every other round to the neckline. You may opt to decrease every third or other odd-numbered round as long as the total number of decreases are worked in the available number of rounds.

UNDERARM JOINS

For a good solid join at the underarm, add one stitch at each side of the sleeve about two to four rows before the finished underarm length. When joining the pieces, knit the extra stitches on the sleeve together with the first and last stitches of the front and back. This action reduces the sleeve stitches to the original number.

Set-In Sleeves

These sleeves take the most planning, but the result is a trim and tailored look with no extra bulk at the underarm.

Armhole Shaping

First, you'll need to calculate the body armhole shaping. Let's stay with the 38" (96.5cm) chest circumference. The armhole depth is the same as for the drop shoulder or modified drop shoulder: one-fourth of the chest circumference, or 9½" (24cm). You'll also need to know the target finished measurement from shoulder to shoulder, which should be between 13" and 14" (33cm and 35.5cm), so let's say 13½" (34cm). Subtract 13½" (34cm) from the width of the front and back, which is 19" (48cm), to get 5½" (14cm). You'll decrease half this amount at each armhole, or 2¾" (7cm) on each side.

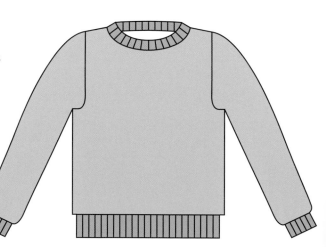

To make a nicely shaped armhole, bind off 1" (2.5cm) at the underarm and then decrease on every other row until you've decreased the appropriate number of stitches, which is determined by your gauge. To work with the measurements presented here and a gauge of five stitches per inch (2.5cm), the total number of stitches to be eliminated for one side of the armhole is fourteen ($2^{1}/_{4}$" [7cm] × 5 stitches per inch [2.5cm] = 13.75 stitches, rounded up to 14). At the beginning of the armhole, bind off 1" (2.5cm), or five stitches. Decrease nine more stitches (14 total stitches to be eliminated – 5 bound off = 9). Decrease one stitch at the armhole every other row nine times. Now you can work even up to the shoulder.

Sleeve Cap Shaping

Now you'll need to shape the sleeve to fit the armhole. Here is one scenario containing all of the information you'll need to know.

The pattern specifies the following:

* Gauge: Five stitches and seven rows = 1" (2.5cm)
* Number of stitches at the widest part of the sleeve (at the underarm): 14" (35.5cm) sleeve width, or seventy stitches (14" [35.5cm] × 5 stitches per inch [2.5cm] = 70)
* Number of stitches to be bound off at the underarm. To match the body, bind off 1" (2.5cm) on each side of the sleeve, ten stitches total.
* Number of stitches needed to shape the top of the cap (usually about 4" [10cm]) = 20 stitches (4" [10cm] × 5 stitches per inch [2.5cm] = 20)
* Armhole depth: We determined previously that this is $9^{1}/_{2}$" (24cm).

With this information we can calculate the necessary decreasing to shape the cap. From seventy stitches we bind off five on each side at the underarm, leaving sixty stitches. We want to end up with twenty stitches to shape the very top of the cap, so we need to decrease forty stitches (60 – 20 = 40).

We need to jump ahead a bit here to figure out our decrease rate. When we shape the top of the twenty-stitch cap, we'll work four shaping rows, reducing the number of stitches by half. Bind off three stitches at the beginning of the next two rows, two stitches at the beginning of the next two rows, and then the remaining ten stitches. The length of this curve is going to be about $4^{1}/_{2}$" (11.5cm), meaning it will consume $4^{1}/_{2}$" (11.5cm) of the armhole, $2^{1}/_{4}$" (5.5cm) from the front and $2^{1}/_{4}$" (5.5cm) from the back. This leaves $7^{1}/_{4}$" (18.5cm), or fifty rows ($7^{1}/_{4}$" [18.5cm] × 7 rows per inch [2.5cm] = 50) over which to decrease the forty stitches.

The curve looks best if the decrease rate is greater at the end, rather than at the beginning. So begin by decreasing one stitch at each side of every fourth row five times (ten stitches and twenty rows) and then decrease one stitch at each side of every other row fifteen times (thirty stitches and thirty rows) for a total of forty stitches decreased over fifty rows.

Saddle Sleeves

Saddle sleeves are worked like other sleeves up to the shoulder, and then they continue in a strip 2" to 4" (5cm to 10cm) wide along the top of the shoulder to the neckline. If your saddle will be 3" (7.5cm) wide, you'll need to reduce the armhole depth on the body front and back by $1^{1}/_{2}$" (4cm).

14 Necklines and Collars

There are several neckline shapes to choose from, most of which will work with both pullovers and cardigans. These shapes can be finished with bands or filled with various types of collars. What follows is not an exhaustive list but a good basis from which you can knit the classics or design your own unique shapes and collars.

Neckline Shapings

A neck is a neck is a neck, but it can be set in a variety of necklines. The choice is largely a matter of personal preference, but you should consider the style and weight of the sweater when deciding on the neckline. For example, you probably wouldn't want to put a scoop neck on a bulky knit sweater that's meant to be worn as an outer garment. (Of course, if you're a fashionista, you may want to do just that, leaving room for one or a dozen scarves!)

Crew Neck

The crew neck follows the line of the wearer's neck. It sits right at the base of the neck and is lower in the front than in the back. The front neckline shaping usually begins about 2" (5cm) below the shoulder line. The back neckline can be straight across in line with the shoulders, or it can be shaped so the center is 1/4" to 1/2" (0.5cm to 1cm) below the shoulder line.

When you've reached the length that is 2" (5cm) below the finished total length, bind off or place on hold a certain number of center stitches to begin the neck shaping. The number of stitches should equal about half of the total neckline width. Then shape the rest of the neckline by removing one quarter of the remaining neck stitches on each side, either with paired decreases or short rows (see Chapter Six). This shaping is done over the final 2" (5cm) to the shoulders.

Crew-Neck Band

There's no special shaping required here. Simply pick up stitches around the neckline, work your chosen band evenly to the desired length and bind off.

V-Neck

V-neck shaping is exactly what the name implies. A V-neck can be just deep enough to show the knot on a preppy tie, it can start at the same point as the underarm and provide a canvas for spectacular jewelry or it can plunge well below the chest on a garment to wear as an over layer (with a shirt underneath, please!). As with the crew neck, the back of the neck can be straight or slightly shaped.

To begin V-neck shaping, work to the length where you want the V to begin, taking into account that you will add some sort of band to the neckline, usually about 1" (2.5cm) deep. Determine the required length from this point to the shoulder and multiply this length by the row gauge to see how many rows you have left to knit. Now figure out how many stitches you have to remove on each side to get to the finished neck width and divide the number of rows still to be knit by the number of decrease rows to determine the decrease rate.

The pattern specifies the following:

* Gauge: Six stitches and eight rows per square inch (2.5 square centimeters)
* Length from beginning of V-neck shaping to shoulder: 6" (15cm) (a shallow V)
* Finished neck width: 6 1/2" (16.5cm)

You have forty-eight rows to work to reach the shoulder (6" [15cm] × 8 rows per inch [2.5cm] = 48). You need to remove forty stitches (6 1/2" [16.5cm] × 6 stitches per inch [2.5cm] = 39 stitches, rounded up to 40), half from each side of the center. You'll remove two stitches from each row, so you need to work twenty decrease rows over the forty-eight rows still to be knit. 48 ÷ 20 = 2.4. Because you can't work decreases over every 2.4 rows, you'll need to spread them out a bit. One solution is to decrease one stitch on each side of the V on every other row sixteen times and then decrease one stitch on each side of the V on every fourth row four times. This is not the only solution, but you get the idea.

V-Neck Band

A V-neck band has to be mitered at the center of the V. If your garment front has an odd number of stitches, you'll have one stitch at the very center of the V, and there are

V-neck with center stitch

V-neck without center stitch

a couple of ways to work the decreases in an added band. You can work double decreases over the center three stitches, or you can work one decrease on each side of the center stitch.

If you do not have a center stitch, place a marker between the two stitches at the center and work one decrease on each side of the marker. (See Chapter Six for paired decrease options.)

If you don't have a center stitch but want to work a center double decrease, simply work a make one increase (see Chapter 6) at the center front when you're picking up stitches.

[183]

Square Neck

A square neckline is usually the width of the back neck, which means that to begin the shaping you'll bind off or place on hold the number of stitches that equals this width at the center front and work straight up on each side from there to the shoulder. The depth of the neckline is again a matter of preference.

Square Neck Band

Square neck bands have mitered corners. Working with a center corner stitch in each corner, you can work the miters in a couple of ways. If you're working with one corner stitch in each corner, you can work to the stitch before the corner and then work a centered double decrease (slip two stitches together knitwise, knit one, pass the slipped stitches over) on the next three stitches. Or, you could work to two stitches before the corner stitch, ssk, knit the corner stitch and k2tog—this will result in a single stitch flanked by decreases leaning toward it.

If you have a space at the corner rather than a stitch, work to three stitches before the corner, ssk, knit two and k2tog. This will result in two corner stitches flanked by decreases leaning toward it. The corners will look like the V-neck band without a center stitch shown on page 183.

Boat Neck

The boat neck is the simplest neckline of all and can be quite flattering, especially over a turtleneck while yachting. The front and back are worked straight across with no neckline shaping and are joined together at the shoulders, leaving a certain number of center stitches bound off and unjoined to form the neck opening.

Henley Neck

Very popular in men's fashion, the Henley neckline is basically a slit down the center front from the neck edge that has a placket for buttons and buttonholes.

Collars

Collars can be added to any of the necklines discussed on the previous pages and can fill the whole neckline or only part of it. Collars can be short, long, ruffled or ribbed. Basically anything goes, and writing an exhaustive survey would be, well, exhausting. Here are some things to consider when working some of the collars we've seen around town.

Turtlenecks

Like most women of a certain age, we love turtlenecks. Usually worked in ribbing from a crew neckline, they can be tight or not so tight, tall or not so tall, straight up or folded over. Generally speaking, the first half (about 5" [13cm]) of the turtleneck should be worked on a needle that's one or two sizes smaller than the body needle, and then the second half is worked on a needle the same size as or one size larger than the body needle—this will allow for a neat fold-over that won't ride up. Before binding off, try the garment on to check the fit and then bind off with a needle that's two sizes larger than the body needle so it will stretch enough to fit over the head. Our sample started with a needle one size smaller than the body needle, continued on a needle one size larger than the body needle and was bound off with a needle two sizes larger than the body needle.

Mock Turtlenecks

Mock turtlenecks are turtlenecks without the fold-over. They should be knit on a needle that's one or two sizes smaller than the body needle and to a height of about 1" (2.5cm) below the chin. Try the garment on before binding off to be sure you're happy with the height and then bind off with a needle two sizes larger than the body needle.

Stand-Up Collars

A stand-up collar, which becomes a mandarin if it doesn't quite meet at the center front, is a great option for either stranded or textured garments, and you can use the same or complementary pattern in the collar. Because it's not worked in rib and won't stretch like a turtleneck, this collar must be worked from a round neckline with live stitches. Calculate the necessary circumference to fit comfortably over the head and then use your gauge to determine how many stitches you'll need. If you don't

have enough stitches in your neckline, work the first row plain, increasing the stitches as necessary.

Once you have the necessary number of stitches, work the collar straight for no more than 2¹/₂" (6.5cm). Work one plain knit row and one plain purl row; this creates a turning ridge. Change to a needle one size smaller than the one you're using and work a facing of 1/1 rib—because the inside of this collar will show, knit this facing to cover stranding or the unattractive back of your pattern stitch. Work one fewer row in the facing as the outside of the collar and join the layers together at the base of the band.

Our sample was worked on the same number of stitches as for the turtleneck, and both the outer Stockinette stitch and the inner rib used the same size needle as the body.

Shawl Collars

Shawl collars can be knit into square necklines or V-necklines. To work one into a square neckline, you can either use live stitches at the center front neck opening (if you have them), pick up stitches at the center front neck opening, or cast on and work the collar separately and sew it in later. All these methods will work, and using live or picked-up stitches only saves sewing along those center front stitches—the collar will have to be sewn to the sides and back of the neck opening anyway. Our sample is worked on a square neckline. The center front of the neckline uses one-third of the total front stitches, but this can vary according to your taste. The center front stitches are put on hold while the rest of the garment front is worked to the shoulders and joined to the back. Knit the shawl collar to fill the hole.

Mark the center back of the neckline and then place the held front stitches on a needle the same size as the body needle. Join a new yarn. Work evenly in pattern (in this case, seed stitch) until the collar is about ¹/₂" (13mm) less than the length from the collar bottom to the shoulder.

Begin to work short rows to curve around the neckline. Begin the short rows from the outer edge of the collar. *Work one-fourth of the stitches, turn, slip one, work back to the outer edge, turn; work half the stitches, turn, slip one, work back to the outer edge, turn; work three-fourths of the stitches, turn, slip one, work back to the outer edge, turn; work all stitches for four rows. Repeat from * until you're completely around the corner and then work evenly over all stitches until you reach the center back. Mark the center back of the collar and then work the other side of the collar in the reverse as with the first side, working short rows to about ¹/₂" (13mm) past the next shoulder. Work even to the bottom of the neckline. Bind off loosely.

Sew the collar to the neck opening, up the front on the right side, across the back and down the front on the left side. Tuck the lower left edge behind the picked-up stitches and sew into place.

Cowls

A cowl-neck collar is another that's worked from a round or crew neckline. The differences between this and a turtleneck lie in both the width and the length—a cowl can grow to be twice as big around and twice (or more) as long. Cowls may or may not be worked in rib. Begin as for a turtleneck, but gradually increase stitch count, needle size or both and work until you reach the desired length. It's a good idea to try on a cowl-neck garment along the way to be sure you get just the right amount of floppiness to suit your personal style.

For our sample, we picked up the same number of stitches as for the turtleneck and the stand-up collar and worked Stockinette stitch in the round from the inside; you need to work from the inside so the cowl folds to the outside with the right side facing outward. The cowl was worked on the same size needle as was used for the body, and after working one-third of the length, the stitches were increased by about 40 percent. The edge was finished with two rows of garter stitch. To keep the edge elastic, we bound off with a needle *three* sizes larger than the cowl needle.

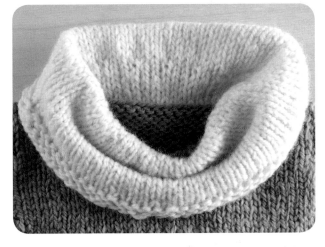

Polo Collars

Polo collars are also worked on a regular crew neckline, usually on cardigans or on pullovers with a Henley front.

We picked up stitches along the neckline with the right side of the garment facing and beginning with the right front. The first row of the collar becomes the right side, even though it's worked off the wrong side of the garment. This is done so the right side is facing out when the collar is turned down. Our sample is worked in seed stitch to match the front placket, and we increased one stitch at each collar end on every other row so the collar points down.

OPEN COLLAR PICK-UP
When picking up stitches for a polo collar such as the one pictured, pick up one or more stitches at the top of each placket to be sure that the transition is smooth. For our sample we picked up one placket stitch on each side.

15 Pockets

The most important elements of pocket planning are ease of entry, comfort and balance on the overall front, or possibly back, of the garment. Yes, we said back! Back pockets are a great place for carrying documents, maps and other essentials while on a motorcycle or bicycle trip.

Pocket Placement

You'll want to place pockets closer to the center front than to the sides of your garment. First, determine how many stitches will be in your pocket. Subtract this number from the number of stitches in half of the garment front—this is the number of stitches in the left or right front if you're working a cardigan, or the number of stitches from the side seam to the center front of the garment. Divide the remaining number of stitches by three and work two-thirds of the stitches between the side and the pocket and one-third of the stitches between the pocket and the center front. This placement will vary for special pockets such as kangaroo or diagonally placed patch pockets, but it's a good one to use for plain old horizontal- or vertical-entry pockets.

> **SIZE MATTERS**
> For a pocket that's meant for hand warming in addition to carrying keys and things, it's important that it is large enough for your hand to fit inside without stretching it. Measure the length and width of your hand and use your gauge to calculate the number of stitches and rows necessary to complete one pocket that will comfortably accommodate these measurements.

Basic Horizontal Pocket

For the purposes of this discussion, we'll refer to the inside of the pocket as the part that's behind the outside of the pocket, which is on public display. It doesn't matter whether you work the inside or the outside of the pocket first—this may change depending on how you're constructing your garment.

Work to the place where you want the bottom of the pocket, ending on a wrong-side row. Thread a tapestry needle with a contrasting colored cotton thread and, with the wrong side facing, run the cotton through the stitches that will become the pocket, plus one extra stitch on each end; these will be used to secure the join of the inside and outside parts of the pocket. Work two rows in pattern, placing markers on the needle to correspond with the beginning and end of the pocket stitches. Slide a small needle (size US 1 [2.25mm] or smaller) through the marked stitches. With the wrong side facing, join a new yarn to the right side of the

inside pocket stitches, leaving a 12" (30.5cm) tail, and work one wrong-side row. If you find it difficult to work the right side of the inside pocket stitches while the outside stitches are still on the needle, place the outside stitches on a string to hold until you've finished the inside pocket. Continue working back and forth on the pocket stitches only until the piece is the depth of the pocket minus your planned pocket border, ending on a wrong-side row. Cut the yarn, leaving a 12" (30.5cm) tail. Place the inside pocket stitches on a string to hold.

Work the garment stitches to the same length as the inside pocket. Thread a tapestry needle with cotton thread and use a running stitch to mark the edges of the pocket onto the wrong side of the outside pocket (body stitches). Place the pocket stitches on a needle so they're ready to knit. With the right side facing, work to the marker and work the next stitch together with the first stitch of the inside pocket. Place the stitches for the outside pocket on hold (all stitches up to one before the next marker), knit the inside pocket to the last stitch and knit the last stitch together with the one remaining stitch from the outside pocket; continue in pattern to the end of the row.

Basic horizontal pocket

Vertical Pocket

The size and placement of a vertical pocket will be the same as the basic horizontal pocket. The difference is that it opens along the side instead of along the top. The inside pocket will consist of the stitches from the side seam to the edge of the pocket closest to the center of the body. The outside pocket will consist of the stitches from the edge of the pocket closest to the side of the body to the center front of the garment.

Work to the place where you want the bottom of the pocket; end on a wrong-side row, placing markers for the beginning and end of the pocket placement. Thread a tapestry needle with cotton thread and, on the inside, run the cotton through the stitches that will comprise the pocket on the wrong side. Work four more rows in pattern. With a small double-point needle (size US 1 [2.25mm] or smaller), pick up the marked stitches on the back of the work. Join a new yarn, leaving a 6" (15cm) tail, and work the picked-up stitches for four rows, the same height as the garment stitches.

Return to the yarn attached to the body stitches and work the body stitches to the pocket marker. Now work the inside pocket stitches from the double-point needle. Cut the yarn attached to the stitches just knit, leaving a 12" (30.5cm) tail. Place the remaining stitches on a string to hold them. Knit the stitches now on the needle—the inside stitches—to the desired pocket depth. Place the stitches on a string to hold them.

Vertical pocket

Diagonal Pocket with Decorative Edge

This pocket is worked essentially the same as the vertical pocket, except that you decrease the outside edge to form a diagonal and work a decorative border along this edge. To calculate the decrease rate, first determine the desired width of the pocket at the bottom and at the top. Use your gauge to translate these widths into numbers of stitches and subtract the top number from the bottom. The result is the number of stitches to decrease. Now translate the intended depth of the pocket into a number of rows and spread the number of stitches to decrease over this number of rows.

It's best to work your decorative edge along with the pocket. Our sample shows a five-stitch border as follows:

Row 1 (RS): K1, p1, twist 2 right, p1.
Row 2 (RS): K1, p2, k2.

The decreases are worked inside this five-stitch border.

When you've finished the body, come back to the pocket and use the 12" (30.5cm) tails to sew the inside pocket to the outside along the marked rows. Place the held stitches on a needle. With the right side facing, leave a 6" (15cm) tail, work the desired border and bind off on a right-side row, leaving a 6" (15cm) tail. Use the tails on each end of your border to stitch it to the body.

Diagonal pocket with
decorative edge

WHERE ARE THE SIDE SEAM POCKETS?

If you're wondering where the side seam pockets are, they've been deliberately omitted. We don't like them, because a garment's side seam is not the right place for a pocket opening; the opening should always be on the garment front. That said, if you're a fan of this type of pocket, consider knitting the lining in a lighter-weight yarn than the garment yarn to reduce bulk—especially if the pocket will be placed anywhere near the hips!

Kangaroo Pouch

A kangaroo pouch is worked the same as a vertical or diagonal pocket except that you have two opening edges that mirror each other. The pouch is placed at the center front of a garment. The edges can be plain, but we think they look best with a decorative edge. Our first sample is a diagonal pouch worked in Stockinette stitch with a two-stitch garter edge. The second sample is vertical and has a Stockinette-stitch diamond on a reverse Stockinette-stitch background. The edges are worked in garter stitch.

Diagonal pouch pocket

Vertical pouch pocket

Patch Pocket

Patch pockets can be any shape and can be placed anywhere you want them, including on sleeves. They can be placed with a vertical, horizontal or diagonal opening. And, of course, they can be as plain or as decorative as you want them. Our sample shows a pocket knitted in a contrasting color, with a decorative slip-stitch pattern and placed on the diagonal.

Afterthought Pocket

If you decide after you've finished your sweater that you'd like to have pockets, you can either work patch pockets and sew them on or work this afterthought pocket, which looks exactly like the basic horizontal pocket.

1 Figure out your pocket depth and width as for other pockets and determine where you want it placed. With cotton threaded on a tapestry needle, mark the edges and top of the pocket placement, minus any top border. Count down the appropriate number of rows to the bottom of the pocket and pick up the inside pocket stitches on the back as for the basic and other pockets, leaving a 12" (30.5cm) tail. Work the inside pocket to the desired depth minus the top border. When you've finished the body, use the tails to sew the inside pocket to the outside along the marked rows.

3 Back the cut yarn out, one side at a time, to the marked pocket edges.

2 Carefully cut the center stitch of the previously marked top pocket placement line.

4 Place the new live stitches onto double-point needles; there will be one fewer stitch on the upper needle than on the lower needle.

Use Kitchener stitch (see Chapter Seven) to join the upper stitches to the inside pocket stitches. Add a border to the lower pocket stitches.

16 Closures

Good finishing techniques are crucial to the success of any knitted garment, and this is especially true when it comes to closures. Whether your garment will include buttons and button bands, a zipper or another decorative closure, here are some techniques that will yield professional-looking results.

Button Bands

Cardigans and Henley necklines that will be buttoned need bands on both edges of the opening. You'll sew buttons to one band and make buttonholes in the other. Here are a few ways to knit the bands.

Vertical Button Bands

If you want to add a vertical button band to a cardigan sweater or vest, you'll need to do a little planning. Vertical button bands can be worked along with the garment or added after the body piece is completed. In both cases, the button band will have the same number of rows as the garment, so the measurements will be precise.

Band Worked Along with the Garment

This is the simplest method. Work both the garment and the band at the same time, but work the band stitches on a smaller needle, usually two sizes smaller than the body needle. With the larger needle, cast on the appropriate number of stitches for the garment and the band—it may help to place a marker between the two sections. Change to a smaller needle and work the lower ribbing or other border to the desired length. Now work the band pattern (rib, Stockinette stitch or

> **BUTTON-BAND EDGE STITCHES**
> When working a button band in a rib, Stockinette stitch, cable or just about any pattern other than seed stitch, work a garter edge stitch to keep the band from rolling in.

whatever you've chosen) with the smaller needles (see the tip on page 197 regarding seed or garter-stitch bands) and then work the garment according to the pattern with the larger needles. Incorporate your chosen buttonholes on the right or left band as you go.

If you don't want to work with two sizes of needles but want to work the band with the garment anyway, we can't stop you. But when you're finished, work a row of slip-stitch crochet along the edge of the button band to firm it up and keep it from stretching.

Band Picked Up from Lower Border

Some knitters find it awkward to work with two sizes of needles at the same time as for the band described on the previous page. Here's a method that will look the same, but the band above the lower rib or border is worked separately and attached while knitting.

Cast on the appropriate number of stitches for the lower border or ribbing, plus the number needed for the band. Work the lower border to the desired length, and on the last wrong-side row, work to the band stitches and place them on a holder. Complete the garment front, working one Stockinette edge stitch at the front.

ATTACHING RIBBED BANDS

If you're working a ribbed band and attaching it to the garment with the crochet hook method, it's best to work with an even number of stitches. Work the edge stitch in garter stitch, then work k1, p1 across and end with k1. This puts a knit band stitch next to the knit body edge stitch. All neat and tidy.

Attaching While Knitting

1 With the wrong side facing, place band stitches on the same size needle used for the lower border or ribbing and work the stitches in pattern. Join the yarn and work one wrong-side row.

2 At the end of the first right-side row of the band, use a small crochet hook to draw the working yarn through the knot above the first edge stitch from bottom to top.

[continued on page 196]

3 You'll have a large loop of yarn on the wrong side, and you'll knit the band with the side of the loop that's attached to the stitches.

4 Work the band in pattern (rib, seed stitch or whatever you've chosen), being sure to pull up any slack when working the first stitch. Work the next row back to the garment edge and use the crochet hook to draw the working yarn through the knot above the next edge stitch from front to back.

Continue in this manner to the end of the garment. If you end on a right-side row, you can continue with the same yarn to pick up stitches around the neckline to work the neck band or collar. When you're finished, slip the cast-on tail through the first edge stitch from front to back and weave it in. Perfection personified!

Knitting and Sewing to Garment

Another option is to knit the band, making sure you knit the same number of rows that there are in the body and then sew the inside band stitches to the body edge stitches.

Band Worked Separately and Attached While Knitting

If you've knit your garment without a band (probably because you couldn't decide what type you wanted), you can still add the same type of vertical band described on page 194. If you've followed the suggestion of working a Stockinette edge stitch along the front edge, you can add a band that looks like it was knit with the garment. Cast on stitches for the band, work one right-side row and attach the band to the garment with a crochet hook as described on page 195 for attaching a band while knitting.

SEED- OR GARTER-STITCH BUTTON BANDS

Although you may choose just about any pattern for a button band, they are not all created equally. For vertical button bands, the row gauge of the band should approximate the gauge of the garment body. A slightly smaller row gauge is okay, but a slightly larger one is not. For example, seed and garter stitches have more rows per inch (2.5cm) than Stockinette stitch. If you've knit a Stockinette body and want a seed or garter border, it may be possible to block the band to match the length of the body, but probably only if you've knit the band on the same size needle as the body.

The difference in row gauge can also be corrected with short rows (see Chapter Six). You could also consider knitting these bands horizontally (see Horizontal Button Bands on page 199). However, if you've knit a garment in seed stitch and the button band in Stockinette stitch, the band will be hopelessly longer than the body, a condition for which there is no known cure. Always do a gauge swatch for both the body pattern and the band pattern when they're different and make adjustments as necessary for a balanced garment.

Double-Faced Stockinette-Stitch Band

Use this band for outdoor garments onto which you want to sew large and possibly heavy buttons—the double layer will help support the extra weight. This is another band that's knit along with the garment. Cast on the appropriate number of stitches for the lower rib or border, plus twice the number of stitches needed for the band, plus one—for a nine-stitch band, cast on nineteen stitches. On wrong-side rows, purl the nineteen band stitches.

On right-side rows, knit nine, slip one purlwise, knit nine. The slipped purl stitch will form a folding ridge in the center of the nineteen stitches.

Note: Work the first row of the Stockinette-stitch band as knit one, purl one; this will prevent the bottom from rolling up. When the garment front is finished, fold the band to the inside and stitch the inside band in place.

Double-faced Stockinette-stitch band, outside

Double-faced Stockinette-stitch band, inside

Bands for Steeked Garments

Bands for steeked garments differ from most other button bands in that they are always worked separately and sewn to the garment and they should always have a facing to hide the cut steek on the inside. This explanation assumes that you have placed the button-band stitches on hold before beginning the steek (see Chapter Seven).

1 Place the band stitches on the same size needles used for the lower ribbing or border and cast on four or five stitches. These stitches form a facing that will be sewn over the cut edge of the steek.

2 Work the band in your chosen pattern and the facing in Stockinette stitch.

3 When you're finished, fold the cut edge to the inside and stitch the band to the body, one stitch in from the sewn edge of the cut steek.

4 Add a basting line on the wrong side four or five stitches (depending on the width of the facing) from the join and sew the edge of the facing to the body along this line.

Horizontal Button Bands

Horizontal button bands are worked after the garment has been knitted. You'll either pick up stitches along the front edge and work to the desired width of the band, or cast on and knit the band and then attach it to the garment. The pick-up or attaching ratio (see Chapter Five) is key here and will depend on the type of band you're knitting. When picking up for bands, begin the right band at the lower edge with the right side facing and begin the left band at the neck edge with the right side facing.

Picked-Up Bands

Do a gauge swatch of your button-band pattern and calculate the pick-up rate (see Chapter Five). Pick up stitches proportionally along the front edge and simply work the band to the desired width and bind off. Our sample shows a seed-stitch band on the right and a garter-stitch band on the left. Both bands are worked on a needle two sizes smaller than the body needle, and both were picked up at a stitch-to-row ratio of two to three.

Because a 1/1 rib pulls in, if you want to work a horizontal ribbed band, the ratio of stitches to rows along the front garment edge is one to one. Using a needle two sizes smaller than the body needle, pick up one stitch in every edge stitch at the center front of the garment. Work 1/1 rib to the desired width and bind off with a needle two sizes larger than you used for the rib.

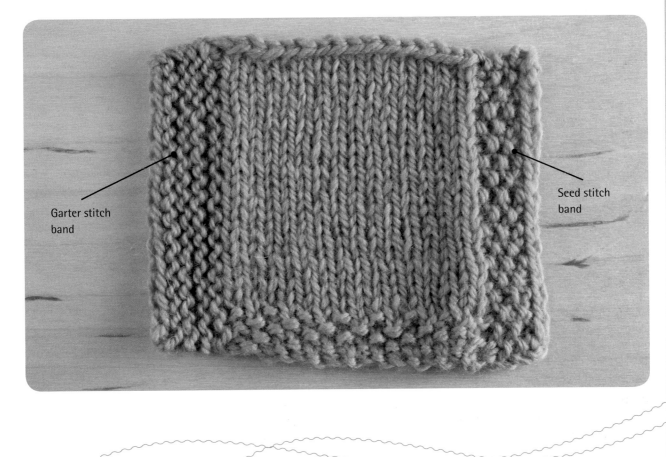

Garter stitch band

Seed stitch band

Crocheted-On Bands

If you work the 1/1 rib band described on the previous page from the outside edge, you'll attach it to the garment between the edge stitch and the next stitch—our sample shows a Stockinette-stitch body, so you'll attach the band between two knit stitches.

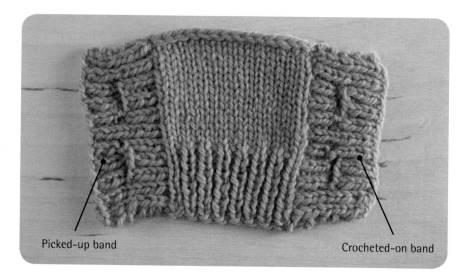

Picked-up band

Crocheted-on band

1 Count the number of rows at the center-front garment edge. Cast on this number of stitches using a needle two sizes larger than you'll use for the rib. Change to the rib needle and work a 1/1 rib to the desired width. Work one row with the larger needle and cut the yarn, leaving a 6" (15cm) tail to be woven in later. Hold the band and the garment edges together with right sides facing. Beginning with the end opposite the cut tail, use a crochet hook to pull the first stitch of the band through the space between the first two garment stitches.

2 Draw the next band stitch through the garment and then through the stitch on the crochet hook.

3 Continue in this manner, pulling stitches through and chaining them off. When you get to the last stitch, pull the tail through the stitch and weave it in.

To work a seed stitch band by casting on and attaching, follow the instructions for casting on and attaching a ribbed band, but pull stitches through the garment following your stitch-to-row pick-up ratio.

Sandwiched Band for Steeked Edge

Here's another way to add a band and clean up after your steeks at the same time.

1 With the right side of the garment front facing, use a needle two sizes smaller than the body needle to pick up and knit stitches along the right front from the hem to the neckline. As with other bands, you'll need to pick up using the appropriate stitch-to-row ratio, and you should pick up the stitches just inside the sewn line of the steek. If you have used the counting thread (see page 107) all along, you know how many rows have been knit to the neckline.

2 Turn and purl one row, then knit one row. Leave the stitches on the needle and trim any excess fabric from the cut edge of the steek. With a new needle and the wrong side facing, pick up and knit one stitch in each of the loops of the initial picked-up and knit row. Turn and purl one row. Place both needles together and knit one stitch from each needle together. You are sandwiching the cut edge between the two rows of picked-up stitches. Turn and work the bands in pattern to desired depth.

Open-Faced Band for Steeked Edge

You can also pick up a band on a steeked edge without sandwiching the cut edge. Simply pick up as for the sandwiched band, knit to the desired depth and bind off.

Buttonholes

As important as the buttons they are paired with, buttonholes can be worked in a variety of ways. For best results, work a buttonhole swatch to determine the number of rows (vertical) or stitches (horizontal) needed to accommodate your chosen button.

I-Cord Buttonhole Band

I-cord makes an attractive finishing edge when it's knit and attached to the garment at the same time. If you leave it unattached for a few stitches at regular intervals up the center front, the "slots" you create become buttonholes.

To work an attached I-cord, cast on three to five stitches onto a double-point needle. Slide the stitches to the other end of the needle, bring the yarn across the back of the stitches and knit to the last stitch. Knit the last stitch together with the edge stitch of the garment.

Cable Button Band

Cable crossings form openings that can be used for buttonholes in either a vertical or staggered alignment. A plain cable offers a center buttonhole only, but with a plaited cable you can place buttons at the center or stagger them at the sides of the cable.

Forgotten Buttonhole

You can find this filed under "Been there, done that!" If you're about 4" 10cm) into a ribbed band and realize you've forgotten a buttonhole, you may be asking yourself, "To rip, or not to rip?" The solution is to make a buttonhole without ripping or cutting.

Mark the spot where the buttonhole should be. From the wrong side, insert a crochet hook under a purl stitch and use it to work chain crochet through the next two purl stitches above the buttonhole; draw a piece of yarn through the remaining loop and secure (shown with pink thread) and pull this yarn upward to open a space for the buttonhole; secure the yarn and weave in the ends. Repeat the process at the bottom of the buttonhole (shown with lavender thread). The number of chain stitches may vary according to the yarn weight and button size.

One-Row Horizontal Buttonhole

This buttonhole can be worked on any type of button band. If worked on a vertical button band, the hole will be horizontal on the garment. You could also work the same buttonhole on a horizontal band, forming a buttonhole that's vertical to the garment. You'll need to know exactly where you want the buttonhole and how many stitches will be in the buttonhole.

Begin by working to the beginning of the buttonhole. Bring the yarn to the front, slip one stitch from the left needle to the right needle, bring the yarn to the back and drop it. *Slip one stitch from the left needle to the right needle and pass the next stitch on the right needle over this stitch. Repeat from * until the desired number of stitches have been bound off for the buttonhole. Slip the last stitch from the right needle to the left needle.

Turn the work and pick up the yarn you previously dropped to the back. Use it to cast on with the cable method (see Chapter Five) the same number of stitches that were bound off. Before placing the last cast-on stitch onto the left needle, bring the yarn to the front; this places a dividing strand between the last stitch and the next-to-last stitch.

Turn the work and slip the first stitch from the left needle to the right needle and then pass the last cast-on stitch over it. Work to the end of the row—buttonhole completed!

Vertical Buttonholes

Work to the bottom of the buttonhole placement, ending with a right-side row. With the wrong side facing, work to the proposed opening, join a new yarn (shown in cream in our swatch) and work to the end of the row. Turn the work and work back to the buttonhole opening, cross the new yarn with the old yarn as for intarsia (see Chapter Eight) and work with old yarn to the end of the row.

Turn and work to the buttonhole opening, drop the old yarn, pick up the new yarn (without crossing the yarns) and work to the end of the row. Continue in this manner for the appropriate height of the buttonhole, ending with a wrong-side row. Work two more rows, crossing the new yarn with the old yarn, and then cut the new yarn. With the wrong side facing, work to the end of the row with the old yarn. Working the new yarn and crossing it with the old yarn for a couple of rows creates a smooth finish, and the buttonhole is more secure because there are no yarn tails right at the beginning or the end of the hole.

REINFORCING BUTTONHOLES
To make sure your buttonholes don't stretch, split your yarn into plies and use one or two to sew a buttonhole stitch around the edges.

One-Stitch Buttonhole

This is a quick buttonhole to make; it's best used with small buttons. On the right side, work to the place where you want the buttonhole, k2tog and work to the end of the row. On the next wrong-side row, work to the decrease, yarn over and work to the end of the row. On the next right-side row, work to the yarn over, knit into the back of the yarn over and work to the end of the row.

NECKLINE BUTTONHOLES
Neckline buttonholes should always be horizontal, even if the others were vertical. This last buttonhole holds the fabric flat and guarantees a neat and tidy look.

Zippers

Zippers can be a little challenging to sew into your knits, but we're not the only ones who love them. A two-row reverse Stockinette-stitch edging will allow the zipper to open and close without a hitch. Take your time and sew carefully. Here's how.

Right Front

With the right side facing and beginning at the lower center-front edge, pick up and knit stitches along the edge to the neckline using your stitch-to-row pick-up ratio (see Chapter Five). Turn and knit one row and then turn and bind off purlwise with a larger needle. Pin and baste the right side of the zipper in place so the edge of the picked-up and knit rows is in the exact center of the zipper. Stitch the zipper in place, sewing in the ditch between the picked-up stitches and the body.

Left Front

Work as for the right front, but begin at the neckline and work to the lower edge.

Optional Casing

If you want to cover the inner zipper tape, use a small needle to pick up and knit three or four stitches along the

neck edge on one side of the zipper. Change to the body needle and work in your chosen stitch for the length of the zipper tape and then bind off. Use a needle and thread to sew one side of the casing to the zipper (not too close to the teeth!). Separate the yarn plies and use two plies threaded on a tapestry needle to sew the facing to the garment at the edge of the tape and across the bottom. Repeat on the other side.

Frogs

We're not really sure how these got their name, but frog closures can add a fabulous decorative element to your garments. You can make them as plain or as fancy as you like.

Our sample uses a three-stitch I-cord formed into three loops—one loop is the buttonhole and the other two are decorative. Pin the frog in place and stitch it to the garment using yarn threaded onto a tapestry needle. To make the button shown here, we held two yarns together and worked as follows: Cast on one stitch. Knit into the front, back, front, back and front of the same stitch, making five stitches from one. Work Stockinette stitch for five rows, beginning and ending with a wrong-side row. On the right side, slip the second, third, fourth and fifth stitches one at a time over the first stitch and off the needle. Cut the yarn and pull the tail through the final stitch. Use the tails to attach the button, shaping it as you go.

17 Finishing and Storing

Congratulations! Your garment is knitted and sewn together, there are no loose ends hanging out and it's almost ready to wear. The final step is to block the garment, which will help straighten out any wiggly lines, even up the stitches and smooth out any bumps. After blocking and wearing, it's important to clean and store your knitted garments to give them a long and beautiful life.

Blocking, Cleaning and Storing Animal Fibers

Animal fibers respond best to full immersion blocking. Fill your sink with tepid water and add a good-quality wool wash, available from sellers of fine yarns. Make sure the soap is completely dissolved and dispersed in the water. Now let your garment take the plunge. It will want to float on top, so coax it down under the water and swish it around until it is completely soaked. Drain the water, fill the sink again and swish the garment around to rinse out the soap. Repeat the rinsing until the soap is completely gone. Squeeze the garment gently several times to remove as much water as possible. Now lay the garment down on a thick towel, making sure there are no creases or folds, and roll up the towel with the garment inside. Squeeze the towel several times to remove more water. You can remove even more water by placing the garment in your washing machine and running it through a spin cycle. Trust us, this is safe. Just be sure you're using a spin cycle and only a spin cycle. Now cover a flat surface with a thick towel or two and lay your garment out to dry. Use your hands to shape the garment, making sure the seams are running straight, the rib is not stretched out, etc. Pat down any bumps and smooth everything out. If you're blocking a sweater, put hand towels in the sleeves to further absorb moisture. Every twelve hours or so, change the towels. Even a thick Aran sweater should be dry and ready to wear within forty-eight hours.

When it's time to clean your garments, follow the same procedure outlined above. If you plan to store your garments for the off-season, it's crucial that you wash and block them before doing so. If you spilled a little Alfredo sauce on the front of your natural-colored sweater, it may not show, but the moths will know it's there and will make a picnic of it. Be sure your garments are completely dry before putting them in storage. If you think your Aran sweater is completely dry, wait at least another day to be sure.

If you don't like the smell of mothballs, don't store your garments with them. Line the chest or box you'll be storing in with newspaper. The ink is known to have a repellent effect, though we're not sure if this is true of the modern soy-based ink. But if your garment is clean and you're storing only for a season, you should be okay. Put white tissue paper over the newspaper, lay your garment(s) on top and layer the paper in reverse on top: white tissue and then newspaper. If you do use insect repellents, put them in a cloth bag and don't let them come into direct contact with the garment.

Blocking, Cleaning and Storing Plant Fibers

Cotton and other cellulosic fibers have characteristics very different from wool, and they don't respond to blocking the same way. Blocking will help finish the knitting to a certain extent, but the changes won't be as dramatic as with wool. Many cotton yarns are

by machine:
Fill with tepid water
Add Eucalan*
Stop machine
Load washables
Squeeze gently
Soak for 30 minutes
By-pass rinse cycle!
Spin water out

by hand:
Fill basin with
tepid water
Add Eucalan*
Squeeze article
gently
Soak 15 minutes
(minimum)
No need to rinse!

*use 5ml /1 tsp. Eucalan per 4l /1 gallon
of water (more for heavily soiled items)

important: always test colour-fastness;
avoid heavy agitation; lay knit articles
flat to dry out of direct heat & sunlight

machine washable, and if this is how you plan to clean your garments, by all means give them a machine wash after knitting and before wearing. Even if the label says "machine wash and dry," we recommend laying your cotton garments flat to dry. Use your fingers to straighten seams and smooth things out.

Follow the same storage guidelines as for wool. Cotton and other cellulosic fibers are particularly susceptible to mildew, so be absolutely sure the items are bone dry before they go into the chest or box.

Special Considerations

It's relatively easy to lay sweaters out to dry and really simple to lay scarves and flat shawls out, so these can be blocked on a tabletop with towels. But some items are a little trickier to deal with.

Blocking Socks

If you're going to knit more than a couple of pairs of socks, invest in a set of sock blockers; your socks will dry faster and snap back into shape with each wash.

Blocking Hats

If you knit a lot of hats, you might consider investing in a head form. If you place your damp hats on a head form to dry, they won't dry with any unwanted creases or folds.

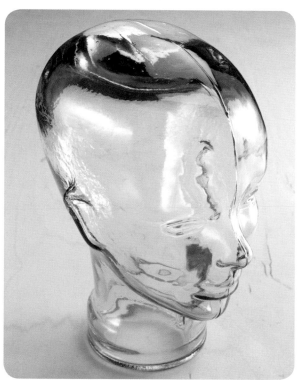

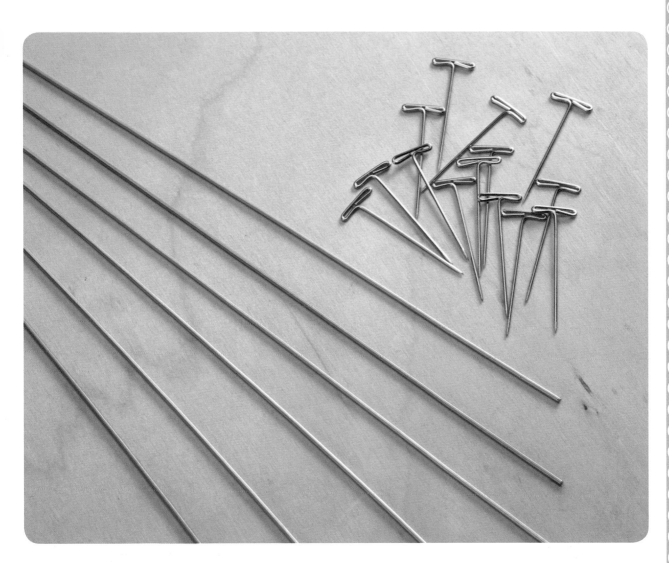

Blocking Large Items

Most of us don't live in mansions, so blocking an afghan or an oversize shawl can pose a problem. Consider using the space under your bed. Get under there with the vacuum and make sure everything's spic and span, lay down towels and spread your item on the towels. Close the door to keep pets out of the room.

Blocking with Wires

Lace shawls will almost always benefit from being blocked with long blocking wires made for this purpose. If you use some other type of wire, make sure it's made of stainless steel.

Insert wires along each edge of your damp piece. If the edge is straight, i.e., it doesn't have an added shaped edging, insert a wire along the edges by passing through all the "knot" stitches. If the edge has a shaped edging, insert the wire through the outermost stitch of each pattern repeat.

Use stainless steel T-pins to pin the wires to a foam blocking board (if the piece is too large for a blocking board, place it on a towel-covered rug); stretch to size the piece as desired, making sure everything is smooth and placing the T-pins at equal distances along the wires.

Part V

Project Lessons

Presented here are eight projects designed to illustrate some of the techniques we've discussed in the previous sections of the book. Rather than simply present instructions, we've added notes to explain why we did what we did and to allow you to make other choices. Each pattern is presented in one size only; at the end of the instructions for the sample size you'll find a section that will direct you through the steps of altering the size of the garment.

* Faux Earflap Hats have a two-color braid and a checkerboard color pattern.

* Beady Cable Gloves have perfectly placed beads inside a double-crossing cable.

* Double-Knit Mitts let you explore two-color double knitting.

* Diamond Central Scarf shows you how to attach a lace edging around corners.

* Stranded Lattice Socks explore stranded knitting and a short row heel.

* Austin's Jacket is loaded with details including pockets and a zipper.

* Ambrosia Sweater involves multi-directional knitting, pick-up ratios and set-in sleeves.

* Lisdoonvarna covers many Aran techniques including balancing patterns.

We hope you have someone to knit each of these projects for, and that you will gain enough knitting know-how to fearlessly alter or design your own unique garments.

Faux Earflap Hats

Here's a little lesson in gauge. Both sizes of this hat use the same number of stitches and the same needle size. So what's different? This time it's the yarn weight. The Vamsegarn used for the larger version is a worsted weight while the Strikkegarn used for the smaller hat is a DK weight. Knit on the same size needle, the worsted has fewer stitches per inch than DK, resulting in a larger hat. (See Chapter One for more information about yarn weights and gauges.)

Yarn

Size 24" (61cm):
Nordic Fiber Arts Vamsegarn (100% wool; 87 yds [80m] per 1.75oz [50g]):
- **Colorway 1:** 2 skeins V03 Light Grey Heather (A); 1 skein each V13 Grey Heather (B), V14 Charcoal Grey Heather (C), V36 Black (D)
- **Colorway 2:** 2 skeins V13 Grey Heather (A); 1 skein each V80 Lime Green (B), V56 Bright Pink (C), V95 Purple (D)

Size 22" (56cm):
Nordic Fiber Arts Strikkegarn (100% wool; 115 yds [105m] per 1.75oz [50g]):
- **Colorway 1:** 2 skeins 103 Light Grey Heather (A); 1 skein each 136 Black (B), 174 Red (C), 114 Charcoal Grey Heather (D)
- **Colorway 2:** 2 skeins 4-60 Bone (A); 1 skein each 7-61 Olive Green (B), 144 Berry Red (C), 198 Yellow Green (D)

☆ *The theory here is to choose four colors—the main color, A, and three contrasting colors, B, C, and D. One set of instructions can be used for all hats; after choosing your colors, assign a letter to each color and follow the instructions. Or get wild and do your own thing.*

Finished Size

24" (61cm) circumference
22" (56cm) circumference

Needles

Set of five US 6 (4mm) dpns or size required to obtain gauge
Three US 6 (4mm) 16" (40cm) circular needles
One US 6 (4mm) straight needle for cast on
Size D crochet hook

Gauge

24" (61cm) circumference: 20 stitches = 4" (10cm) in Stockinette stitch
22" (56cm) circumference: 22 stitches = 4" (10cm) in Stockinette stitch

Notions

Cotton waste yarn for cast on
2 stitch holders
Tapestry needle
4 markers

Patterns

TWO-COLOR BRAID 1

Round 1: *K1A, k1b; repeat from to marker.
Round 2: Bring both yarns forward, *purl A with strand B, bring strand A over B, purl B with strand A; repeat from * to marker.

TWO-COLOR BRAID 2

Round 1: *K1C, k1A; repeat from to marker.
Round 2: Bring both yarns forward, *purl C with strand A, bring strand C over A, purl A with strand C; repeat from * to marker.

CHECKERBOARD PATTERN 1 (in the round)

Round 1: K1C, k2A, *k2C, k2A; repeat from * to last stitch, k1C.
Round 2: K1C, p2A, *k2C, p2A; repeat from* to last stitch, k1C.

CHECKERBOARD PATTERN 2 (in the round)

Round 1: K1D, k2B, *k2D, k2B; repeat from * to last stitch, k1D.
Round 2: K1D, p2B, *k2D, p2B; repeat from * to last stitch, k1D.
Round 3: K1B, k2D, *k2B, k2D; repeat from * to last stitch, k1B.
Round 4: P1B, k2D, *p2B, k2D; repeat from * to last stitch, p1B.
Round 5: Repeat Round 1.
Round 6: Repeat Round 2.

Crown

Using a provisional cast on (see Chapter Five), a straight needle and A, cast on 120 sts. With a circular needle, knit 1 row. Place a marker and join, being careful not to twist stitches. Work in Stockinette stitch until piece measures 3" (8cm) from beginning.

☆ *We choose a provisional cast on here because once we've finished the Crown, we'll go back and use the live stitches to work the Inner and Outer Bands. While you could pick up stitches from a regular cast on, you would seriously limit the stretch in the fabric where you need it most.*

Decreasing for the Top of the Crown

Work Crown decreases as follows, changing to dpns when necessary.

☆ *Because you'll have fewer and fewer stitches as you decrease, you'll eventually have too few to fit the circular needle. When you get to this point, transfer the stitches, evenly divided, onto four double-point needles and knit with the fifth.*

Round 1: *Sl 1 as to knit, k19, repeat from * to marker—120 sts.
Round 2: *K2tog through the back loops, k18, repeat from * to marker—114 sts.
Round 3: *Sl 1 as to knit, k18, repeat from * to marker—114 stitches.
Round 4: *K2tog through the back loops, k17, repeat from * to marker—108 sts.

☆ *We call this technique Elongated Slip-Stitch Decreases. It results in evenly tensioned stitches and also forms a stylish pinwheel pattern.*

Continue in this manner, working 1 fewer stitch between the slip sts on odd-numbered rounds and 1 fewer stitch between the decs on even-numbered rounds, until you've worked 10 dec rounds total and 60 sts remain.

Work top of Crown as follows, removing marker when necessary.

Round 1: *Sl 1 as to knit, k2tog, psso, k7; repeat from * to end of round—48 sts.
Round 2: *Sl 1 as to knit, k2tog, psso, k5; repeat from * to end of round—36 sts.
Round 3: *Sl 1 as to knit, k2tog, psso, k3; repeat from * to end of round—24 sts.
Round 4: *Sl 1 as to knit, k2tog, psso, k1; repeat from * to end of round—12 sts.

Cut yarn, leaving a 6" (15cm) tail. Thread tail onto tapestry needle, draw needle through 12 remaining sts twice, pull up tight and fasten off. Weave in end.

☆ *The decreasing through most of the Crown top was worked on every other round. When you get to the top, if you were to continue decreasing every other round you'd end up with a point. To flatten out the top, double decreasing is accelerated to every round.*

Inner Band

With WS of Crown facing, remove provisional cast on and place stitches and an end-of-round marker on a circular needle.

☆ *You'll now be knitting in the opposite direction of the original cast on. When the Band folds to the outside of the hat, the RS will be facing.*

Inc Round: Join B, k5, M1L, *k10, M1L; rep from * 10 more times, end k5—132 sts.

☆ *Here we increase the number of stitches by 10 percent to compensate for the two-color stranded work to be used in the Outer Band pattern, which will pull in and knit up at a smaller gauge. The M1L (make one left-leaning) increase is described in Chapter Six.*

Work even in Stockinette stitch for 1" (2.5cm). Purl 2 rounds— this is the turning ridge for the Inner Band. Knit 1 round.

Outer Band

Join A and work Two-Color Braid 1. Cut B, join C and work Two-Color Braid 2. Work Checkerboard Pattern 1. Work Two-Color Braid 2. Cut A and C, join B and D and work

Checkerboard Pattern 2. Cut B and D, join A and C and work Two-Color Braid 2. Work Checkerboard Pattern 1. Slip the next 38 sts to a circular needle. This is the back of the hat.

☆ *Working this way places the color join (or seam) at the left side of the Right Earflap where it will hardly be noticeable, rather than locating the blip at the center back of the hat.*

Earflaps (worked straight)

Left Earflap

Place next 22 sts on a dpn. Join yarns A and D. Work Rows 1–26 of Earflap Chart and place remaining 4 sts on a holder. Place next 50 sts on a circular needle. This is the front of the hat.

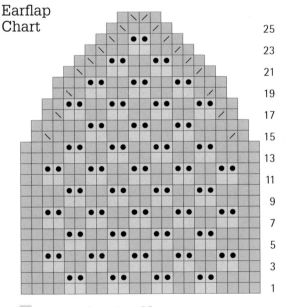

Earflap Chart

25
23
21
19
17
15
13
11
9
7
5
3
1

☐ Knit with Color A on RS

☐ Knit with Color D right side; purl with Color D on WS

● Knit with Color A

╱ K2tog on RS
P2tog on WS

╲ Ssk on RS
Ssp on WS

Right Earflap

Place the next 22 sts on a dpn. Join yarns A and C.
Work Rows 1–26 of Earflap Chart and place remaining 4 sts on a holder.

Edging Braid

With a circular needle and beginning at the left side of the Right Earflap, work Round 1 of Two-Color Braid 2 on all live and picked-up stitches as follows: work 38 sts, place marker; with dpns, pick up and knit 21 sts along right side of Left Earflap, k4 held sts, pick up and knit 21 sts along left side of Left Earflap, place marker; with circular needle work 50 sts, place marker; with dpns pick up and knit 21 sts along right side of Right Earflap and k4 held sts; with dpns pick up and knit 21 sts along left side of the Right Earflap, place marker—180 sts.

☆ *The pick-up ratio along the sides of the Earflaps is four for five: You pick up four stitches and skip one. This is a generous pick-up rate to ensure that the flaps lie flat and don't cup.*

Work Round 2 of Two-Color Braid 2 as follows: *Ssk, work to 2 sts before next marker, k2tog, slip marker, ssk, continue in pattern to 2 sts before next marker, k2tog, slip marker; repeat from * 1 more time. Cut C and join B, work Two-Color Braid 1 over remaining 172 sts, removing all markers. Bind off in Round 1 of Two-Color Braid 1.

☆ *Decreases are worked on both sides of the Earflap to tighten the perpendicular join between the Earflap and the Band.*

Finishing

Weave in all ends. Steam press area where Crown and Inner Band meet along the turning ridge. With crochet hook and color of choice, work a 9" (23cm) chain beginning at the center top of each Earflap; tie the ends in a knot. Tie the chains together in a bow at the top of hat. Add tassels if desired.

Size 24" (61cm) in Colorway 1

Size 24" (61cm) in Colorway 2

Size 22" (56cm) in Colorway 2

Beady Cable Gloves

A 3/2 eyelet ribbed cuff flows seamlessly into a 5/2 beaded cable pattern for the back of the hand. The glove shown is knitted at a gauge of six stitches to the inch (2.5cm) and will fit an average woman's hand. The yarn used for the model can be knit at five stitches per inch (2.5cm) for a larger glove; a finer yarn can be knit at seven stitches per inch (2.5cm) for a smaller glove. Two stitches cross in front of three for an all-knit cable of unusual depth, and a single bead sits in the center of each cable.

Finished Size

Approx 7¾" (19.5cm) circumference

Yarn

Louet Gems Sport Weight (100% machine washable merino wool; 225 yds [206m] per 3.5oz [100g]): 1 skein Crabapple

Needles

Set of 5 US 3 (3.25mm) and 4 (3.5mm) dpns or size needed to obtain gauge

Gauge

12 sts and 14 rows = 2" (5cm) in Stockinette stitch using US 4 (3.5mm) needles

16 sts and 17 rows = 2" (5cm) in cable pattern using US 4 (3.5mm) needles

Notions

Big eye beading needle or dental floss threader
50 size 6° seed beads
Cable needle (cn)
Tapestry needle
Waste yarn

Abbreviations

C1/3/1: Slip 4 sts to cable needle and hold in back; knit 1 from left needle; slip 3 sts from cn back to left needle; holding cn in front, k3 from left needle; k1 from cn.

kfbf: Knit into the front, back and front of the next stitch—2 sts increased.

S2kp: Slip 2 sts tog kwise, k1, pass 2 slipped sts over.

SS1B (slipstitch 1 bead): Bring yarn to front, slip 1 stitch, slide up a bead, bring yarn to back ready for next stitch, leaving bead in front of the slipped stitch.

Patterns

RIB (MULTIPLE OF 5)

Rounds 1 and 2: *P2, k3; rep from * to end of round.
Round 3: *P2, s2kp; rep from * to end of round.
Round 4: *P2, (k1, p1, k1) in the next stitch; rep from * to end of round.
Repeat Rounds 1–4 for pattern.

☆ *The "(k1, p1, k1) in one stitch" double increase produces the required number of stitches and a decorative eyelet. The s2kp double decrease adjusts the stitch count and produces a single centered stitch that flows to the center of the five-stitch cable.*

BEADY CABLE (MULTIPLE OF 7 + 5)

Round 1: *C1/3/1, p2; rep from * 3 more times, C1/3/1—33 sts.
Rounds 2 and 3: *K5, p2; rep from * 3 more times, k5.
Round 4: *K2, SS1B, k2, p2; rep from * 3 more times, k2, SS1b, k2.
Rounds 5 and 6: Rep Rounds 2 and 3.
Repeat Rounds 1–6 for pattern.

☆ *The C1/3/1 cable is worked with all knit stitches, which works very well with the slipstitch beading technique—when a bead is slipped over a purl stitch, the purl bump may push the bead to one side or the other. There's nothing wrong with that, but the perfectionists among us will have a problem if some beads lean to the right while others lean to the left.*

Beady Cable Chart

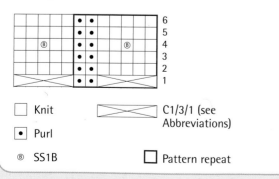

☐ Knit	⧓ C1/3/1 (see Abbreviations)
• Purl	
ⓑ SS1B	☐ Pattern repeat

Right Glove

String 25 beads onto the yarn and slide them down a couple of yards (see Chapter Eleven).

☆ *There's no need to string the beads for the second glove now—you'll be breaking the yarn many times between now and then, and you can string them after you've finished this glove.*

Cuff

Cast on 50 sts and divide onto 4 dpns, being careful not to twist the sts. Work Rounds 1–4 of Rib 7 times. Cuff measures approx 3" (7.5cm).

☆ *Use the regular long-tail cast on here. When you join to work in the round, you'll have knit stitches on the outside. Mittens and gloves are best worked with five dpns—you can work with the back-of-hand stitches on two needles and the palm stitches on the other two needles. The cuff can be shortened or lengthened by working more or fewer repeats of the rib pattern.*

Next Round: *P2, k1, kfbf, k1; repeat from * 4 more times, p2, k3, pm, k1, pm, k to end of round; knit first 2 sts of round onto last needle worked to change start of round. You now have 33 back-of-hand sts and 27 palm sts.

☆ *The back-of-hand stitches need to be increased to accommodate the five-stitch cable pattern. Because cable patterns pull in (see Chapter Nine), increasing ten stitches does not widen the fabric. Placing the increases in the center stitch of the three-stitch part of the rib allows the cables to grow seamlessly from the center of the rib. You shift two stitches from the back stitches to the palm stitches so the back-of-hand begins and ends with a cable. The thumb gusset is placed three stitches into the palm, not worked directly on the side, which is more in line with hand anatomy.*

Hand

Round 1: Work Row 1 of Beady Cable chart on back-of-hand sts, k to marker, sm, M1R, k1, M1L, sm, k to end of round.

Round 2: Work Row 2 of Beady Cable chart on back-of-hand sts, k to end of round.

Round 3: Work Row 3 of Beady Cable chart on back-of-hand sts, k to end of round.

Round 4: Work Row 4 of Beady Cable chart on back-of-hand sts, k to marker, sm, M1R, k to next marker, M1L, sm, k to end of round.

Round 5: Work Row 5 of Beady Cable chart on back-of-hand sts, k to end of round.

Round 6: Work Row 6 of Beady Cable chart on back-of-hand sts, k to end of round.

Continue as established, working Beady Cable chart on back-of-hand sts and Stockinette st on palm, increasing at the beg and end of thumb gusset every 3rd round until there are 15 thumb gusset sts. Work 1 round even in established patterns.

☆ *The thumb gusset is worked with a right-leaning increase (M1R) at the start and a left-leaning increase (M1L) at the end so the increases lean with the shaping. You don't have to count the three-round shaping repeats for the thumb gusset; because the cable is worked over six rounds, you only need to remember to increase the gusset in the same round that you work a cable crossing (Round 1 of the pattern) or slide a bead (Round 4 of the pattern). All palm stitches are worked in Stockinette stitch.*

Next Round: Work even in established patterns to marker, remove marker, place 15 thumb gusset sts on string to hold, remove marker, cast on 1 st, k to end of round. You now have 33 back-of-hand sts and 27 palm sts.

☆ *Once the increased gusset stitches are removed, we need to replace the one palm stitch that was included in those stitches. The backward-loop cast on will be the most invisible for this purpose. Though it is somewhat difficult to work on the first row, it's only one stitch, so it's not a problem.*

Continue in patterns as established until you have worked 5 repeats of Beady Cable chart.

Next Round: *(C1/3/1, but instead of knitting the 3 center sts work s2kp), p2; rep from * 3 more times, (C1/3/1, but instead of knitting the 3 center sts work s2kp), k to 5 sts

before end of round. Place rem 5 sts and first 6 sts from next round on a string to hold for Little Finger. Cast on 3 sts and rejoin to work in the round.

☆ *Once the cable pattern is finished, we need to reduce the stitch count to compensate for the lack of take-up by the cables (see Chapter Nine). To maintain pattern continuity, make a double decrease at the center of the pattern, which mirrors the double increase made at the beginning. After removing the stitches for the Little Finger, three new stitches fill the gap for the space between the fingers. Again, use the backward-loop cast on.*

Work to Finger Bases

Round 1: *K3, p2; repeat from * 2 more times, k3; k to end of round.

Round 2: Repeat Rnd 1.

Round 3: *S2kp, p2; repeat from * 2 more times, s2kp; k to end of round.

Round 4: *(K1, p1, k1) in the next st, p2; repeat from * 2 more times, (k1, p1, k1) in the next st, k to end of round.

☆ *Once the stitches for the Little Finger have been isolated, you need to work a short distance to reach the base of the other fingers. In this case, four rows will make the right length; the Stockinette stitch gauge would be too wide at this point, so we'll make the transition to the fingers with four rounds of the cuff rib.*

Ring Finger

K6, place the next 27 sts on waste yarn to hold, cast on 3, knit remaining 9 sts—18 sts for Ring Finger. Divide onto 3 dpns and knit until Ring Finger is ⅛" (3mm) from desired finished length. Decrease for top of Ring Finger as follows:

Round 1: *K1, k2tog; repeat from * to end of round—12 sts.

Round 2: Knit.

Round 3: *K2tog; repeat from * to end of round—6 sts.

Cut yarn, leaving a 6" (15cm) tail. Thread tail onto tapestry needle, draw through rem 6 sts, pull up snugly and fasten off on the wrong side.

☆ *The Ring Finger uses six back-of-hand stitches, six palm stitches, the three stitches cast on after isolating the Little Finger and three new cast on stitches, which fill the gap between the fingers.*

Middle Finger

Place 6 held front sts and 6 held back sts on needles. Join yarn to held palm sts and knit them, pick up 5 stitches along the Ring Finger cast on (see Tip below), knit 6 back sts, cast on 3. Knit 1 round even. On next round, knit to the 5 picked-up stitches, ssk, k1, k2tog, and k to end of round. Finish as for Ring Finger.

No-Hole Pick-Up

When picking up stitches between the fingers, pick up 1 extra stitch before and after the cast-on stitches. Knit the two extra stitches for one round, then decrease them on the following round. This will help to prevent holes from forming at the base of the fingers.

Index Finger

Place rem 15 held sts onto needles. Join yarn and pick up 5 from the Middle Finger cast on. Work as for Middle Finger.

Little Finger

Place held 11 sts onto needles. Join yarn and pick up 5 stitches along the Ring Finger cast on. Knit 1 round even. On next round at the 5 picked-up stitches, ssk, k1, k2tog. Knit until finger is 1/8" (3mm) from desired finished length. Decrease for top of Little Finger as follows:

Round 1: *K1, k2tog; repeat from * to last 2 sts, k2—10 sts.
Round 2: Knit.
Round 3: *K2tog; repeat from * to end of round—5 sts.

Cut yarn, leaving a 6" (15cm) tail. Thread tail onto tapestry needle, draw through rem 6 sts, pull up snugly and fasten off on the inside.

Thumb

Place 15 held thumb sts on needles. Pick up 5 sts over gap. Work as for Middle Finger.

Left Glove

Set up and work cuff as for Right Glove.

Next Round: *P2, k1, kfbf, k1; repeat from * 4 more times, (p2, k3) to last 2 sts, pm, k1, pm, k1; knit first 2 sts of round onto last needle worked to change start of round. You now have 33 back-of-hand sts and 27 palm sts.

☆ *The left glove is worked as a mirror image of the right glove, so the thumb gusset is placed at the end of the palm stitches instead of the beginning.*

Hand

Work Hand as for Right Glove.
Continue as for Right Glove until 5 repeats of Beady Cable pattern are complete.

Next Round: *(C1/3/1, but instead of knitting the 3 center sts work s2kp), p2; repeat from * 3 times, (C1/3/1, but instead of knitting the 3 center sts work s2kp), k to end of round.
Next Round: *K3, p2; repeat from *2 more times, k2; place next 11 sts on waste yarn to hold for Little Finger, cast on 3, rejoin round, k to end of round.

Knit to 5 sts before end of round. Place rem 5 sts and first 6 sts from next round on waste yarn to hold for Little Finger. Cast on 3 sts and rejoin to work in the round.

☆ *Note that the previous two rounds are altered slightly from right glove to place the little finger on the opposite side of the glove.*

Work to Finger Bases
Work as for Right Glove.
Work Fingers and Thumb as for Right Glove.

Finishing

Weave in all ends, using tails at base of Fingers and Thumb Gusset to close up any holes that may have formed despite your best efforts. Block.

Preventing Gaps in the Thumb Gusset

1 Place held thumb gusset stitches onto three double-point needles and join yarn.

2 Pick up and knit one stitch between the last held stitch and the cast-on stitch, then pick up and knit one more stitch before the cast-on stitch.

3 Pick up and knit the cast-on stitch, then pick up and knit two stitches between the cast-on stitch and the first held stitch. Knit all picked-up stitches on the first round. On the next round, ssk the first two picked-up stitches, knit one, knit the last two pick-up stitches together.

Double-Knit Mitts

Mittens are the perfect canvas for double knitting. Not only will you create really, really warm mittens, you can change the look by turning them inside-out. Or is that outside-in? Your choice!

Finished Size

Approx 8" (20.5 cm) circumference

Yarn

Regia Silk 4-Ply (55% merino wool, 25% nylon, 20% silk; 219 yds [200m] per 1.75oz [50g]): 2 skeins 053 Blue Denim

Crystal Palace Panda Silk (52% bamboo, 43% superwash merino wool, 5% silk; 204 yds [187m] per 1.75oz [50g]): 2 skeins 3204 Natural Ecru

☆ *There's no reason or message for using two different yarns here. Our source did not have a natural color of the Regia in stock, so we paired it up with Panda Silk.*

Needles

Set of 5 US 2 (2.75mm) dpns or size needed to obtain gauge
1 straight US 2.5 (3mm) needle for cast on

☆ *Because the mitten begins with an elastic rib that only has to fit over the palm width, the cast-on stitches don't need to be on a needle that's two sizes larger as we usually recommend. Although the pattern is written for knitting on five dpns, you can adapt it to knit with four dpns, two circulars, one long circular for magic loop, whatever you'd like!*

Gauge

14 sts and 20 rows = 2" (5cm) in Stockinette double knitting

Notions

Tapestry needle
Waste yarn for holder

Cuff

With blue yarn and straight needle, cast on 62 stitches using the long-tail method. Divide the stitches evenly onto 4 dpns and join into a round, being careful not to twist the stitches. Place a marker for the end of the round.

☆ *For this mitten we casted on sixty-three stitches and used the extra-stitch joining method (see Chapter Seven). You can't exactly divide sixty-two stitches evenly; we worked with sixteen stitches on three needles and fourteen stitches on one needle.*

Following the instructions for double-knitting cast-on method 2 (see Chapter Eight), join ecru and set up for double knitting—124 stitches. Work k1, p1 rib for 2½" (6.5cm).

☆ *If you've cast on correctly, you'll have alternating blue and ecru stitches on the needles, beginning with blue and ending with ecru. To work k1, p1 rib in double knitting, with both yarns back k1 blue; with both yarns front, p1 ecru; with blue front and ecru back, p1 blue, k1 ecru; repeat from * to end of round.*

Thumb Gusset

Set Up for Right Mitten

The round begins at the side of the hand opposite the Thumb, and there are 31 back-of-hand stitches followed by 31 palm stitches. Work 1 round in Stockinette stitch, placing a marker before and after 4th palm stitch.

Set Up Left Mitten

The round begins at the side of the hand with the thumb, and there are 31 back-of-hand stitches followed by 31 palm stitches. Work one round in Stockinette stitch, placing a marker before and after 3rd palm stitch from end of round.

Begin Patterns and Thumb Gusset

Begin Chart A over back-of-hand stitches, work Chart B over palm stitches and work Chart C over Thumb Gusset stitches as you increase the Thumb Gusset as described below.

☆ *Following a chart in double knitting can be a bit challenging, so we recommend stopping and admiring your work often on both sides to make sure everything looks okay. A quick way to spot a mistake is seeing more than two stitches of the same color side-by-side—go back immediately and make the correction. A common mistake is to have one or the other yarn in the wrong place when working a stitch. This is a mistake you can't fix after the fact, so be vigilant.*

Thumb Gusset Increase Round: M1R after the first marker, M1L before the second marker.
Work this increase every 3rd round until you have 19 Thumb Gusset stitches.

☆ *Note that the Thumb Gusset increases are worked on same rounds as the pattern rounds of Chart B. This should make it easier to keep track of when you should increase.*

When you have 19 Thumb Gusset stitches, thread them onto waste yarn, cast on 1 stitch and rejoin the round.
Continue working patterns as established until you've worked Rounds 1–41, then Rounds 20–43, of Chart A.

Chart A Work Rounds 1–41, then work Rounds 20–43.

Chart B

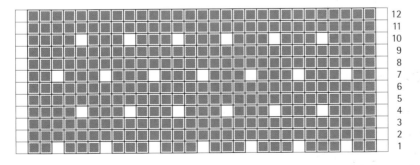

Chart C

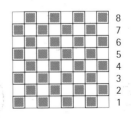

Shape the Mitten Top

Continue with Chart B on palm sts and work with MC only on back-of-hand sts. Maintaining the 3-stitch stripe pattern on each side of the mitten, decrease on both sides of the stripes every other round until you have 12 sts remaining.

☆ *This is another opportunity to show off with perfectly paired decreases. Following the instructions for decreasing in double knitting (see Chapter Eight), work ssk/ssp after the stripes and k2tog/p2tog before the stripes. The decreases will slant in the direction of the shaping.*

Sk2p (sp2p) the front and back sts that remain between the stripes. Draw up the remaining 8 sts for the inside mitten and outside mitten separately as follows. Thread each tail onto a separate yarn needle and remove the outside sts to one tail and the inside sts to the other. Pass the needle holding the inside sts through the opening to the inside of the mitten. Tighten and finish off the outside sts, then turn the mitten inside-out and tighten up and finish off the inside sts.

Thumb

Use a needle to pick up 5 outside and 5 inside sts (the cast-on stitch and 2 each side), one after the other.

☆ *This maneuver can be a little tricky. Try picking up stitches for the inside and the outside of the mitten separately, i.e., pick up five blue stitches onto one needle, then pick up five ecru stitches onto another needle. Now transfer the stitches to one needle alternating blue, ecru, blue, ecru, etc. The two extra stitches picked up before and after the cast-on stitch help to prevent holes from forming at the base of the thumb gusset. (See Beady Cable Gloves on page 218.)*

Place the held 19 Gusset sts on needles. The round begins at the start of the held sts and ends with the picked-up sts. On the first round, decrease one of the 5 picked-up sts so you can knit the dots in a spiral without a seam line. Work even until Thumb reaches the middle of the wearer's thumbnail or about 1½" (4cm). Work a 3-point decrease as follows, working the decrease stitch in the color appropriate to the first stitch of the decrease pair, i.e., if the knit pair consists of an ecru, then a blue stitch, knit them together with ecru; the purl pair will be a blue, then an ecru stitch, so purl them together with blue.

Round 1: K6, k2tog, k5, k2tog, k6, k2tog.
Rounds 2, 4, and 6: Knit.
Round 3: K5, k2tog, k4, k2tog, k5, k2tog.
Round 5: K4, k2tog, k3, k2tog, k4, k2tog.
Round 7: K3, k2tog, k2, k2tog, k3, k2tog.
Round 8: K2, k2tog, k1, k2tog, k2, k2tog.

Draw up remaining 8 sts on the inside and outside of the Thumb separately and finish off as for top of mitten.

Diamond Central Scarf

This scarf features a large crossing-diamonds panel flanked by four repeats of a very simple six-stitch allover lace. Once the main part of the scarf is finished, you'll pick up stitches around all four sides and add a small picot-like edging.

Finished Size

Approx 9" × 57" (23cm × 145cm), blocked

Yarn

Classic Elite Silky Alpaca Lace (70% baby alpaca, 30% silk; 460 yds [421m] per 1.75oz [50g]): 2 balls 2453 Berry

☆ *The main part of the scarf and about one-quarter of the edging was complete when the first ball came to an end. With two balls you can make a longer and wider scarf. To stick with one ball, consider casting on and beginning with Row 28 of the central motif, knitting seven rather than eight repeats.*

Needles

Two US 2.5 (3mm) circular needles 24" (60cm) long, and two US 2.5 (3mm) dpns for edging or size needed to obtain gauge

Gauge

32 stitches and 40 rows = 4" (10cm) in lace patterns

☆ *Gauge is not critical here. Just find the gauge that produces the fabric you want. Be sure to wash and block your gauge swatch—it will change dramatically.*

Notions

Tapestry needle

First Half of Scarf

Using a provisional method, cast on 61 stitches. Beginning with Row 1, work Chart A for 4 full repeats, ending with Row 56. Purl 1 row, decreasing 1 stitch on each side of the main center panel.

☆ *There are two edge stitches on each side of the Scarf. These edge stitches are worked in Stockinette stitch, slipping the first of every row purlwise with the yarn in the back.*

Place markers between the lace borders and the center panel as indicated by the red lines on the chart. To be sure you're staying on track, count stitches on every plain purl row: Slip 1, purl 14, purl 31, purl 15. This way you'll know if you've made a mistake in the lace and won't have far to back up to correct it.

The simple lace borders are worked over thirteen stitches. When you begin to work the entire row in this pattern, the repeat becomes a multiple of 6 + 1 as indicated on Chart B. You need to eliminate one stitch from the center panel and one stitch from the border to the left of the center panel, which you do on the purl row following Row 56.

Maintaining the 2 edge stitches on each side of the scarf, work Rows 2–16 of Chart B on all stitches. Place stitches on hold.

☆ *You don't want to bind off here. Once the other side of the scarf is knitted, you'll knit the edging onto these stitches and stitches picked up along the long edges. Binding off would tighten the ends; working with live stitches keeps everything fluid.*

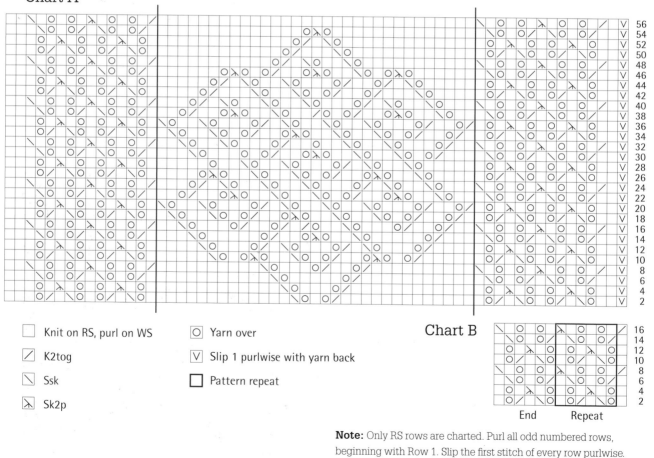

Chart A

☐	Knit on RS, purl on WS	Ⓞ	Yarn over
╱	K2tog	Ⓥ	Slip 1 purlwise with yarn back
╲	Ssk	☐	Pattern repeat
⋏	Sk2p		

Chart B

End   Repeat

Note: Only RS rows are charted. Purl all odd numbered rows, beginning with Row 1. Slip the first stitch of every row purlwise.

Second Half of Scarf

Place stitches from provisional cast on onto a needle. Repeat the instructions for the first half of the scarf, ending with Row 16 of Chart B and leaving the stitches on the needle.

☆ *As discussed in Chapter Five, you'll lose one-half a stitch from each end of the Scarf, so you'll have to increase one. It works out best in this lace design to increase the one stitch right in the center when working the first purl row.*

Edging

With the needle holding 59 end stitches, place a marker, then pick up and knit 236 chain stitches along the first long edge. With the same needle, place a marker and knit held 59 stitches on the opposite end. With second needle, pick up and knit 236 chain stitches along second long edge, place a marker, then knit 59 stitches from the first needle. You now have 295 stitches on each needle.

☆ *You have 240 chain stitches on each side. To pick up 236, skip four chains evenly spaced. The lace Edging has a six-row repeat; the last stitch of every other row will be knit together with a live stitch on the edge of the main body, and you need one extra stitch on each side in the corners. From the 236 chain stitches, subtract one for each corner. The 234 chain stitches divided by three tells you you'll work seventy-eight repeats along this edge. For the short ends, subtract one stitch for each corner from the fifty-nine stitches for fifty-seven stitches, which means you'll work nineteen repeats along these edges.*

Break the yarn. With RS facing, slip the first stitch (a corner stitch) from the needle you'll be starting on to the other circular needle. Cast on 4 stitches onto a dpn and knit 1 row, working the last stitch together with the first stitch on the circular needle. Turn and work Row 1 of the edge chart, using the circular needle to knit the stitches from the dpn. Turn and work Row 2, knitting the last stitch of the Edging together with the next stitch of the Body. Continue in this manner until you reach the first corner, 1 stitch before the marker, ending with Row 1.

Scarf Edging Chart

				⌒	⌒	⌒	⌒	6
5	⊻	•	•	○	╱	○	•	•	4
3	⊻	•	○	╱	○	•	•		2
1	⊻	○	•	○	•				

☐ Knit on RS   ╱ K2tog

• Knit on WS   ○ Yarn over

⌒ Bind off   ⊻ Slip 1 purlwise with yarn front

Turning the Corner

Work Rows 2–6, but knit the Edging together with a Body stitch at the end of Row 4 only; on Rows 2 and 6 simply turn the work without attaching. Work Rows 1–6 of the Edging, and knit the Edging together with the next corner stitch, the one after the marker, on Row 4 only.

Now you may resume working the Edging as before, turning the corners as described above when you come to them. When you've finished the last corner, bind off 4 stitches and sew them together with the 4 cast-on stitches.

Weave in all ends and block.

Stranded Lattice Socks

Here's an example of making the most of a variegated yarn—a solid color is used for the background stitches, and the multicolored yarn is used for the pattern, making the simple design appear to be more complex than it is.

Finished Size

Approx 8" (20.5cm)
    circumference, foot and leg
    length as desired

Yarn

Classic Elite Alpaca Sox (60%
    alpaca, 20% merino wool,
    20% nylon; 450 yds [411m]
    per 3.5oz [100g]): 1 skein
    each 1847 (Blue) and 1872
    (Gold/Green/Blue)

Needles

Set of 5 US 2.5 (3mm) dpns or
    size needed to obtain gauge
One US 5 (3.75mm) straight
    needle for cast on

Gauge

16 sts = 2" (5cm) in stranded
    pattern

Notions

Cotton waste yarn, about 1 yd
    (1m)
Tapestry needle

Abbreviations

MC: Main color, solid
CC: Contrasting color, variegated

Cuff

With US 5 (3.75mm) straight needle and MC, cast on 64 sts, divide onto 4 US 2.5 (3mm) dpns and join into a round.

☆ *For this sock we casted on sixty-five stitches and used the extra-stitch joining method (see Chapter Seven).*

With MC, work 1 round of k2, p2 rib.
Next Rnd: *K2 CC, p2 MC; repeat from * to end of round.
Repeat this round 9 more times.

☆ *The rib uses CC for knit stitches and MC for purl stitches. Because the CC is variegated, purl stitches would create contrasting bumps on the right side, which are not very attractive. But when the variegated CC is knit, the transition from one color to the next is smooth.*

Leg

Beginning with Round 1, work stranded colorwork following the Latticework Chart until sock measures 8" (20.5cm) or desired length to top of Heel, ending 16 stitches before the end of the round.

Note: The rounds begin and end at the center back.

☆ *There will be a bit of a blip between the pattern repeats at the join, and if you place this at the back it will hardly be noticeable. You could place the beginning/end of the round at one side, but unless you are careful every time you put the socks on, you could be wearing the blip at the outside of the leg, which would be only slightly less obvious than wearing it down the center front.*

Latticework Chart

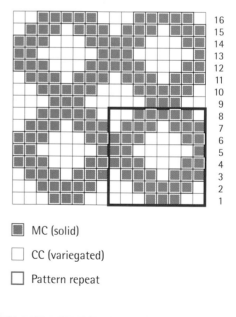

■ MC (solid)

☐ CC (variegated)

☐ Pattern repeat

Set Up for Heel

With waste yarn, knit the 16 stitches before and after the center back. Now go back and pick up the working yarns and work the row in pattern as established.

☆ *We tried working a regular short row heel, but because of the stranding the stitches were a bit sloppy. So we opted for this at-the-end heel, which is much neater.*

Foot

Continue in pattern as established until sock measures 4" (10cm) less than desired finished Foot length.

☆ *Foot length is measured from the back of the Heel to the tip of the longest Toe, and normally you'd measure the sock the same way and knit to 2" (5cm) less than the finished measurement. But because we have no Heel in our sock at this point, we need to allow an extra 2" (5cm) for the Heel, plus 2" (5cm) for the Toe.*

Shape Toe

Work Dot pattern and decrease as follows.

Dot Chart

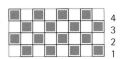

☆ *You'll need to make some adjustments to the Dot pattern on decrease rounds. When you reach the first decrease stitches, knit them together with the next color in sequence, i.e., if the stitch before the decrease was worked in MC, k2tog with CC; then work the next knit stitch in MC, which will be the same as the stitch of the previous round. Work the next knit stitch in CC, which will also be the same as the stitch of the previous round, then work the ssk with MC. Now you can continue in Dot pattern to the next set of decreases and repeat the sequence.*

Round 1: *K13, k2tog, k1; k1, ssk, k13; repeat from * once more.
Round 2: Knit.
Repeat Rounds 1 and 2, working 1 fewer st before and after the decreases until 32 stitches remain. Knit the next 8 stitches to end at the side of the Toe. Graft the remaining two sets of 16 stitches together with Kitchener stitch (see Chapter Seven).

☆ *Because the end of the round is at the center back, once you've reached the desired number of stitches you'll need to knit to the side of the toe for seaming; in this case you'll need to knit eight more stitches.*

Heel

Carefully remove the waste yarn at the Heel, placing 32 live stitches onto the lower needle and 31 stitches onto the upper needle. This can be a little tricky because of the 2-color pattern. The best way is to thread the stitches on both sides of the waste yarn row onto needles, then remove the waste yarn. If you find you have a large loop on the needle that should be a stitch (Figure 1), remove the loop, twist it (Figure 2) and place the newly formed small loop on the needle (Figure 3).

☆ *Knitting onto waste yarn and returning for live stitches is much like doing a provisional cast on (see Chapter Five): Because of the nature of the knit stitch, you will be one stitch short on the "top" of the row of knit stitches, or the row that's closest to the Toe.*

Join MC and CC at the side of the lower stitches and work the 16 stitches before the center back in the last round of the pattern worked on the other stitches.

☆ *When we stopped to knit the waste yarn for the Heel, we did not finish the last round but rather stopped sixteen stitches before the end of the round. Finish the round now.*

Work 1 round in Dot pattern, increasing in the 3rd quarter of the stitches so there are 64 heel stitches. Work decrease Rounds 1 and 2 as for Toe until 32 stitches remain. Work the first 16 stitches of the round again so the working yarn is at the side of the heel. Join the two halves of the heel together with Kitchener stitch.

☆ *To prevent holes from forming in the corners where the picked-up stitches meet, pick up an extra loop after the sixteenth stitch and knit it together with the sixteenth stitch; pick up an extra loop before the seventeenth stitch and knit it together with the seventeenth stitch; pick up an extra loop before the forty-eighth stitch and knit it together with the forty-eighth stitch; pick up an extra stitch before the forty-ninth stitch and knit it together with the forty-ninth stitch.*

Figure 1: Stranding formed a large loop that needs to be tightened to form a stitch.

Figure 2: Place the loop on a spare needle and twist it.

Figure 3: Place the newly formed stitch on the needle.

Finishing

Weave in all ends. Wash and block.

☆ *It's best to block these socks on sock blockers. Both the toe and the heel were formed with a relatively large seam of Kitchener stitch, and we want these seams to form nice rounded shapes, not flat ones.*

Austin's Jacket

This jacket is designed to teach many lessons—creating textural changes with variations on K2/P2 patterns, making vertical pockets and a button band, working a zipper closure, and matching patterns at side seams. It is a timeless, classic pattern, one that you could size for adults and children.

Finished Size

32" (81cm) chest circumference

Yarn

Nordic Fiber Arts Strikkegarn (100% wool; 115 yds [105m] per 1.75oz [50g]): 7 skeins 174 Red

Needles

US 3 (3.25mm) straight needles
US 6 (4mm) straight needles or size required to obtain gauge

Gauge

22 sts and 34 rows = 4" (10cm) in Stockinette stitch

Notions

3 stitch holders
Two ³/₈" (1cm) buttons
Tapestry needle
14" (36cm) jacket zipper or one of appropriate length
Sewing needle
Coordinating sewing thread

Stitch Patterns

K2/P2 RIB

Row 1: K2, *p2, k2; rep from * to end of row.
Row 2: P2, *k2, p2; rep from * to end of row.
Repeat Rows 1–2 for pattern.

Chart 1: Ribbing to Box Stitch

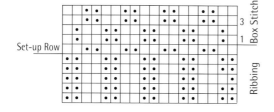

K2/P2 BOX STITCH

Rows 1: K2, *p2, k2; rep from * to end of row.
Rows 2 and 4: Knit the knits and purl the purls.
Row 3: P2, *k2, p2; rep from * to end of row.
Repeat Rows 1–4 for pattern.

K2/P2 DIAGONAL RIB

Row 1: (RS) *P2, k2; rep from * to end of row.
Row 2 and all WS rows through 8: Knit the knits and purl the purls.
Row 3: P1, *k2, p2; rep from * to last st, p1.
Row 5: *K2, p2; rep from * to end of row.
Row 7: K1, *p2, k2; rep from * to last st, k1.
Repeat Rows 1–8 for pattern.

Chart 2: K2, P2 Diagonal Rib Shoulder Pattern

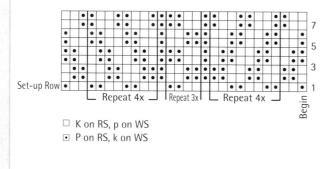

□ K on RS, p on WS
⊡ P on RS, k on WS

Back

With larger needles and using the long-tail knit/purl method (see Chapter Five), cast on 86 sts. Change to smaller needles and work k2, p2 rib for 15 rows, ending with a RS row.
Next Row (WS): P1 (edge stitch), k1 *p2, k2; rep from * to last 2 sts, ending k1, p1 (edge stitch).

☆ *This is a one-row change over of the current rib pattern to a set up for the Box Stitch. Working just this single row while still using the smaller rib needle produces a smooth transition.*

You will notice that there is now one edge stitch and only one stitch in the first and last repeats of the Box Stitch. There is good reason for this: When seaming the garment, the edge stitches will be consumed by the seam and the single Box Stitch on each side of the back will match up with the single Box Stitches on the seam side of both fronts.

Change to larger needles. Maintaining the edge sts, begin with Row 1 of Box Stitch and work until piece measures 11" (28cm) from beginning. Mark this last row at each end for the underarm. Continue in pattern for 2" (5cm), ending on a RS row. Maintaining edge sts, knit 6 rows (3 garter ridges), ending with a RS row.

☆ *We're using a garter ridge pattern separation here because we'll change from a K2/P2 Box Stitch pattern to a K2/P2 Diagonal Rib pattern.*

With WS facing, work Set-Up Row, then p1 (edge st), follow Chart 2 to work Diagonal Rib over 35 sts, place marker, k1, (k2, p2) 3 times, k1, place marker, work Diagonal Rib over 35 sts, p1 (edge st). Continue even in patterns as established until piece measures 6¼" (16cm) straight up from bottom of garter ridge, ending on a RS row.

☆ *If you choose to alter this pattern, remember that the K2/P2 Rib and Box Stitch patterns are multiples of four plus two. The Diagonal Rib can be worked on any number of stitches maintaining the k2, p2 pattern. This works because you are working from the center panel toward both armholes. The Diagonal Rib moves to the right and left of the center fourteen stitches—one reverse Stockinette stitch, twelve Box Stitches and one reverse Stockinette stitch. When finished, the Diagonal Rib stitches form right and left arrowheads when the front and back shoulder stitches are knit together.*

Shape Neck and Shoulders

Next Row (WS): P1 (edge st), work 30 sts in Diagonal Rib, place center 24 sts on a holder, join another ball of yarn and work rem 30 sts in Diagonal Rib. Dec 1 st at each Neck edge every other row twice. Place 28 sts plus 1 edge st on holders for each shoulder.

☆ *Once you put the center back Neck stitches on a holder, you'll have to work each side of the Neck separately. Begin by working the right Shoulder, which has the new ball of yarn attached. To decrease at the Neck edge, you'll work a RS row to the last two stitches, then k2tog. Work two decrease rows, then purl one row and place stitches on a holder. To work the left Shoulder, you'll begin with right side facing; k2tog, knit to the end of the row. Work two decrease rows, then purl one row and place all stitches on a holder. You have now worked the same number of rows on both the right and left Shoulders.*

Pocket Linings (make two)

Cast on 24 sts and work in Box Stitch for 10 rows. Place on holders and set aside.

☆ *This vertical square Pocket is one of the simpler ones to knit. For a new learning challenge, see Chapter Fifteen for six other versions of pockets and choose a substitute.*

Left Front

With larger needles and using the long-tail knit/purl method (see Chapter Five), cast on 46 sts and work K2/P2 Rib as for Back, ending with a RS row.

Next Row (WS): Pfb, *p2, k2; rep from * to last 2 sts, k1, p1 (edge stitch). With RS facing, change to larger needle and work in Box Stitch for 10 rows. Keep the edge stitches on each side in Stockinette stitch throughout.

☆ *The new increased stitch at the center front edge will be used later to establish the vertical casing that will fold over the zipper.*

Place Pocket

With RS facing, k1 (edge st), work 16 sts in Box Stitch, place rem 30 sts on a spare needle, then work 24 sts of Pocket Lining—41 sts on needle. Work in Box Stitch for 44 rows or approx 6" (15cm) from beginning of pocket. Place these sts on a spare needle. Return to the 30 sts on the first spare needle. With RS facing, join yarn and work in Box Stitch with edge sts on each end for 44 rows. Place these sts on a spare needle.

☆ *Since you're working in Box Stitch, counting the rows is easy. Each pattern change represents four rows, so you'll count eleven patterns.*

Join the Pieces

With needle holding 41 sts and RS facing, k1 (edge st) and work 16 sts in Box Stitch. Place needle holding 30 sts in front of first needle and, continuing in pattern, work 1 st from front needle tog with 1 st from back needle across 24 sts; work last 6 sts in pattern, k1 (edge st). Continue in pattern as established until same length as Back to underarm marker. Place a marker for left front underarm. Work until same length as Back to garter st pattern. Knit 6 rows (3 garter ridges). Change to Diagonal Rib and work until 4¼" (11cm) measured straight up from bottom of garter ridge, ending with a RS row.

☆ *This is where the front neckline will start. The front neckline needs to be lower than the back; in this case it begins 2" (5cm) lower.*

Shape Neck and Shoulders

Next Row (WS): Work 11 sts and place on holder for Neck, work in pattern to end of row. Continue to work in pattern and dec 1 st at Neck edge every other row 7 times, maintaining an edge stitch. When same length as back, place 29 Shoulder sts plus 1 edge st on a holder.

You could work the decreases two ways here. If you want to decrease on RS rows, work to the last 3 sts and k2tog, knit the edge stitch. If you'd rather decrease on WS rows, work to last 3 sts and p2tog, purl the edge stitch.

Right Front

Cast on 54 sts and work in K2/P2 Rib for 4 rows. With RS facing, work 3 sts, work a 2-stitch one-row buttonhole (see Chapter Sixteen) on next 2 sts, work to the end. Work 5 more rows, work another buttonhole as before. Work 3 more rows, then bind off 8 sts in pattern. Work until same length as Left Front ribbing, ending with a RS row.

☆ *The eight extra stitches cast on for the rib and then bound off form an overlapping tab at the bottom of the sweater. You've placed two buttonholes on this tab.*

Next Row (WS): P1 (edge st), k1, *k2, p2; repeat from * to last stitch, pbf. Work as for Left Front, reversing shaping.

☆ *You'll often see "reversing shaping" used as a shorthand instruction and it means exactly that. In this case, you work the Right Front the same as the Left Front except that the center front will be on the right end of the piece when the RS is facing. So, you'd begin the first shaping row, which is a WS row, by working to the last eleven sts and placing them on a holder for the neck. Then, to work Neck decreases on the right side, you'd knit the edge stitch, ssk and work to the end of the row; to work them on the wrong side you'd work to the last three stitches, ssp and purl the edge stitch.*

Join Shoulders

With RS together, place Shoulder sts on spare needles and join the sts of Fronts and Back tog with three-needle bind off (see Chapter Five).

☆ *Here you'd place the Right Front Shoulder stitches on one needle and the right Back stitches on another needle. Hold the pieces so the right sides are together and the needles are pointing in the same direction, then bind off. Repeat on the left side.*

Sleeves (make two)

With small needle and WS facing, pick up and purl 84 sts between underarm markers.

☆ *Picking up with the smaller needle produces a smooth transition.*

Next Row: Change to larger needle. K1 (edge st), *p2, k2 across row, ending p2, k1 (edge st).

Continue working in Box Stitch, dec 1 stitch inside the edge stitch every 4 rows 26 times—32 sts remain. Work until piece measures 13½" (34cm). Change to smaller needles and work K2/P2 Rib for 2" (5cm). Bind off with larger needles in pattern.

☆ *Picking up the stitches for the Sleeves along the armhole means that there are two fewer seams to sew, something that most knitters will appreciate! Because the pattern is simple, you'd have to look very closely to see that the Sleeves are knit in the opposite direction from the body. Don't try this on a sweater with a definite up-and-down pattern!*

Neck

With WS facing, place 11 sts from Left Front holder on smaller needle; join yarn, pick up and purl 13 sts up Left Front to Shoulder, pick up and purl Shoulder st, pick up and purl 4 sts down left Back, purl 24 sts from Back holder, pick up and purl 4 sts up right Back to Shoulder, pick up and purl Shoulder st, pick up and purl 13 sts down Right Front, purl 11 sts on holder—82 sts.

☆ *Note that when we're putting everything together for the Neck we don't work the eleven stitches at the Left Front; these were already worked on the WS before they were placed on the holder. However, the Right Front stitches were placed on a holder without being worked on that wrong side row, so we need to purl them now to match the Left Front.*

The only thing that's not self-explanatory here is the number of stitches to pick up between the held stitches and the shoulder seam. Here we use a ratio of one for one in this short area to ensure that the neckline stays loose and comfortable.

Turn and work k2, *p2, k2, rep from * to end. Continue to work in K2/P2 Rib for 1" (2.5cm), ending on a WS row. Bind off in pattern.

Zipper Placket

Left Side

With smaller needle, RS facing and beginning at top left, pick up and knit every other st (this is a 1 for 2 ratio; see Chapter Five) along the long edge, ending above bottom ribbing. Turn, change to larger needles and knit 1 row; turn and bind off purlwise.

Right Side

With smaller needle, RS facing and beginning at bottom right above ribbing, pick up and knit every other st along the long edge, ending at Neck edge. Turn, change to larger needles and knit 1 row; turn and bind off purlwise.

☆ *You should have the same number of stitches along the Right and Left Fronts. There should be no question since you worked the same number of rows, but it's a good idea to count and be sure they're the same.*

Sew in Zipper

Baste zipper in place behind Zipper Placket and sew in place (see Chapter Sixteen). Take your time and work carefully.

Finishing

With WS facing, pick up and purl 30 sts along Pocket edges and work in K2/P2 Rib for 4 rows. Bind off in pattern. Tack the edges of the Pocket border down to the sweater Body. Sew side with mattress stitch (see Chapter Seven), matching the single Box Stitch pattern. Sew Sleeve seams with mattress stitch. Sew Pocket linings to Body on the inside (see Chapter Fifteen). Sew buttons opposite buttonholes. Weave in all ends.

Ambrosia Sweater

This sweater is knitted with Ambrosia from Knit One, Crochet Too, and we think the name suits the sweater perfectly. Knitted in every direction—side-to-side, bottom-up and top-down—it features a lovely openwork pattern for the bodice and a leaf pattern for the waist that is then altered to create a flared skirt.

Finished Size

Bust 36" (91.5cm), waist 26" (66cm), hips 36" (91.5cm)

Yarn

Knit One, Crochet Too Ambrosia (70% baby alpaca, 20% silk, 10% cashmere; 137 yds [125m] per 1.75oz. [50g]): 12 skeins color 633 Cornflower

Needles

US 3 (3.25mm) and US 4 (3.5mm) circular needles 24" (61cm) long, or sizes needed to obtain gauge
US 2.5 (3mm) circular needle 24" (61cm) long for front bands
US 6 (4mm) needle of any type for skirt bind off

Gauge

18 sts and 32 rows = 4" (10cm) in Miniature Leaf pattern using US 4 (3.5mm) needles, washed and blocked
25 sts and 32 rows = 4" (10cm) in Large Leaf pattern using US 3 (3.25mm) needles, washed and blocked

☆ *The pattern for the top is very open and stretchy by nature, and a little more so with the size 4 needle. Be sure and measure the gauge swatch in several places.*

Notions

Twelve $^{7}/_{16}$" (1cm) buttons with shanks
Twelve $^{5}/_{8}$" (1.5cm) flat buttons
Sewing needle and coordinating thread

Stitch Patterns

LARGE LEAF (MULTIPLE OF 14)

Row 1 (RS): *K3, k2tog, k1, yo, p2, yo, k1, ssk, k3; rep from * to end of row.

Rows 2, 4, 6, and 8: *P6, k2, p6; rep from *.

Row 3: *K2, k2tog, k1, yo, k1, p2, k1, yo, k1, ssk, k2; rep from * to end of row.

Row 5: *K1, k2tog, k1, yo, k2, p2, k2, yo, k1, ssk, k1; rep from * to end of row.

Row 7: *K2tog, k1, yo, k3, p2, k3, yo, k1, ssk; rep from * to end of row.

Repeat Rows 1–8 for pattern.

MINIATURE LEAF (multiple of 6)

Rows 1 and 3 (WS): Purl.

Row 2: *K3, yo, sk2p, yo; rep from * to end of row.

Row 4: *Yo, sk2p, yo, k3; rep from * to end of row.

Repeat Rows 1–4 for pattern.

SEED STITCH (worked over an even number of sts)

Row 1: *K1, p1; rep from * to end of row.

Row 2: *P1, k1; rep from * to end of row.

Repeat Rows 1–2 for pattern.

Large Leaf

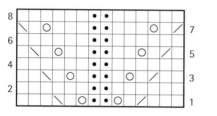

- ☐ Knit on RS, purl on WS
- • Purl on RS, knit on WS
- ╱ K2tog
- ╲ Ssk
- ◯ Yarn over
- ☐ Pattern repeat

Miniature Leaf

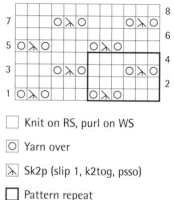

- ☐ Knit on RS, purl on WS
- ◯ Yarn over
- ⅄ Sk2p (slip 1, k2tog, psso)
- ☐ Pattern repeat

Special Abbreviations

Twr (twist 1 right): K2tog but leave on needle, knit the first st again and drop both from needle.

Twl (twist 1 left): Go behind the sts on left needle and knit the second st and leave it on needle, then knit the first st and drop both from needle.

Waistband

With US 3 (3.25mm) needle, cast on 26 sts using a provisional method and purl 1 row.

Row 1 (RS): K2, p1, twr, p1, work large leaf, p1, twl, p1, k2.

Row 2: P2, k1, p2, k1, work Large Leaf pattern, k1, p2, k1, p2. Work 13 full repeats of Large Leaf pattern and bind off with decreases as follows: K3, k2tog, k1, k2tog, k4, k2tog, k4, k2tog, k1, k2tog, k3—21 sts.

☆ *The Large Leaf pattern is something like a cable, which means it splays. In order to keep things straight at the center front of the Waistband, you need to reduce the number of stitches.*

Remove provisional cast on and, with WS facing, purl 1 row. Work 13 repeats in the other direction. Bind off with decreases as described above.

☆ We used the crochet over the needle cast on. As discussed in Chapter Six, when the cast-on is removed you'll have one fewer stitch than you casted on, and in this case the center has only one purl stitch instead of two. Purl one row and M1 before the remaining center purl. When you've finished the thirteen repeats in each direction, you'll have worked 212 rows: 208 rows in patt + 2 BO rows + 2 CO rows = 212 rows.

Bodice

With US 3 (3.25mm) needle, pick up and knit 141 sts along top of Waistband. Change to US 4 (3.5mm) needle and purl 1 row, placing a marker on the 36th and 106th sts—these are the side "seams." Maintain 2 edge sts at beg and end of each row and these seam sts in Stockinette st throughout.

☆ To begin the top we want to begin with a width of about 30"–31" (76cm–79cm), then increase to the full 36" (91.5cm) between the pickup and underarm.

30" (76cm) × 4.5 stitches per inch (2.5cm) = 135 stitches.

The pattern is a multiple of 6 + 3 for symmetry (we want to begin and end with the same three-stitch part of the repeat) and we'll need two edge stitches on each side of the front, and one to form each side "seam."

Beginning with the 135 stitches, subtract three and divide by six to determine the number of pattern repeats: twenty-two pattern repeats. This step ensures that you have an even number of repeats. If you don't, add or subtract to a multiple of six. Add four edge stitches and two side seam stitches to the 135 for a total of 141 stitches to be picked up.

We determined earlier that we have 212 edge stitches along the Waistband. The difference between 212 and 141 is seventy-one, so we'll pick up all but seventy-one of the

Waistband stitches. To determine where to skip stitches, divide the total, 212, by the number of stitches to skip, seventy-one, to get 2.98, which rounds to three. This means you'll skip every third stitch, giving you a pick-up rate of two for three.

Row 1: K2, work Miniature Leaf pattern to marked st, k the marked st, work Miniature Leaf pattern to next marked st, k the marked st, work Miniature Leaf pattern to last 2 sts, k2—145 sts.
Row 2: Purl.
Row 3: Rep Row 1.
Row 4: Rep Row 2.
Row 5: K2, work Miniature Leaf pattern to marked st, M1R, k1, M1L, work Miniature Leaf pattern to next marked st, M1R, k1, M1L, work Miniature Leaf pattern to last 2 sts, k2.
Row 6: Purl.

☆ It's important to maintain the four-row Miniature Leaf pattern while increasing every sixth row. This can be somewhat confusing; when you increase on Row 5 of the Bodice, you'll be working Row 1 of the pattern. Row 6 of the Bodice will be Row 2 of the pattern, etc. Just be sure you increase every sixth row and repeat Rows 1–4 of the pattern.

Repeat Rows 1–6 five more times, incorporating the increased sts into patt when possible—165 sts. Work even in patts as established until piece measures 5½" (14cm) above band, ending with a RS row.

Divide for Fronts and Back

Next Row (WS): Purl 35 and place on hold for Left Front. BO 13 for underarm. Purl 69 and place on hold for Back. BO 13 for underarm. Purl 35 and place on hold for Right Front. Break yarn.

☆ The goal here is to set aside stitches for the underarm and divide the remaining stitches evenly for the Front and Back. We want about 3" (7.5cm) for each underarm: 3 × 4.5 = 13.5, rounded down to thirteen stitches for each underarm. Subtract the underarm stitches from the total: 165 − 26 = 139. Divide the 139 remaining stitches by two and round to get sixty-nine stitches for the Back and thirty-five stitches for each Front.

Back

Place 69 Back sts on needle. With RS facing, join yarn. Maintain 2 edge sts each side, continue in patt, dec 1 st at each armhole edge every other RS row 4 times—61 sts. Maintain 2 edge sts at each armhole edge, continue in patt until piece measures 13½" (34.5cm) from band, ending with a RS row.

Next Row (WS): Purl 19 and place on hold for left Shoulder, BO 23 for back Neck, purl 19 and place on holder for right Shoulder.

☆ *Because this is a fitted sweater, and because the fabric in the bodice is very stretchy, the armholes, shoulders and neck are going to be a bit smaller than those for a less-fitted sweater of a firm fabric. We've determined that the armhole depth will be 7" (18cm). We want to get to a Neck width of 5" (12.5cm) and a Shoulder width of between 4" (10cm) and 4½" (11.5cm). The Neck will consume twenty-three stitches (5" × 4.5 sts = 22.5, rounded up to 23) and each shoulder will consume nineteen stitches (4.25" × 4.5 sts = 19.125, rounded down to 19). Add the Neck and Shoulder stitches to get sixty-one stitches. We have sixty-nine back stitches, so we'll decrease four more at each armhole.*

Left Front

Place 35 held sts on needle. With RS facing, join yarn. Maintain 2 edge sts at armhole and 2 edge sts at center front, continue in patt and dec 1 stitch at armhole edge every other RS row 4 times—31 sts. Maintain 2 edge sts at armhole and front edge, continue in patt until piece measures 10½" (26.5cm) from top of waistband, ending with a RS row.

☆ *Work the armhole shaping to match the back. When the piece measures 10½" (26.5cm) from the Waistband it's time to shape the Neck. The width will be the same as the Back, 5" (12.5cm), and the depth will be 3" (7.5cm). The Neck width will be the same as the Back plus one (the Front has one more stitch than the back) so we'll eliminate twelve stitches on the Left and the Right Fronts. Bind off eight and decrease four to equal twelve.*

Next Row (WS): BO 8 purlwise, purl to end of row.

Maintaining 1 Stockinette st at Neck edge, continue in patt as established, dec 1 st at Neck edge every RS row 4 times—19 sts. Work even to length of Back. Join Shoulders with three-needle BO.

Right Front

Place 35 held sts on needle. With RS facing, join yarn. Maintain 2 edge sts at armhole and 2 edge sts at center front, continue in patt and dec 1 stitch at armhole edge every other RS row 4 times—31 sts. Maintain 2 edge sts at armhole and front edge, continue in patt until piece measures 10½" (26.5cm) from band, ending with a WS row.

☆ *Work Right Front same as Left Front, reversing shaping. (See Austin's Jacket on page 244 for an explanation of reverse shaping.)*

Next Row (RS): BO 8 knitwise, work in patt to end of row. Maintaining 1 Stockinette st at Neck edge, continue in patt as established, dec 1 st at Neck edge every RS row 4 times—19 sts. Work even to length of back. Join shoulders with three-needle BO.

Skirt

With US 3 (3.25mm) needle, pick up and knit 188 sts along bottom of band.

Setup Row (WS): P1, k1, *p6, k2, p6, k1, p1, k1; repeat from * to last 16 sts, p6, k2, p6, k1, p1.
Begin Large Leaf pattern with p1, k1, p1 between each repeat and maintain edge sts in rib as established. Work 1 full repeat of Large Leaf pattern, ending with Row 8.

☆ *The skirt will be worked in the Large Leaf pattern with three stitches between each repeat and four edge stitches. We'll be increasing in every other repeat to make the hip measurement and add flare to the skirt. Because we want the Fronts to remain straight for buttoning, the repeats on each side of the center front will maintain the original stitch counts. We'll begin with approximately 26" (66cm) of stitches, which is the Waistband measurement. The three stitches between the Large Leaf repeats are worked in rib, and they are nearly invisible when the fabric lies flat; but they'll be there to allow for a slightly larger hip measurement. With the added (nearly invisible) stitches between the pattern repeats, the gauge works out to be about seven stitches per inch (2.5cm). 26" (66cm) × 7 stitches per inch (2.5cm)*

= 182 sts. Pattern is a multiple of 14 + 3 stitches between each pattern. We divided 182 stitches by seventeen for 10.7 and decided on eleven pattern repeats.

So here's what we need:
Two edge stitches, (ten pattern repeats, plus three between for 170), fourteen for final repeat, two edge stitches. 2 + 170 + 14 + 2 = 188 sts.

To determine the pick-up rate, subtract 188 from the 212 stitches along the edge of the Waistband. We need to skip

twenty-four stitches. Divide 212 by twenty-four for 8.8, which rounds to nine. We need to skip every ninth stitch, so the pick up rate is eight for nine.

Begin Increases

It would take far too many words to describe how to do the increases, so here they are in chart form. Increase using the lifted stitch method on each side of every other Large Leaf, beginning with the second and ending with the tenth,

Increasing Large Leaf 1

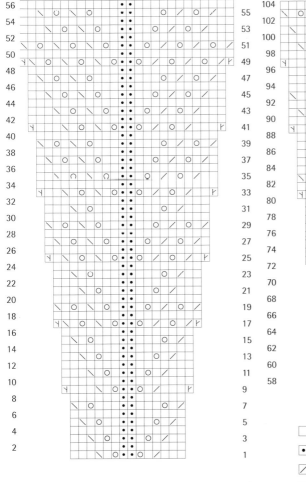

Increasing Large Leaf 2

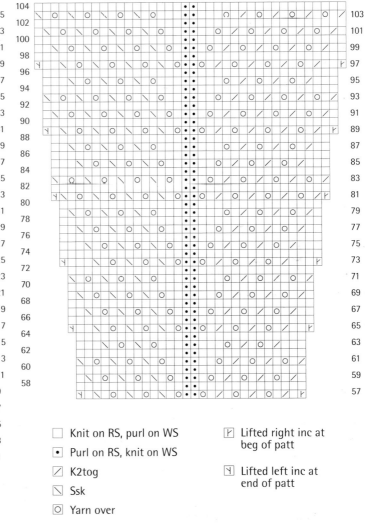

☐ Knit on RS, purl on WS	⊬ Lifted right inc at beg of patt
• Purl on RS, knit on WS	� Lifted left inc at end of patt
⟋ K2tog	
⟍ Ssk	
○ Yarn over	

continuing the pairs of 1 dec/1 yo where possible. Work until 13 repeats of the Large Leaf pattern have been worked from the Waistband and you have 308 sts, ending with Row 104. Work 2 rows seed st, bind off in pattern with size US 6 (4mm) needle.

Sleeves (make two)

CO 43 sts using the long-tail method and US 3 (3.25mm) needle. Purl 1 WS row. Maintaining 2 Stockinette st edge stitches on each side, work Miniature Leaf pattern, increasing 1 st each end every 6th row 11 times—65 sts; then every 8th row 7 times—79 sts, working the stitches into pattern when possible. Work even if necessary until Sleeve measures 16" (40.5cm).

☆ *The Sleeve doesn't need to be quite as stretchy as the bodice, so we went down a needle size, working with a gauge of five stitches per inch (2.5cm). Although you'll pick up stitches along the bottom of the sleeve to add a cuff, we don't use a provisional cast on here because we need the stability of a regular cast on. For balance, the Miniature Leaf pattern is set up as a multiple of 6 + 3.*

Shape Cap

BO 6 sts at beg of next 2 rows—67 sts.
BO 2 sts at beg of next 4 rows—59 sts.
Maintain 1 Stockinette st edge st on each end while working decreases as follows.
Dec 1 st at each end of this and every other RS rows 3 times—51 sts.
Dec 1 st at each end every other RS row 10 times—31 sts.
BO 3 sts beg next 2 rows—25 sts.
BO 2 sts beg next 4 rows—17 sts.
Knit 1 row, BO purlwise on WS.

☆ *What we've done is shape a bell curve for the cap, adding a plain knit row for stability at the shoulder. See Chapter Thirteen for an explanation of shaping a sleeve cap.*

Cuff

Pick up and knit into the 43 CO sts. Purl 1 row, inc 15 sts evenly spaced—58 sts.

☆ *Because the Cuff will be in the form of a slight ruffle, we want to increase 3" (7.5cm), being sure we have the correct number of stitches for two edge stitches and four repeats of the Large Leaf pattern, which in this case is fifteen. Patterns are usually written this way, without saying exactly where to do the increasing. We have forty-three sts, which is not evenly divisible by fourteen (which is the number of spaces between the fifteen increases)—that would be way to easy! So in this case, fifteen stitches evenly spaced would be worked as follows:*

(P3, M1) 4 times, (p2, M1) 3 times, (p3, M1) 2 times, (p2, M1) 3 times, (p3, M1) 3 times, p4. What's the key to figuring that out? Pencil and paper. Make little lines for the original forty-three stitches and add stitches between until you get the right balance. This is not perfect, but it's close enough. There's probably a mathematical way to figure this out, but this works for us. Be sure you have a good eraser!

Maintaining 1 Stockinette st at each end, work 4 Large Leaf patterns over 56 sts. Work 2 full repeats, work 2 rows of seed st, bind off in pattern.

Sew underarm Sleeve seam with mattress stitch. Fit the Sleeve into the armhole, matching the Sleeve underarm seam with the body side "seam" stitch. Pin the Sleeve in place, easing gently and evenly if necessary. Sew in place.

Front Bands

Left Front Band

With US 2.5 (3mm) needles and RS facing and beg at left Neck edge, use smaller needle to pick up and knit 166 sts along front edge to bottom of Skirt. Pick up rate is approx 2/3. Work seed st for 10 rows, bind off in pattern.

☆ *The pick-up rate is worked out here by gauge. The seed stitch band needs to be the same length as the center front of the sweater. Determine the length of the band, do a seed stitch gauge, count the rows in the sweater depth and do the math (see Chapter Five for pick-up rates).*

Right Front Band

With RS facing and beg at right bottom edge, use smaller needle to pick up and knit 166 sts along front edge to Neck.

Work seed st for 4 rows. On the next row (WS), work 2-st one-row buttonholes (see Chapter Sixteen) as follows: Seed 3, make buttonhole, *seed 12, make buttonhole; rep from * 4 times, (seed 6, make buttonhole) twice, **seed 12, make buttonhole; rep from ** 3 times, seed 19. Work 5 more rows in seed stitch, bind off in pattern.

☆ *There's an extra buttonhole added at the waistband to prevent what we like to call "gaposis."*

Collar

With RS facing and beg at right Neck edge, pick up and knit 2 sts at Right Front Band, 33 sts to Shoulder seam, 23 sts along back neck to Shoulder seam, 33 sts to Front Band, and 2 sts at Left Front Band—93 sts.

☆ *For the collar we pick up two stitches in the band so the collar covers the join between the sweater and the band, then pick up the eight bound-off center front stitches and twenty-three more stitches up to the shoulder to accommodate the Right Front neck shaping; pick up stitch for stitch along the Back neck, then mirror the right pick-up rate for the Left Front neck.*

Set-up Row 1 (RS): Knit, increasing 9 sts evenly spaced—102 sts.
Set-up Row 2 (WS): Purl.

☆ *Because the Collar pattern has a right and wrong side, once we've picked up the stitches along the right side of the sweater, we have to reverse direction and make the right side of the Collar on the wrong side of the sweater.*

Row 1 (RS): P1, k1, M1, work Large Leaf pattern to last 2 sts, M1, k1, p1—104 sts.
Row 2: Work 3 sts in seed st, work Large Leaf pattern to last 3 sts, work 3 sts in seed st.
Row 3: Work 3 sts in seed st, M1, work Large Leaf pattern to last 3 sts, M1, work 3 sts in seed st—106 sts.
Row 4: Work 4 sts in seed st, work Large Leaf pattern to last 4 sts, work 4 sts in seed st.

Continue in this manner, increasing at the inside of the seed st blocks on RS rows, until 2 full repeats of large leaf pattern have been worked and you have 10 seed sts at each side of the collar.

Next Row (RS): Work 10 sts in seed st, M1, work seed st to end of row.

☆ *Because the entire row becomes seed stitch here, we want an odd number of sts so the piece begins and ends with the same stitch, in this case a purl.*

Work 3 more rows of seed st, then bind off loosely in pattern.

Finishing

Weave in all those nasty ends. Use heavy sewing thread to sew buttons to Left Band corresponding to buttonholes on Right Band as follows: Place the shank button on the front and the flat button on the back, sandwiching the band between, and sew securely. Block lightly.

☆ *A note on storage: If you ever hang your knits on padded hangers, don't try it with this sweater. The skirt is heavy and will stretch the top way out of shape. In fact, the design works because the waistband is snug to the body, taking all the weight of the skirt away from the bodice. Fold this one up nicely and put it in a drawer. That's if you can bear to take it off!*

Changing the Size

Altering this sweater is pretty straightforward, except perhaps for the skirt, which has a high stitch count in the pattern repeat. But let's start at the beginning.

Altering the Waistband

The waistband is knit side to side, and the current width given will work for all sizes. The row gauge is eight stitches per inch (2.5cm), so each eight-row pattern repeat will add 1" (2.5cm). So, for a 28" (71cm) waist, knit two extra eight-row repeats; for a 30" (76cm) waist, knit four extra eight-row repeats, etc.

Altering the Bodice

Like the waistband, this is pretty straightforward. The pick-up rate at the top of the waistband will be the same as for the given size, but you'll pick up more or fewer stitches based on the length of the waistband. Refer to the sample to remember that you'll pick up enough stitches to accommodate approximately 15 percent more in width than you have in the waistband—the bodice immediately blouses out from the band. Be sure you pick up the right multiple: the pattern is a multiple of 6 + 3, plus two edge stitches and two side seam stitches.

  The armhole shaping will stay close to the sample, give or take a few stitches. To adjust the depth, simply knit more or fewer rows. Adjust the neck and shoulder width from the original as necessary, using the following as a guide: For every 4" (10cm) of added bust width, add about $1/2$" (1cm) to the shoulder width and neck width. This is not exact and the actual number should match those on your measurement sheet (see Chapter Twelve).

Altering the Skirt

The skirt is a little tricky to alter, mainly because of the 14 + 3 repeats of the Large Leaf pattern used. Because the skirt requires an odd number of leaf patterns, you'd need to add two repeats to upsize and work it the way it's currently written. That's a difference of slightly more than 5" (12.5cm), which will work out great if your waistband is 31" (79cm). But you may want to add only 2" to 3" (5cm to 7.5cm). The best way to do this is to add a couple of stitches between the Leaf motifs. For example, using a repeat of 14 + 5 (working p2, k1, p2 between the Leaf patterns instead of p1, k1, p1) would add twenty stitches, or about 3" (7.5cm) to the hip measurement. And if you refer back to the pattern you'll remember that because the stitches between the Leaf motifs are worked in rib fashion, they will expand or contract to accommodate more or less width. Once you've figured out the pick-up rate and have the correct number of stitches, you can work the skirt as for the sample.

Lisdoonvarna Aran

Aran sweaters, named for the Aran Islands in Ireland where they originated, usually use a combination of cables set apart by fields of reverse stockinette, seed, or other allover patterns. Arans also usually include a large center panel.

Finished Size

46" (117cm) chest circumference

Yarn

Cascade Yarns Cascade 220 (100% Peruvian Highland Wool; 220 yds [200m] per 3.5oz. [100g]): 9 skeins color 8010

Needles

US 6 (4mm) needles
US 8 (5mm) needles or size required to obtain gauge
US 6 (4mm) 16" (40cm) circular needle

Gauge

20 sts and 25 rows = 4" (10cm) in Stockinette stitch

Notions

Cable needle (cn)
Markers
Tapestry needle
Stitch holders

Planning Your Sweater

There's a lot that goes into the planning of a cable sweater, and we hope that after reading through and working this one you'll have the confidence to design your own. Once you get to the knitting, the best advice we can give you is to stop often and admire your work. If you see that you've crossed a cable to the right that should have been crossed to the left within a couple of rows of the error, it's not nearly as daunting to make the correction as it is if you only notice the mistake several inches later.

Cables on the right and left of a center panel are usually mirror images. This is important to keep in mind when you're following a chart that shows the patterns through the center panel and then instruct you to follow the chart back in the reverse direction—make sure that a right-turning cable on one side of the center panel is balanced by a left-turning cable on the other side.

Choosing Your Stitch Patterns

To begin planning, look through your stitch pattern books and choose a center panel and a couple of cables and allover patterns that you like. The best way to figure out how to combine the patterns is to knit a strip of each one that's, say, four or six inches long. Yes, that's a lot of knitting, but you want to get it right. Make one photocopy of the center panel and two of the other cables and cut away the background. Lay the center panel down and position the other cables to the right and left until you get a composition you like.

If you're new to Aran sweater design, it may be best to choose cables that are a multiple of two, four, six, eight or twelve rows. If you choose a center panel of twenty-four rows, all cable can be used on either side of the center panel—multiple repeats of these patterns will end on the same row as the center panel.

Determining the Stitch Count

Now that you've chosen your patterns, you need to figure out how to make them work for the desired garment size. One of the most important things about designing an Aran sweater is figuring out how many stitches you'll need to cast on for the ribbing and increase after the ribbing to compensate for the cable take-up (discussed in Chapter Nine) and exactly where

to work those increases. Here's a formula that works every time.

First determine the size of your finished garment and divide by two to get the width for the front and back. Work a Stockinette stitch gauge in your chosen yarn and multiply the number of stitches in one inch by the number of inches in the back. Round to an even number and work the ribbing on this number of stitches.

Choose the cables you want to use and note the stitch count of each cable, then multiply the number of stitches in the cable by .6666. Round the result to an even number. This is the number of stitches from the rib that will be the basis for the cable and you'll need to increase to the number needed for the cable on the first row. For example, if you're going to work a six-stitch cable, multiply 6 by .6666 to get 3.999. Round this to four; wherever you're placing a six-stitch cable you'll use four rib stitches and increase them to six. To work an eight-stitch cable, you'd use five stitches and increase them to eight.

For this 46" (117cm) sweater we started with 116 stitches: 23" (58cm) for the back × 5 stitches per inch (2.5cm) = 115, rounded up to 116. The pattern consists of four six-stitch cables, two twelve-stitch cables and one thirty-stitch center cable.

* The six-stitch cables will each use four ribbing stitches, increased to six; this adds eight stitches.
* The twelve-stitch cables will each use eight ribbing stitches, increased to twelve; this adds eight stitches.
* The thirty-stitch cable will use twenty stitches increased to thirty; this adds ten stitches.

The total number of stitches to be increased is twenty-six; 116 + 26 = 142 stitches for half the body.

Now that you know how many stitches need to be increased, you'll want to place those increases exactly where they're needed—where the cables will be placed. Draw a chart or plot the stitches to show exactly where the cables will be placed. This is explained thoroughly in the pattern notes, following the increase row in the sweater instructions and illustrated in the chart.

Length of Garment

The next item to be considered is the overall length of the garment from the cast-on edge to the back neck. Multiply this length by your row gauge. This will give you the approximate number of rows in the garment. Divide this number by the number of rows in your center panel and round the number to full pattern repeats. If you need to make adjustments, add or subtract from the ribbing depth.

The Finished Neckline

Another important consideration is the finished look at the neckline. Perhaps there are six pattern repeats in your row count for your desired length. If you begin at Row 1 of a given pattern you may need to end with a half or partial pattern to begin neckline shaping, and this could be unattractive. If you know this could be a problem beforehand, you can start in the middle of a pattern repeat at the bottom and end with a full pattern at the neckline.

Vertical Placement

The 24-row cable pattern we chose for the center panel fits into the back measurement with six full repeats, so no matter where you begin in the cable pattern following the rib, you'll end in the same place at the neckline. However, you also need to consider the front of the sweater, where the neckline is going to be about 2" (5cm) lower than in the back. In this case, we decided to make the front neckline end just after the cable crossings, so the half pattern repeat where the six bound cables grow from the ribbing is at the bottom, and at the top we have a cable that looks finished. Of course this is a matter of personal preference; if you like the look of the half cable at the top, that's your choice to make. If you understand how the patterns work, you can plan the design to work however you want. Liberating, yes?

Once you've got the patterns and sizing all worked out, choose a ribbing and cast on!

Pattern Stitches

K1, P1 TWISTED RIB
(worked back and forth for body and cuff ribbing)

All rows: *K1B (knit 1 in back of stitch), p1; rep from * to end of row.

K1, P1 TWISTED RIB
(worked in the round for neck ribbing)

Round 1: *K1B (knit 1 in back of stitch), p1; rep from * to end of round.
Round 2: *K1, p1B (purl 1 in back of stitch); rep from * to end of round.

DOUBLE SEED

Row 1: *K1, p1; rep from * to end of round.
Rows 2 and 4: Knit the knits and purl the purls.
Row 3: *P1, k1; rep from * to end of round.

TWIST 2

Row 1: K2tog and leave sts on needle, knit the first stitch again and drop both sts from needle.
Row 2: P2.

2/2 LEFT CABLE

Row 1: Place 2 sts on cn and hold in front, k2 from left needle, k2 from cn.
Row 2: P4.

2/2 RIGHT CABLE

Row 1: Place 2 sts on cn and hold in back, k2 from left needle, k2 from cn.
Row 2: P4.

6-STITCH LEFT PLAITED CABLE

Row 1: Place 2 sts on cn and hold in front, k2 from left needle, k2 from cn, k2 from left needle.
Rows 2 and 4: P6.
Row 3: K2, place 2 sts on cn and hold in back, k2 from left needle, k2 from cn.

6-STITCH RIGHT PLAITED CABLE

Row 1: K2, place 2 sts on cn and hold in back, k2 from left needle, k2 from cn.
Rows 2 and 4: P6.
Row 3: Place 2 sts on cn and hold in front, k2 from left needle, k2 from cn, k2 from left needle.

☆ *Look closely at the two Plaited Cables and you'll see that Row 1 of the Left Plaited Cable and Row 3 of the Right Plaited Cable are the same and Row 3 of the Left Plaited Cable and Row 1 of the Right Plaited Cable are the same. This is what makes them a mirror image.*

3/3 RIGHT CABLE

Row 1: Place 3 sts on cn and hold in back, k3 from left needle, k3 from cn.
Row 2: P6.

3/3 LEFT CABLE

Row 1: Place 3 sts on cn and hold in front, k3 from left needle, k3 from cn.
Row 2: P6.

K3/P2 LEFT CABLE

Row 1: Place 3 sts on cn and hold in front, p2 from left needle, k3 from cn.
Row 2: Knit the knits and purl the purls.

Lisdoonvarna Chart

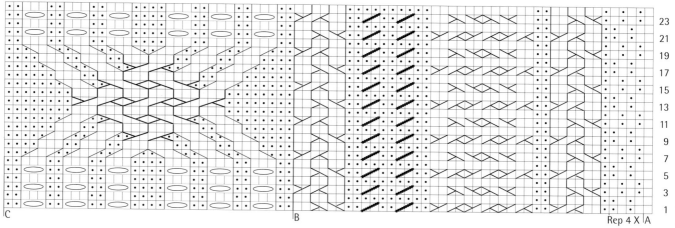

Work the wrong-side increase row from instruction in the text. For succeeding rows, work A to C, then B to A.

Pattern Stitches (continued)

K3/P2 RIGHT CABLE

Row 1: Place 2 sts on cn and hold in back, k3 from left needle, p2 from cn.
Row 2: Knit the knits and purl the purls.

BASKET WEAVE STITCH
(right side of sweater [or sleeve] as it faces you)

Row 1: 2/2 Left Cable 3 [6] times.
Rows 2 and 4: Purl.
Row 3: K2, 2/2 Right Cable 2 [5] times, k2.
Rep Rows 1–4 for pattern.

BASKET WEAVE STITCH
(left side of sweater [or sleeve] as it faces you)

Row 1: 2/2 Right Cable 3 [6] times.
Rows 2 and 4: Purl.
Row 3: K2, 2/2 Left Cable 2 [5] times, k2.
Rep Rows 1–4 for pattern.

CENTER PANEL

Special abbreviation: B3 = bind 3. See Chart Key
Row 1: (B3, p2) twice, B3, p4, B3, (p2, B3) twice.
Row 2 and all even rows: Knit the knits and purl the purls.
Rows 3–6: Rep Rows 1 and 2 twice more.

Row 7: 3/2 Left Cable 3 times, 3/2 Right Cable 3 times.
Row 9: P2, 3/2 Left Cable twice, 3/3 Right Cable, 3/2 Right Cable twice, p2.
Row 11: P4, 3/2 Left Cable, 3/3 Left Cable twice, 3/2 Right Cable, p4.
Row 13: P6, 3/3 Right Cable 3 times, p6.
Row 15: P4, 3/2 Right Cable, 3/3 Left Cable twice, 3/2 Left Cable, p4.
Row 17: P2, 3/2 Right Cable twice, 3/3 Right Cable, 3/2 Left Cable twice, p2.
Row 19: 3/2 Right Cable 3 times, 3/2 Left Cable 3 times.
Rows 21–24: Rep Rows 1 and 2 twice.
Rep Rows 1–24 for pattern.

Lisdoonvarna Sleeve Chart

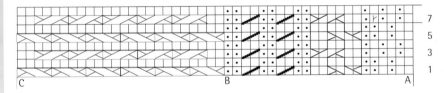

Lisdoonvarna Key

⬭ Bind 3 (B3) = Slip 1 st with yarn at back of work, k1, yo, k1, psso the k1, yo, k1

☐ Knit on RS, purl on WS

▣ Purl on RS, knit on WS

☑ Right leaning increase; work as left leaning when working chart from B to A

⬩ 2/2 Right Cable
Place 2 sts on cn and hold in back, k2 from left needle, k2 from cn

⬩ 2/2 Left Cable
Place 2 sts on cn and hold in front, k2 from left needle, k2 from cn

⬩ 3/3 Right Cable
Place 3 sts on cn and hold in back, k3 from left needle, k3 from cn

⬩ 3/3 Left Cable
Place 3 sts on cn and hold in front, k3 from left needle, k3 from cn

⬩ K3/P2 Right Cable
Place 2 sts on cn and hold in back, k3 from left needle, p2 from cn

⬩ K3/P2 Left Cable
Place 3 sts on cn and hold in front, p2 from left needle, k3 from cn

 2-Stitch Twist
K2tog and leave sts on needle, knit the first stitch again and drop both sts from needle

Back

With larger needles and using the long-tail knit/purl method (see Chapter Five), cast on 116 sts. Change to smaller needles and work K1, P1 Twisted Rib pattern for 3" (8cm) or desired length. End with a RS row.

☆ *Since you're going to sew seams up the sides of this garment, you'll want the ribbing to align so there is no visible interruption. This is explained in Chapter Five, but here it is again. Begin the rib on the RS with two knit stitches and end with one knit stitch. If you do this on both the front and the back, when you join the seams you'll have two knit stitches from one edge going to one knit stitch on the other edge. Seaming with mattress stitch consumes one stitch from each edge, so you'll end up with a knit stitch and a purl stitch together, with no interruption in the rib.*

Here's how you'd work the K1, P1 Twisted Rib:

Row 1: K1, *k1B, p1; repeat from * to last st, k1.
Row 2: *P1, k1B; repeat from * to last 2 sts, p2.

We're working with 116 stitches and have designed a pattern of cables and twisted stitches with purl-two separators. The cables will consume fifty-two stitches; the two Twist 2 panels with separators consume twenty stitches, and the remaining purl-two separators consume eight stitches for a total of eighty stitches. Subtract this from the 116 stitches to get thirty-six; divide by two for eighteen stitches on each side of the sweater to work in the pattern of your choosing, in this case double seed stitch.

Increase Row (WS): P1 (edge stitch), beginning with a knit st, work 16 sts in Double Seed pattern, k1, pm (place marker), p1, M1PL, p2, M1PL, p1, pm (this is a 6-Stitch Plaited Cable), k2, pm, p1, (M1PL, p2) 3 times, M1PL, p1 (this is the Basket Weave Stitch), pm, (k2, p2) twice, k2 (this is two Twist 2 repeats with 2-stitch purl separators), pm, p1, M1PL, p2, M1PL, p1, pm (this is a 6-Stitch Plaited Cable), k2, M1PL, p1, k2, M1R, p2, M1PL, k2, M1PL, p2, M1R, k2, M1R, p2, M1PL, k2, M1PL, p2, M1R, k2, p1, M1PL, k2 (this is the Center Panel), pm, p1, M1PL, p2, M1PL, p1, pm (this is a 6-Stitch Plaited Cable), pm, (k2, p2) twice, k2 (this is two Twist 2 repeats with 2-stitch purl separators), pm, p1, (M1PL, p2) 3 times, M1PL, p1 (this is the Basket Weave Stitch), k2, pm, p1, M1PL, p2, M1PL, p1, pm (this is a 6-Stitch Plaited Cable), pm, k1, beginning with a knit st, work 16 sts in Double Seed pattern, p1 (edge stitch)—142 sts.

☆ *When setting up patterns, it's helpful to place markers before and after the cables. There will be twenty-six increases on the first wrong-side row after the rib, and it's important that they're placed in the area of the cable take-up.*

For this sweater you can plot a series of numbers as follows:

18 | 6-st cable | 2 | 12-st cable | 10 | 6-st cable | 2 | 30-st cable | 2 | 6-st cable | 10 | 12-st cable | 2 | 6-st cable | 18

This string of numbers tells us exactly where the cables are placed and therefore where to increase. So, for the set-up row, which is worked on the wrong side, you'll purl the edge stitch followed by sixteen in Double Seed, followed by one knit stitch, which will be a purl separator on the right side. Now you've reached the first cable, which is a six-stitch cable; we've already determined that we'll use four ribbing stitches for the cable, so we have to increase two stitches here. To increase evenly over the four stitches and end up with six stockinette stitches on the right side for the cable, increase purlwise as follows: P1, M1PL, p2, M1PL, p1. Now you knit two stitches, then work the increases for the twelve-stitch cable.

On the first right side row, you'll work cable crossings for the six- and twelve-stitch cables, so it doesn't really matter whether you make right- or left-leaning increases; they will disappear into the crossing. But the center panel will be worked for several rows before crossing, so we've worked mirror-image right- and left-leaning increases for this panel.

Follow the chart to work all patterns as follows:

K1 (edge stitch), 16 sts in Double Seed, p1, Left Plaited Cable, p2, Basket Weave Stitch, 10-st panel of Twist 2 with purls, Right Plaited Cable, p2, Center Panel, p2, Left Plaited Cable, 10-st panel of Twist 2 with purls, Basket Weave Stitch, p2, Right Plaited Cable, p1, 16 sts in Double Seed, k1 (edge stitch).

Continue working the patterns as established until piece measures 17" (43cm) from beginning or desired length to underarm, ending with Row 6 of the Center Panel. Mark this row on the Center Panel so you'll know where to end for the front armhole. Bind off 8 sts at the beginning of the next 2 rows—126 sts.

Work 4 rows even in patts as established with an edge stitch at each end of the row.

Begin Raglan Decreases

Row 1: K1 (edge stitch), p1, k2tog, work in established patts to last 4 sts, ssk, p1, k1 (edge stitch).
Row 2: Knit the knits and purl the purls.
Repeat these 2 rows 7 more times—110 sts.
Next Row: K1 (edge st), p1, work the Left Plaited Cable, p2, k2tog, work in established patterns to the last 2 sts of the Basket Weave Stitch on the other side of the Center Panel, ssk, work in patterns to last 2 sts, p1, k1 (edge stitch).
Next Row: Knit the knits and purl the purls.

Continue in this manner, working the decs on the outer edges of the Basket Weave panels, until the piece measures 9" (23cm) from underarm. Place remaining 66 sts on holder for back Neck.

☆ *Working decreases in this way really shows that you know your stuff. You began by binding off half the Double Seed pattern area. Then you decreased until the Double Seed was completely consumed. Now, rather than interrupt the 6-Stitch Plaited Cable, you shift the decreases to the other side of these cables and make them after and before the p2 separators. Then you continue decreasing until you've consumed the Basket Weave stitches and continue through the Twist 2 panels. Notice how the plaited cable follows the angle of the decreases.*

Front

Work as for Back for 14 fewer rows, ending on Row 9 and with 80 sts. With WS facing, work 22 sts in pattern, place center 36 sts on hold for front Neck, join new yarn, and work to end of row. Working each side separately, dec 1 st at each Neck edge 1 stitch in from edge stitch every other row 7 times as you continue to work raglan armholes to match back, ending on Row 24. Place remaining 8 sts on each side on holders.

Sleeves (make two)

With larger needles and using the long-tail knit/purl method (see Chapter Five), cast on 56 sts. Change to smaller needles and work K1, P1 Twisted Rib for 3" (8cm) or desired length. End with a RS row.

☆ *Use the same trick here that you used for the Front and Back so you'll have perfectly matching ribs at the seams.*

Increase Row: With WS facing, p1 (edge stitch), beginning with a knit st work 4 sts in Double Seed pattern, k1, pm, M1PL, p2, M1PL, pm (this is a 6-Stitch Plaited Cable), pm, (k2, p2) twice, k2 (this is two Twist 2 repeats with 2-stitch purl separators), pm, p1, (M1PL, p2) 7 times, M1PL, p1 (this is the Basket Weave Stitch), pm, (k2, p2) twice, k2 (this is the two Twist 2 repeats with 2-stitch purl separators), pm, p1, M1PR, p2, M1PR, p1, pm (this is a 6-Stitch Plaited Cable), k1, pm, work 4 sts in Double Seed pattern, p1 (edge stitch)—68 sts.

☆ *The same methods used for the Back and Front of the sweater apply here for calculating how many stitches you'll need to increase to compensate for cable take-up and where to place those increases.*

Continue in established patterns, increasing 1 st at inner edge of Double Seed pattern every 8 rows, until you have 92 sts. Work even in patterns until Sleeve measures 20" (51cm) from beginning. Bind off 8 sts at beginning of next 2 rows.

Work the Double Seed decreases as for the Back, then work decreases on the other side of the 6-Stitch Plaited Cables and make them after and before the p2 separators every 4 rows instead of every 2 rows until 38 sts remain. Place sts on hold.

☆ *Here you're using the same technique employed for the Back: Once the Double Seed area is consumed, you're keeping the 6-Stitch Plaited Cable at the edge intact and working the decreases on the other side.*

Neck

Use mattress stitch to join the Front and Back to the Sleeves along the raglan edges, working from the underarms to the Neck edge. At the end of each seam there will be 2 live knit seam sts—8 sts in all. When you begin to work the first decrease round, work each of these live knit sts together with the adjacent purl stitch. Keep these sts live and place them on the needle for the Neck with the others as follows:

Onto a circular needle slip live sts as follows: 38 left Sleeve sts, 8 left Front sts, 36 front Neck sts, 8 right Front sts, 38 right Sleeve sts and 66 Back sts, pm—194 sts.

Join new yarn.

First Decrease Round: Beginning with the left Sleeve, k2tog (1 Sleeve and 1 seam st); k1, k2tog twice, k1; k1, k2tog, (k1, k2tog, k1) 4 times, k2tog, k1; k1, k2tog twice, k1; k2tog (1 Sleeve and 1 seam st); k2tog (1 seam and 1 Front st); k1, k2tog twice, k1; pick up and knit 7 sts down left Neck edge; (k1, k2tog) 3 times; (k1, k2tog twice, k1) 3 times; (k2tog, k1) 3 times; pick up and knit 7 sts up right Neck edge; k1, k2tog twice, k1; k2tog (1 Front and 1 seam st); k2tog (1 seam and 1 right Sleeve st); k1, k2tog twice, k1; k1, k2tog, (k1, k2tog, k1) 4 times, k2tog, k1; k1, k2tog twice, k1; k2tog (1 Sleeve and 1 seam st); k2tog (1 seam and 1 Back st); k1, k2tog twice, k1; k2, k1, k2tog twice, k1; k2tog, (k1, k2tog, k2) 3 times; (k2, k2tog, k1) 3 times; k2tog; k1, k2tog twice, k1; k2, k1, k2tog twice, k1; k2tog (1 Back and 1 seam st)—148 sts.

☆ *Just as we had to increase from the ribbing for the cables to compensate for take-up, we have to decrease the cables at the other end to return to ribbing. The principle is the same, decreasing where the cables are.*

Second Decrease Round: *K2, (k4, k2tog) 12 times; repeat from * once more—124 sts.
Round 1: *K1b, p1; rep from * to end of round.
Round 2: *K1, p1b; rep from * to end of round.
Rep Rounds 1 and 2 for 3" (8cm).

Fold the neckband in half and sew the live sts to the second decrease round. Sew side and Sleeve seams. Weave in all ends.

Changing the Size

Designs for Aran sweaters are very specific and not the easiest ones to alter to your desired fit. However, it can be done! One way is to work at a different gauge. If you want a sweater that is a little bit bigger, knit with fewer stitches per inch (2.5cm); if you want a sweater that's a little bit smaller, work with more stitches per inch. These gauge changes can be minor, using the same yarn specified in the pattern and altering the needle size by one up or down. Or, these changes can be dramatic by substituting different weights of yarn—a DK or sport weight yarn will give you a smaller sweater and a bulky yarn will yield a larger garment. You can also make alterations in the allover patterns. For example, for this sweater you could work a few more or fewer stitches in the Double Seed stitch area, purl more or fewer stitches between the cables, or work more or fewer purls between the Twist 2 stitches.

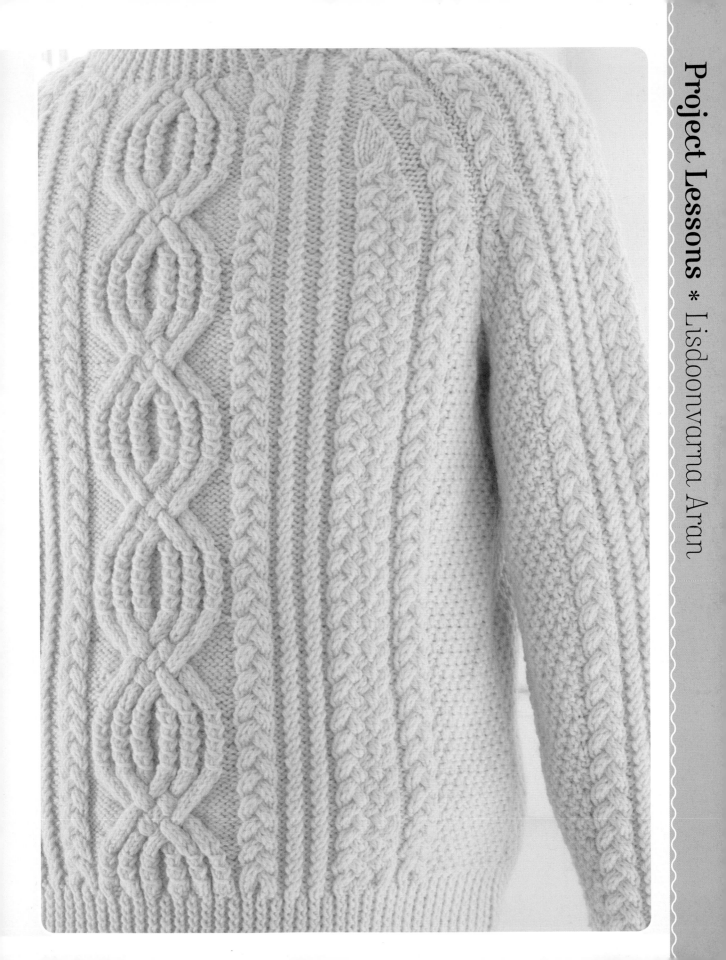

Resources

Yarns

Classic Elite Yarns
122 Western Avenue
Lowell, MA 01851-1434
978.453.2837
www.classiceliteyarns.com

Knit One, Crochet Too, Inc.
91 Tandberg Trail, Unit 6
Windham, ME 04062
207.892.9625
www.knitonecrochettoo.com

Cascade Yarns
1224 Andover Park E
Tukwila, WA 96188
206.574.0440
www.cascadeyarns.com

Crystal Palace Yarns
160 23rd Street
Richmond, CA 94804
www.straw.com

Regia Yarn - Westminster
Fibers
165 Ledge Street
Nashua, NH 03060
800.445.9276
www.westminsterfibers.com

Louet North America
3425 Hands Road
Prescott, ON, Canada
K0E 1T0
613.925.4502
www.louet.com

Nordic Fiber Arts
4 Cutts Road
Durham, NH 03824
603.868.1196
www.nordicfiberarts.com

Notions

A Feibusch Corp
27 Allen Street
New York, NY 10002
888.947.7872
Zippers in all colors and lengths

Bibliography

Parkes, Clara. *The Knitter's Book of Yarn: The Ultimate Guide to Choosing, Using, and Enjoying Yarn*, New York: Potter Craft, 2007.

Singer, Amy R. *No Sheep for You: Knit Happy with Cotton, Silk, Linen, Hemp, Bamboo & Other Delights*, Loveland, CO: Interweave Press, 2007.

Stanley, Montse. *Knitter's Handbook: A Comprehensive Guide to the Principles and Techniques of Handknitting*, Pleasantville, NY: Reader's Digest, 2001.

Walker, Barbara G. *A Treasure of Knitting Patterns*. New York: Charles Scribner's Sons, 1968; Pittsville, WI: Schoolhouse Press, 1998.

———*A Second Treasury of Knitting Patterns*. *New York*: Charles Scribner's Sons, 1970; Pittsville, WI: Schoolhouse Press, 1998.

Index

About the Authors

Dorothy T. Ratigan's career in fiber arts spans more than forty years, and in that time she's done it all. From bargello to beadwork, crewelwork, crochet, cross-stitch, embroidery, knitting, needlepoint, tatting and weaving, Dorothy has designed, stitched, edited and taught it all.

This adventure with needlework began with the skills that her mother, Peg, and her aunts, Nell and Delia, brought from Ireland and passed on to her. Dorothy has designed or edited for many major fiber magazines, craft book publishers and yarn companies. As president and co-owner of Pine Tree Knitters she designed knitted skiwear, oversaw a production staff and marketed finished items to L.L. Bean, Eddie Bauer and others.

Dorothy got to the bottom of her love of fiber with her recently published *Knitting the Perfect Pair: Secrets to Great Socks* (Krause Publications). Publication of *Knitting Know-How* fulfills her long-held desire to share what she's learned from and with the knitting world.

Judith Durant is author of *Knit One, Bead Too, Never Knit Your Man a Sweater* and *Ready, Set, Bead!*, co-author of *Beadwork Inspired by Art: Impressionism, Beadwork Inspired by Art: Art Nouveau* and *The Beader's Companion* (with Jean Campbell), and editor of Storey's *One-Skein Wonders* series, which includes *Sock Yarn One-Skein Wonders, Luxury One-Skein Wonders, Designer One-Skein Wonders* and *One-Skein Wonders*.

Judith received a B.F.A. in costume design for theater and worked as a costume artisan for theater and television in New York City before beginning a publishing career with Drama Book Publishers, a publisher of technical theater books. She is former craft book editor for Interweave Press and one of the founding editors of *Interweave Knits*. She has contributed designs and articles to *Cast On, Creative Knitting Magazine, Interweave Knits, Beadwork* and *PieceWork* magazines, and had a regular column in *Beadwork* for five years. Her mother taught her to knit when she was eight years old.

Acknowledgments

Thanks to Stacy and all the folks at Cascade Yarns for providing yarn for swatching and photos and for Lisdoonvarna and for staying with us as we changed our minds about colors and amounts; to Hélène Rush of Knit One, Crochet Too for providing the yarn for Ambrosia; and to Deborah Gremlitz of Nordic Fiber Arts for providing the yarn for Austin's Jacket and Faux Earflap Hats.

Thanks to the team at Krause Publications: Jennifer Claydon for championing the work and getting us to contract; Rachel Scheller for keeping track of all the details and putting them all together; Christine Polomsky for the step-by-step photography; Sue Cleave for the book design; the sales and marketing folks who will help us sell the book; and to anyone we've missed who helped bring the book to fruition.

Knitting Know-How. Copyright © 2012 by Dorothy T. Ratigan and Judith Durant. Manufactured in China. All rights reserved. No part of this book may be reproduced in any form or by any electronic or mechanical means including information storage and retrieval systems without permission in writing from the publisher, except by a reviewer who may quote brief passages in a review. Published by Krause Publications, a division of F+W Media, Inc., 10151 Carver Road, Blue Ash, Ohio 45242. (800) 289-0963. First Edition.

www.fwmedia.com

16   15   14   13   12   5   4   3   2   1

Distributed in Canada by Fraser Direct
100 Armstrong Avenue
Georgetown, ON, Canada L7G 5S4
Tel: (905) 877-4411

Distributed in the U.K. and Europe by F&W MEDIA INTERNATIONAL
Brunel House, Newton Abbot, Devon, TQ12 4PU, England
Tel: (+44) 1626 323200, Fax: (+44) 1626 323319
Email: enquiries@fwmedia.com

Distributed in Australia by Capricorn Link
P.O. Box 704, S. Windsor NSW, 2756 Australia
Tel: (02) 4577-3555

SRN: W1583
ISBN-13: 978-1-4402-1819-4

Editor: Rachel Scheller
Designer: Sue Cleave
Production Coordinator: Greg Nock
Photographers: Christine Polomsky, Marissa Bowers

Metric Conversion Chart

To convert	to	multiply by
Inches	Centimeters	2.54
Centimeters	Inches	0.4
Feet	Centimeters	30.5
Centimeters	Feet	0.03
Yards	Meters	0.9
Meters	Yards	1.1

Put your knitting knowledge to the test with gorgeous patterns and new techniques!

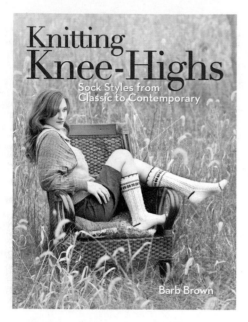

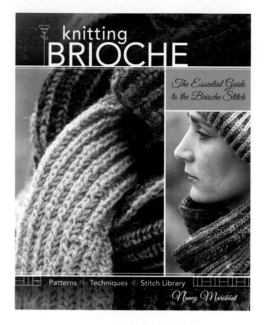

Knitting Knee-Highs

Barb Brown

If you love knee-high socks, you know there are never enough knee-high patterns to keep your needles going. Inside *Knitting Knee-Highs*, you'll find knee-high patterns featuring intricate colorwork, twisting and twining cables, lovely lacework and beautifully textured stitches inspired by beloved knitting traditions. From casting on at the knee to grafting the toe stitches, Barb Brown will lead you step-by-step through creating a fabulous pair (or pairs!) of knee-high socks.

Knitting Brioche

Nancy Marchant

Knitting Brioche is the first and only knitting book devoted exclusively to the brioche stitch, a knitting technique that creates a double-sided fabric. This complete guide will take you from your first brioche stitches to your first project, and even to designing with brioche stitch. Whether you're new to brioche knitting or experienced at "brioching," author Nancy Marchant provides the information and inspiration you need.

For more inspiring books like these, plus knitting tips, tricks and inspiration, visit store.marthapullen.com.

Join the online crafting community!

f facebook.com/fwcraft

@fwcraft